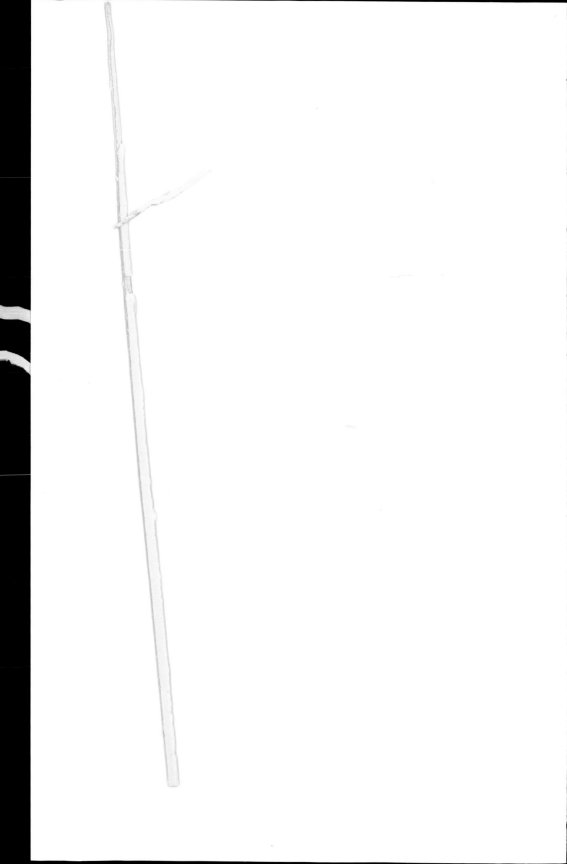

MEDICARE
SECONDARY PAYER
COMPLIANCE
The Liability Case

SECOND EDITION

Roy A. Franco
Jeffrey J. Signor

JURIS

Questions About This Publication

For assistance with shipments, billing or other customer service matters, please call our Customer Services Department at:

1-631-350-2100

To obtain a copy of this book, call our Sales Department:

1-631-351-5430
Fax: 1-631-351-5712

Toll Free Order Line:

1-800-887-4064 (United States & Canada)

See our web page about this book:
www.jurispub.com

ISBN 978-1-57823-327-4

Juris Publishing, Inc.
71 New Street
Huntington, New York 11743
USA
www.jurispub.com

CONTENTS

PREFACE

When we first wrote this book, Medicare Secondary Payer Compliance was at its infancy for liability settlements, judgments, and awards. The plaintiff bar widely disbelieved the applicability of the Medicare Secondary Payer Act to the personal injury claim; and the defendant (through their insurance companies or themselves) took on the burden of education on behalf of Medicare. Facing significant penalties for failure to report information electronically to Medicare and a deadline to meet such reporting obligations which moved several times; confusion was also added to the mix.

Since our first edition a lot has changed in the area of Medicare Secondary Payer Compliance. Most vendors in this space have changed their focus from exclusively pushing Medicare Set Asides to more broadly assisting with Medicare Secondary Payer Compliance. Reporting requirements are now in place and this has shifted insurance carriers and self insureds from building claim systems to communicate with Medicare to implementing processes that mitigate their exposure from Medicare for the data being reported. Medicare intends to use the data it collects to recover payments it made for medical items and services related to the personal injury claim. It also plans to coordinate benefits. Insurance carriers and self insureds cannot rely upon compliance being managed by the plaintiff when it comes to repaying and protecting Medicare. Such compliance efforts must be managed using a proactive approach.

The purpose of the second edition, like the first, is to use our guidance as a resource guide. It provides a historical context of the law, and breaks down the Medicare Secondary Payer Act into three parts. In each section the authors share their best practices for compliance. Two underlying themes run throughout the book – develop a proactive approach and seek cooperation of both sides to the liability claim.

Medicare Secondary Payer exposure is best mitigated when there is a single voice to Medicare. If information being delivered by all sides to Medicare is not consistent, Medicare will process the information to improve its recovery effort. Further, if data is inconsistent, Medicare may coordinate future benefits resulting in the Beneficiary being denied benefits for treatment that are not related to the claim.

The Centers for Medicare and Medicaid Services is charged with keeping the Medicare Trust Fund whole. It will continue to refine its procedures to further that goal. The applicability of the Medicare Secondary Payer Act to the liability claim is here to stay. Understanding its etiology and applicability to the claim and planning for its mitigation is critical. Our book is designed to help anyone wishing to improve their understanding of this law, and provides situations to consider when resolving the liability claim.

The topic of Medicare Secondary Payer compliance can be dense and confusing. We take pride in staying on top of the topic by reviewing current case law and Medicare Alerts, and by having our own hands in day-to-day management of MSP issues for our clients. The second edition was written with the practical approach in mind. We have combined some chapters and entirely removed others in order to provide the industry with a clear, practical approach to the subject matter. We hope you like our book!

ABOUT THE BOOK

The liability arena has no shortage of seminars and educational meetings to learn about the topic of Medicare Secondary Payer compliance. Most such meetings involve a level of fear to push a practitioner towards compliance with the law. In fact, many such seminars and meetings involve a presenter citing to the penalty of "$1,000 per day per claim..."

There is an easier way to learn about and remember what it takes to comply with the MSP Act. There are three "buckets" of compliance, comprised of 1. Conditional Payments – Re-paying Medicare; 2. Protecting Medicare's interests – Future medical component; and 3. Reporting to Medicare at the time of settlement, judgment or award.

Even though two years have passed since the first writing of this book, the law continues to be embryonic, and the entire industry is grappling with compliance to it.

Chapter 1 provides an overview of Medicare Secondary Payer Act, including some of the policies surrounding its creation and implementation. Entitlement programs have taken on increased political meaning, but their very existence depends upon aggressive recoupment by Medicare and its contractors. The framework of benefits is also discussed in this chapter. The liability practitioner will be wise to study it and thereby gain an understanding of the background and framework of Medicare, and make use of the practice tips set forth in this chapter.

Chapter 2 discusses conditional payments and the process through which a liability practitioner must go to repay Medicare. Medicare employs an ICD-9 Code language and the authors extensively lay out recommendations for learning the language that Medicare recognizes. The chapter also offers more practice tips and practical recommendations. The labyrinth of acronyms and pathways utilized by the MSPRC and COBC must be understood before real progress can begin at the case-handling level. Chapter 2 embarks the reader on this journey and appendices 42 and 43 provide respectively, a graphic representation of the necessary steps toward compliance and a list of the acronyms used in the industry.

In Chapter 3, the reader is shown step-by-step how to report a settlement, judgment or award, as mandated by Section 111 Reporting, aka MMSEA, aka MIR, aka SCHIP Extension Act, aka Mandatory Reporting. The technical aspects of Section 111 Reporting are explained in great detail in Chapter 3.

The 800-pound gorilla is tackled in Chapter 4: Future incident-related treatment and how to manage the exposures in an area of the law that sparsely addresses this topic. The authors present perspectives and recommendations on this topic that are not found in the typical seminar. The industry, and Medicare, are both growing on this topic and the information set forth in Chapter 4 will keep the liability practitioner in touch with hands-on and practical methods of compliance.

Chapter 5 covers the ways to dispute and appeal conditional payment letters. It is extremely difficult to directly commence suit against Medicare. Chapter 5 cites to case law and shows the reader how to dispute Medicare's stated amount owed, and again recommends practice tips to use when presenting such disputes to Medicare and all appellate levels contained within the Medicare framework of administrative appeals.

Chapter 6 offers the reader our thoughts on what lies on the horizon. The embryonic nature of the MSP Act, insofar as Section 111 Reporting and compliance with Medicare is sure to hit the desks of most liability practitioners, will involve a process through which change and education are a must. Finally, we discuss where some of the potential paths taken by the MSP Act may lead.

It is our hope that practitioners will enjoy and benefit from their discussion. Readers' comments to improve the book are always welcome. Please direct comments to engage@francosignor.com.

ABOUT THE AUTHORS

Roy A. Franco

Roy A. Franco is a principal of Franco Signor LLC a Liability Medicare Secondary Payer Compliance group with offices located in Kenmore, New York; Bradenton, Florida; Charlotte, North Carolina; and Denver, Colorado. Before co-founding the company, Mr. Franco worked for Safeway Inc., a Fortune 50 grocery retailer. During his 15-year career with Safeway, he was the Director for the Company's self-administered liability claims operation. Having more than 1700 retail facilities in 26 states, as well as a complement of distribution centers and manufacturing plants, there was no lack in the variety and type of tort claims falling within his area of responsibility.

As Mr. Franco progressed in his career with Safeway he was exposed to Medicare and its relationship to the resolved liability claim. This journey began in early 2003, when his Portland office contacted him to discuss two non-represented claims that had been previously settled and closed. These claims were being reopened because of letters received from one of Medicare's contractors stating that Medicare was owed money for past medical items and services related to the liability claim. This original inquiry started an odyssey that continues to serve as a basis for Mr. Franco's passion to reform the law.

Initially, he worked to build processes within his organization that would identify Medicare beneficiaries and promptly reimburse Medicare. However, he quickly learned that Medicare had its own timetable. Liability claims do not improve with age, and the reimbursement methodologies adopted by Medicare were a challenge. When Medicare consolidated its contractors on October 1, 2006, the time with which to deal with Medicare went from a few months to closer to one year – an unacceptable time period to hold funds from Medicare beneficiaries who were also Safeway's customers. The reimbursement process became disruptive and a change had to occur – but how?

Beginning in 2006, Mr. Franco embarked upon a grass roots campaign to bring about reform. He started the Medicare Secondary Payer Act Reform Task Force in San Francisco, and by the spring of 2007, published a white paper to enlist support (*Easy Solutions to Help Resolve Medicare Reimbursement Issues for Beneficiaries and Insurers*, May 4, 2007). Engaging brokers, attorneys, insurance representatives and self-insureds throughout the State of California, he developed a weekly forum to discuss the problem and potential solutions. His efforts led to an invitation to Washington DC to meet with the American Insurance Association (AIA) and present his concerns. On a napkin at a local Washington DC Starbucks, Mr. Franco, along with his defense attorney, Jonathan Klein, conceived the Medicare Advocacy Recovery Coalition or MARC. The basic premise: the industry needed a "voice" beyond the insurance carriers. Their simple goal: to join forces with the insurance industry to bring about meaningful change.

Since meeting with the AIA in the fall of 2007, Mr. Franco has been engaged with the liability industry to promote awareness and support reform of the Medicare Secondary Payer Act. He has advocated change on three levels: Legislative, Regulatory and Common Law Advocacy. The MARC group was formalized into a coalition as of November, 2008 and is currently pending its non-profit status. Franco Signor LLC is a steering committee member of MARC and active contributor.

Mr. Franco is a frequent lecturer at professional and business conferences, as well as, a featured speaker at continuing legal education for various bars. He has authored two nationally published articles with his partner, Jeff Signor. He serves as an industry resource on the topic, and is often quoted in national publications such as Business Insurance and BNA.

Mr. Franco holds a Bachelor of Arts in both Business Administration and Economics (BA '83) and a Juris Doctorate from Santa Clara University School of Law (JD '87). He is a member of the State Bars of California and Hawai'i and has practiced in the fields of civil litigation, real estate transactions, labor relations and worker's compensation.

He previously held a membership with the Risk Insurance Management Society, serving as the Golden Gate Chapter Vice-President, legislative liaison and Delegate to the National House of

CHAPTER 1

MEDICARE SECONDARY PAYER COMPLIANCE –
Overview

1.0   The Reality of Entitlement Programs – There Is No Free Lunch!

1.0.1.   Social Security and Medicare

Social Security and Medicare[1] are separate and distinct entitlement programs supported by tax revenue, both projected and realized. Trustees have evaluated the financial health of these entitlements and have provided some disturbing projections.[2] Swift political action is necessary to avert potential collapse of these programs. Regrettably, our elected officials lack the appetite to deal with this issue directly. As a consequence, a patchwork of laws, regulations, policies and case law has developed which was never fully vetted with the industry it impacts and has created unintended consequences for all parties resolving the liability claim involving Medicare payment for related items and services.

In 2011, the percentage of tax revenue to support both Social Security and Medicare was 13%. It is projected to increase to 27% by 2020, and almost double again to 49% by 2030. Support for Medicare and Social Security will start to level off in 2040, by which time 61 cents of every tax dollar collected will be needed to support Social Security and Medicare. The projected impact of the U.S. budget is unsustainable and not what was intended by the original architects of these entitlement programs. Such programs were never intended to be "pay

---

[1] Established in 1965, Medicare was the responsibility of the Social Security Administration, an agency within the Department of Health, Education & Welfare (HEW). The Health Care Financing Administration (HCFA) was established in 1977 under HEW to coordinate Medicare and Medicaid. In 1980, HEW was dissolved and replaced by two departments – Department of Education and Department of Health & Human Services (HHS). HCFA remained the responsibility of HHS and its name was changed in 2001 by its administrator, Tom Scully to Centers for Medicare & Medicaid Services (CMS).

[2] http://www.ssa.gov/OACT/TR/2012/trTOC.html.

1

as you go." Trust Funds were established to provide for future benefits without adverse impact to the U.S. Budget. However, over time these Trust Funds became an easy way to fund other government programs and loans were allowed against them. Today, the actuarial shortfall between projected benefit payments to Medicare beneficiaries as compared to the expected tax revenues is $89 trillion. It is unrealistic to expect this shortfall to work out on its own. Something will have to give and our government realistically has three options to solve this conundrum:

1. Increase taxes to cover the shortfall of the entitlement programs;
2. Reduce entitlement benefits to match projected revenues; or
3. Identify and create programs that reduce or transfer the risk for entitlement payments.

In today's political climate, the first two options are unlikely. Congress has no appetite to increase taxes or reduce benefits. Rather, it is more likely there will be legislation to continue to cut taxes and enhance Medicare benefits to attract support from each party's constituents. While this further exacerbates the problem, it is a probable outcome, which will no doubt lead to the implementation of regulations and policies under the last option, the one that has the least probable cause for political fallout. Taxpayers can all agree that the Medicare Trust Fund should not be subject to fraud, waste or abuse. Amendments to the law to improve repayment in that regard included the possibility of a *qui tam* provision which was entertained during the Affordable Health Care Act committee mark-ups.[3] The point is that implementing the third option is easy. It is fair and right for the Trust Fund to be made whole. However, having only this option to solve this gaping chasm is like the little boy who has his fingers in the dike. After a point, the solution is absurd and the outcomes result in more harm than good.

Two formidable forces prevent dealing directly with this issue. No new taxes, in the name of protecting job investment and the graying Americans who are unwilling to relinquish any benefits previously promised. A compromise is necessary but difficult to see on the horizon.

---

[3] "Medicare Qui Tam: A Health Care Bill Surprise," by Walter Olson, Overlawyered Blog, July 17, 2009.

As each day passes, perhaps positions will change. What will not change are the approximately 49 million people presently enrolled in the Medicare program with an expected 5 million to join the rolls by the end of 2012.[4] The number of Medicare enrollees will easily reach 70 million before the end of the next decade as the baby boomers retire. Not only are the numbers of Medicare beneficiaries staggering, but their lifestyles are changing. Healthy measures are being promoted and seniors every day increase their amount of physical activity. Beneficiaries are living longer, further taxing the system. The shortfall between promised benefits and collected revenues could easily exceed the $89 trillion projection. A satisfactory solution must be found, but until then the limited approach by the government will result in the development of incremental programs that create a dynamic environment for the foreseeable future. The liability industry must be prepared for it, otherwise the ability to have a final settlement is nothing but certain.

1.0.1.1.   Medicare Entitlement

Medicare is a health insurance program for people eligible in any of the following situations. Enrollment is required before benefits will take effect to people who are:[5]

- Age 65 or older,
- Under the age of 65 on Social Security Disability Income for more than 24 months,
- Receiving Social Security Disability Income for 1 month to pay for amyotrophic lateral sclerosis (ALS or Lou Gehrig's disease); and
- Of all ages with end-stage renal disease (permanent kidney failure requiring dialysis or a kidney transplant).

All Medicare beneficiaries, upon enrollment, are assigned a Health Care Identification Number (HICN). Although enrolled, the individual is not a Medicare beneficiary until eligible. Consequently, an assigned HICN does not automatically translate to Medicare beneficiary status. In order to confirm status, it is wise to contact Social Security or the

---

[4] Fiscal Year 2010 Budget in Brief, http://www.hhs.gov/asrt/ob/docbudget/2010 budgetinbriefp.html.

[5] Please refer to www.cms.hhs.gov for more information on this topic.

Coordination of Benefits Contractor for the date of eligibility. MSP compliance only applies to a Medicare beneficiary, not a potential Medicare beneficiary.

1.0.1.2. Medicare Benefits

One form of Medicare coverage is a **Part A** benefit, which implicates Hospital Insurance. Most people receive premium-free Part A because they or a spouse already paid for it through their payroll taxes while working. Medicare Part A (Hospital Insurance or HI) helps cover inpatient care in hospitals and skilled nursing facilities (but not custodial or long-term care). It also helps cover hospice care and some home health care. Beneficiaries must meet certain conditions to receive these benefits.

If a person is not eligible for premium free Part A then it can be purchased either during the seven month period that begins three months before that person's 65th birthday and ends three months after the Claimant's 65th birthday, or from January 1 through March 31 of each year. There was once a special enrollment period if the person had group health coverage through himself or his spouse's employer or union but that coverage is no longer available.

Part A Medicare pays all covered costs except the Medicare Part A deductible and co-insurance. These deductibles and co-insurance amounts may impact whether Medicare will have a reimbursement claim for a particular case. For example, if the Medicare beneficiary was hospitalized in 2009 for a single day and received no further treatment, the Medicare beneficiary may be responsible for the entire cost. The deductible in 2009 was $1,068 and may cover the entire cost of the stay. While an insurance company or self insured would still be required to report any settlement, award, judgment or other payment, there may be no conditional payment that is owed back to Medicare.

Part B Medical Insurance arises when people of Medicare age or disability pay a monthly premium for Part B. Medicare Part B (Supplemental Medical Insurance, or SMI) helps cover physician and other supplier items/services as well as hospital outpatient care. It also covers durable equipment, a variety of outpatient care services such as clinical lab services, physical and occupational therapies, some preventive services, and some home health services not otherwise covered by Part A.

Part B coverage is optional and not all persons purchase it. The general enrollment period for Part B is January 1 through March 31 of each year. If the Claimant does not sign up for Part B when first eligible, then a penalty is assessed. Since this coverage is optional, it is always a best practice to secure the Health Insurance Card from the Medicare beneficiary to determine what coverages they have selected. This will have a bearing on what is owed in the reimbursement claim to Medicare.

The Part B is subject to a deductible and co-pays which can be found at www.medicare.gov (under "Search Tools," select "Find out What Medicare Covers").

Part A and **Part B** may best be described as "traditional Medicare." As Medicare will pay for items and services under these coverage parts, the MSP law applies and requires reimbursement back to Medicare once responsibility to pay for such items and services is demonstrated by a settlement, judgment or award.

Part C coverage is implicated through Medicare Advantage Plan Coverage. Medicare Advantage Plans are health plan options (like HMOs and PPOs) approved by Medicare and run by private companies. These plans are part of the Medicare Program and are sometimes called "Part C" or "MA plans." These plans are an alternative to the fee-for-service Part A and Part B coverage and often provide extra coverage for services such as vision or dental care. These are private plans. Medicare pays a flat rate to the private plan for each beneficiary that is covered. Those eligible for Part A and enrolled in Part B may enroll in Medicare Advantage but must reside within the service area of the plan selected. For more information the liability practitioner may visit www.medicare.gov. However, the liability practitioner should be aware that the Secretary has assigned her rights under the Act to these private companies for their reimbursement. *See* 42 U.S.C. §1395 w-22(a)(4) and 42 C.F.R. §422.108.

Whether these private plans are afforded the same reimbursement rights as Medicare has been called into question. At least two U.S. District Courts have ruled against such plans.[6] The issue turns on whether the rights of the Secretary of the U.S. Department of Health

---

[6] *Humana Medical Plan, Inc. v. Reale* 2011 U.S.Dist. LEXIS 8909 (Florida, 2011) and *Para v. PacifiCare of Arizona, Inc.,* 2011 U.S. Dis. LEXIS 33310 (Arizona, 2011).

and Human Services are the same as those of the United States. As Congress used both terms in the MSP law, the Courts have held it was meant to have a different meaning. Only the United States is entitled to seek a reimbursement claim, the Secretary does not have that authority. In response, Medicare issued a memorandum supporting these Medicare Advantage Plans' right of reimbursement. However unless there is further clarification by Congress or the Courts, it is difficult to know if the Memorandum will be respected.[7] Notwithstanding, the Third Circuit Court of Appeals in *Avandia Marketing, Sales Practices and Products Liability Litigation GlaxoSmithKline, LLC & GlaxoSmithKline, PLC Humana Medical Plan, Inc. and Humana Insurance Company, individually and on behalf of all others similarly situated, Appellant, 2012 U.S. LEXIS 13230, U.S. Court of Appeals, Third Circuit* has found otherwise. Breathing life into the Medicare Secondary Payer Act Private Cause of Action (42 U.S.C. §1395y(b)(3)(a)), the *Avandia* Court found Medicare Advantage Plans, including Part D Prescription Plans have a right to sue primary plans in federal court.[8] How the conflict will ultimately resolve within the Circuits will take time.

---

[7] Department of Health & Human Services – Center for Medicare & Medicaid Services Memorandum Re: Medicare Secondary Payment Subrogation Rights, dated 12/5/2011.

[8] In *Avandia Marketing, Sales Practices and Products Liability Litigation GlaxoSmithKline, LLC & GlaxoSmithKline, PLC Humana Medical Plan, Inc. and Humana Insurance Company, individually and on behalf of all others similarly situated, Appellant, 2012 U.S. LEXIS 13230, U.S. Court of Appeals, Third Circuit,* 42 U.S.C. Section 1395y(b)(3)(A) was expanded to include Part C and Part D Plans as Plaintiffs. Prior to this legal decision, the private cause of action was believed to be reserved for the Medicare beneficiary. However, the Third Circuit Court of Appeals pointed out that the language of the provision was not restrictive, and since Congress took no action to limit this provision when it amended Medicare to include Part C and Part D, that it was their intention to allow such Plans the right to sue.

In previous decisions attempting to create a cause of action for MA Plans, the focus was on whether the rights of the United States to seek reimbursement or subrogation under the Medicare Secondary Payer Act were the same for the MA Plan. These cases cited to 42 C.F.R. Section 422.108 which affords the MA Plan the same rights as the Secretary to recover from a primary plan or individual under the MSP regulations. The MA Plan believed its right was clear, but Courts pointed out consistently that there is a clear distinction between the rights of the Secretary and those of the United States. As such, 42 U.S.C. Section 1395y(b)(2)(B)(iii) (Reimbursement Claim) and 42 U.S.C. Section 1395y(b)(2)(B)(iii) (Subrogation Claim) was not intended for MA Plans. Medicare has

Prescription Drug Coverage **(Part D)**: Starting January 1, 2006, Medicare prescription drug coverage became available to everyone with

---

limited jurisdiction to pursue claims and therefore, the Secretary had no right to file lawsuit for reimbursement or subrogation. *See* 28 U.S.C. Section 1331.

Avandia takes a different path from prior cases. Essentially, the MA Plan concedes that it is not entitled to the rights of the United States; and instead looks to the MSP private cause of action – 42 U.S.C. Section 1395y(3)(A) for relief. In ruling for the MA, the Court of Appeals determined first that the private cause of action provision was unambiguous in that it was not limited to any particular plaintiff (except qui tam plaintiffs) and provided a clear cause of action for the MA Plan to recover damages. Alternatively, the Court determined that even if the provision were unambiguous, under the *Chevron deference*, the Medicare regulations and subsequent memoranda made clear that MA plans (and Part D Plans) have recovery rights.

In reaching a decision that the MSP private cause of action was clear and unambiguous with regard to its applicability to MA Plans, the court reviewed briefly the purpose of the Medicare Secondary Payer Act, the Medicare Act as well as the role MA Plans were to serve to reduce Medicare costs. Of important note is the Court's recognition that the private cause of action provision was part of the original MSP Act when it was adopted on December 5, 1980 and was never amended. The turning point for the Court was the meaning of the term "subchapter" as used in describing payments under the Medicare Secondary Payer Act. The primary plan argued that the term applied only to the Medicare Secondary Payer Act, in particular payments made by traditional Medicare, and therefore could not possibly cover payments made by the MA. The MA argued that it applied to the entire Act which would include payments by Part C, and the Court agreed after its analysis of how the Medicare Act used the term. After reaching that conclusion and finding that Congress did not alter the MSP private cause of action when Part C was added, the Court found reason enough to believe that the private cause of action would be applicable to the MA.

The Court pushed its decision over the finish line based on two important policies. First, to effectuate the purpose of the Medicare Secondary Payer Act which is to curb skyrocketing Medicare costs; and second, to improve upon Part C, which was also put in place to curb Medicare costs by creating competition for Medicare beneficiaries by private insurance. If the MA were not allowed to recoup benefits that should have been paid by other responsible parties, its costs go up, and so does Medicare.

In supporting its decision further, the Court took the added step of assuming the MSP private cause of action was ambiguous. Applying the *Chevron deference*, the Court attempted to close any loopholes. Finding that Congress granted Medicare the authority to promulgate regulations, the Court then identified 42 C.F.R. Section 422.108 which provides MA with the same MSP recovery powers. Although 42 C.F.R Section 422.108 is permissive in how it is written, the Court found it an appropriate clarification supporting MA private cause of action rights. Further CMS Memorandum issued last December further clarifies CMS position that MA plans and Prescription Plans be allowed to recover. In this instance, the memo is on par with a regulation for Chevron purposes and which may not be viewed in the same way by other circuits. See for instance, *Humana Medical Plan v. Reale*, 2011 U.S. Dist. LEXIS 8909 (S.D. Fla. Jan. 31, 2011).

Medicare. Private companies provide the coverage. Those eligible for Part A may enroll and most (except qualified low income individuals) will pay a monthly premium. Medicare drug plans are run by insurance companies and other private companies approved by Medicare. Each State offers different plans and these plans can vary in cost and drugs covered.

Medicare Part D drug plans have a list of drugs covered by the plan called a "formulary" that must always meet Medicare's requirements. Each plan has its own formulary. Even if a drug is on the plan's list, there may be special rules for filling the prescription e.g., prior authorization, quantity limits, or step therapy. Each plan must have a procedure whereby medication that is not on the formulary may be considered as an exception but this process requires a physician's statement in support.

However, traditional Medicare does not provide coverage for certain types of drugs. These include benzodiazepines, barbiturates, drugs for weight loss or gain, over-the-counter medications, cough and cold medication, vitamins, weight control drugs and drugs for erectile dysfunction. Some plans may choose to cover these medications as an added benefit.

Part D is subject to a coverage gap, commonly referred to as the "donut hole." Most plans have these gaps and some for higher premiums do not, however some drugs even in those plans may not be covered, so referral to the summary plan description is important. The "donut hole" is important as it may have a bearing on a possible reimbursement claim to Medicare. Thus it is an important consideration as deductibles and co-pays are under Part A and Part B.

Based on how Courts have reacted thus far with regard to Medicare Advantage Plans (Part C), we anticipate a similar result should Part D actively pursue reimbursement. However, it is questionable whether Medicare can make the case that it may collect on behalf of Part D providers under the MSP law. 42 U.S.C. §1395 w-22(a)4 evidences Congressional intent to authorize Medicare to provide for a process for reimbursement by Part C Medicare Advantage Plans; but it does not mention Part D Prescription Plans. 42 C.F.R. §422.108 is the Secretary's implementing regulation to equate her rights under the Medicare

Secondary Payer Act to Part C Plans, but cannot do the same for Part D, as Part D was not enacted at the time the regulation was put in place. It is therefore a stretch in the author's opinion that *Chevron* deference is to be given the same weight to Part D as it has been given to Part C-Medicare Advantage. The *Avandia* decision may not ultimately hold for Part D Prescription Plans without further Congressional intervention.

Practice Tip: Part D is provided by private insurance companies and is much like Part C. However, Part D does not have similar implementing statutes and regulations (See 42 U.S.C. §1395 w-22(a)(4) and 42 C.F.R. §422.108) that confers authority under the Act to the private carrier to seek reimbursement. This may be a fatal flaw for a drug carrier that attempts to utilize the Act for repayment.

Exclusions: Medicare has various coverage and payment rules which determine whether a particular item or service will be covered and/or reimbursed. To learn more about what may be covered or not, the publication *Medicare & You*, issued annually by Medicare to every beneficiary, is a good source of helpful information. Another source for information is www.medicare.gov as well as the Act itself.[9] The liability practitioner should become familiar with what is excluded by Medicare as it will obviously have bearing on the reimbursement claim as well as on situations where future medical should be considered.

1.0.2.   Medicare Secondary Payer – Preserving the Financial Integrity of Medicare

The Medicare Secondary Payer Act (Act) (See Appendix 1) is a program created by Congress to preserve the financial integrity of the Medicare Trust Fund. Medicare is prohibited from making payment for medical items and services if it expects payment or reasonably expects payment to be made by another plan. It defines a plan as liability insurance, including self insurance, where responsibility to pay has been demonstrated. Such plans takes a primary position with regard to the

---

[9] 42 U.S.C. §1395y(a).

payment of medical items and services where it is obligated to make payment because of settlement (whether or not liability is admitted or there is a judgment or award). Just like the private sector, this law gives Medicare the authority to recover its payments caused by another's tort. While the tort is being sorted out, Medicare could pay for medical items and services, but on the condition it is paid back when there is a settlement, judgment or award. Any payments Medicare makes during this claim analysis or "litigation period" are identified as conditional payments.

Medicare and private entities seeking repayment of their claim differ in several ways. Fault is not considered by Medicare when it seeks reimbursement or subrogation under the Act. The Medicare demand is always 100 percent of the payments for medical items or services related to the personal injury claim. While adjustments may be made to the government's recovery claim for Medicare beneficiary procurement costs and attorney's fees,[10] there are no other reductions, and legal defenses do not exist unless recovery can somehow be shown to exceed the Secretary's authority under the Act.[11] Medicare's claim is not a lien. It is a reimbursement claim that accrues after a settlement is reached, an Award is made after hearing, or Judgment is pronounced after trial. This nuance of reimbursement claim versus lien is important as it provides a right of priority of the proceeds over all others. Finally, notice is not necessary by Medicare to preserve its claim. All parties to the transaction are responsible to reimburse Medicare, and it does not matter if the funds have already been exhausted for other purposes.

There is no free lunch. The Medicare beneficiary cannot claim damages paid for by Medicare and expect to keep the benefit after such claim accrues. The cost to Medicare must be reimbursed. In the past, Medicare has had difficulty identifying those situations in which it should not pay or be reimbursed. However, with recent changes to the Medicare Secondary Payer Act, Medicare's ability to become aware of such situations has been perfected. Medicare has now started to collect data on liability cases that have resolved involving Medicare beneficiaries. It will no doubt use this information to coordinate

---

[10] 42 C.F.R. §411.37.

[11] *Haro v. Sebelius*, 2011 WL 2040219 (D. Ariz. May 9, 2011).

benefits (a.k.a. stop making payments) and seek reimbursement.[12] Medicare is making up for over 30 years of non-compliance, and given the financial status of the Trust Fund, the expectation is that Medicare will be a standard piece of the liability claims process going forward.

Practice Tip: The Medicare trust fund is under-funded and Congress is looking for ways to make the fund solvent. Expect penalties for non-compliance with the Act to become more stringent and retroactive for maximum fund recovery. Therefore, always approach settlements with the Medicare beneficiary carefully. Complete all three aspects of MSP Compliance, as explained more fully in this book, and include provisions in your documents that address Medicare that will insulate both you and your client from liability. Never ignore and avoid Medicare or its contractors.

1.1. Historical Overview of the Act

1.1.1. Medicare Act

Medicare was enacted to provide health insurance for qualified elderly and disabled persons.[13]   This law never intended to cover or be responsible for work-related injuries or illnesses.[14] Consequently, the Act carved out responsibility for industrial accidents and required reimbursement by Worker's Compensation insurance should Medicare make a payment. These payments were referred to as mistaken payments because Congress never intended Medicare to cover such expenses. No provision was made with regard to how Medicare became aware of such industrial accident claims and no penalties existed if such claim was later brought to Medicare's attention. Good faith was the only standard, and the Medicare Trust Fund paid for medical items and services that should have been covered by worker's compensation plans.

The law as originally written also made no provision for Group Health Plans. If a situation occurred where an elderly or disabled person

---

[12] MMSEA Section 111 Medicare Secondary Payer Mandatory Reporting Users Guide Ver. 3.3, page 15.

[13] 42 U.S.C. §§1395 *et seq.*

[14] Pub. L. No. 89-97, 42 U.S.C. §426a.

was covered under private contracts of health insurance, how benefits were to be coordinated with Medicare became an issue. The conflict was resolved when Group Health Plans amended their private contracts of insurance to take a secondary payment position should an insured be also covered by Medicare. Congress did not anticipate this problem, which led to debate to correct this and other inequities in order to preserve the Medicare Trust Fund.

1.1.2. Medicare Secondary Payer Act (Omnibus Reconciliation Act of 1980)

On December 5, 1980, Congress passed the Medicare Secondary Payer Act. Using as a blueprint the Medicare Act's reimbursement provisions for Worker's Compensation, the law required liability Group Health Plans, Workers' Compensation, liability insurance, no-fault, and automobile liability insurance to be designated as primary payers in certain situations. Congress acted in order to preserve Medicare's financial integrity, curb skyrocketing Medicare costs, and reverse the payment order so that these insurers are primary payers where there is overlapping insurance coverage.[15] The law provided immediate relief for the Medicare Trust Fund with regard to Group Health Plans, but had little impact with regard to the Non-Group Health Plans (workers' compensation, liability, automobile liability, and no-fault). It was probably as intended because Congress itself did not believe that the savings would ever amount to much, which is why most paid no attention when it became law.[16]

In brief, the law prohibited Medicare from making payment for an item or service where the plan has paid or is reasonably expected to make payment promptly. However, Medicare was allowed to make payment *conditionally*[17] to the extent a plan has <u>not</u> made payment or was reasonably <u>not</u> expected to make payment. Furthermore, if

---

[15] *Wall v. Leavitt,* 2008 WL 4737164 (E.D. Cal.) at 10.

[16] *See* H.R. Rep.No. 96-1167, at 522 (1980).

[17] A "conditional payment" means Medicare made a payment for which another payer is claimed to be responsible. *See* 42 C.F.R. §411.52. Conditional payments are payments made for Medicare-covered services or portions of services that are not paid under other coverage that is or was primary to Medicare. *See* 42 C.F.R. §411.21.

Congress an opportunity to push for the power to require electronic reporting of claims by Primary Plans to Medicare. As a result, Section 111 of that legislation was conceived which provided enough benefit to cover the expense of the law through improved recoveries, better coordination of benefits, and penalties for non-compliance with reporting.

The MMSEA amends the Act by adding two sections to the statute — short in length but powerful in effect — imposing a specific reporting requirement for plans, otherwise characterized as primary payers. Section 111 of the Act imposes a new duty to report all settlements, awards, judgments or other payments made that involve a Medicare beneficiary. Failure to comply with the reporting requirement results in a penalty of $1,000 per day for each claim. The provision certainly got the attention of the plans, but more importantly, it provided the government a method by which to obtain perfect knowledge of all liability claims involving a Medicare beneficiary. It also helped to pay for the Act, with the Congressional Budget Office projecting revenue of $1.4 billion from fines and penalties and about $10 billion from increased recoveries over the next ten years.[25]

It is important to understand that this new obligation did not change or otherwise alter a Plan's responsibility under Act but simply imposed a new duty of reporting. The provision was added to the Act and is therefore a separate and distinct obligation under the statute. Other obligations of the Act are still in effect; it is the coupling of the new reporting requirement with the prior obligations that potentially will impact bringing finality to a liability case.

The MMSEA left the form and manner of reporting to be later determined by the Secretary of Health and Human Services ("HHS"). By virtue of HHS's division of labor, the determination falls upon CMS for implementation and enforcement. The implementation process at CMS remains ongoing at the time this book went to publication, but is sufficiently far along to understand where the problems may lie for the liability claim practitioner. We will cover Section 111 implementation issues later in this book, but it is important to note that the outcome of the implementation will be accomplished through

---

[25] See http://www.cbo.gov/ftpdocs/78xx/doc7861/m_m_schip.pdf.

program directives. This means that CMS has the power to internally control and direct the implementation of Section 111, without much say from the industry.

The Act has been a work in progress for about three decades. The MMSEA appears to provide the government with all the tools it needs to perfect its recovery efforts, but it would be foolish to believe further amendments are not forthcoming. As mentioned earlier, the government has limited options to remedy the funding problems it has for its entitlement programs. It is more likely than not that those later amendments will seek new powers to streamline the process and avoid making payment where a plan is responsible. What specific authority asked for next would be anyone's guess, but the liability industry needs its own watchdog to monitor those issues. An organization that has stepped up to serve that purpose is the Medicare Advocacy Recovery Coalition ("MARC"),[26] a grouping of interested parties and organizations that represent all sides of the industry. While the liability arena is an adversarial process, the Medicare component of it should not be treated similarly. There are no sides to Medicare, and if a party erroneously uses it as an attempt to gain advantage then finality will be elusive. The cooperation of all sides is required.

Practice Tip: The evolution of the Act has been deliberate by the government. Each step taken has increased the government's involvement in the liability case. Although Medicare is never a party to the case, the practitioner must resolve the potential claims of the government, or otherwise face new liabilities that ripen upon receipt or payment of the settlement, award, judgment or other payment. In addition to the above-mentioned statutes and case law, careful consideration must be paid to the regulations set forth in Title 42, Part 411 (See Appendix 4) that further detail liabilities and set forth requirements for compliance. Reporting is only required by a Primary Plan.

---

[26] To learn more about MARC, please visit http://www.marccocalition.com.

1.2. The Three Parts of MSP Compliance

The new reporting law took the liability industry by surprise. No longer was it possible to lay responsibility for compliance at the feet of the Medicare beneficiary or his attorney. The Primary Plan (i.e., liability insurance, no-fault, automobile insurance, including self insurance) had a responsibility to report the settlement, judgment or award electronically to Medicare. The fact that Medicare would know about the liability claims increased the Primary Plan's responsibility to be certain of compliance with all aspects of the Act. Thus, the Primary Plan was compelled to take the lead role in ensuring compliance with Medicare because it ultimately was responsible to Medicare. Also, as the potential deep pocket, the primary plan wanted to be certain its liability for the claim was complete and relying on the Medicare beneficiary to complete compliance created too many variables for claims to possibly be re-opened and litigated.

Under the Medicare Secondary Payer Act, there are three compliance buckets; Medicare reimbursement, reporting and protecting Medicare's future interest. Each requires separate attention and review and non-compliance with the law occurs if any one bucket is not considered. Not every claim will require full compliance, but every claim will require full consideration and documentation evidencing how a compliance decision was reached.

1.2.1. Reimburse Medicare

42 U.S.C. §1395y(b)(2)(ii) is the starting point of this analysis. Reimbursement is required to Medicare if it is demonstrated that a primary plan has or had a responsibility to make payment with respect to such item or service. Responsibility is demonstrated by a judgment, a payment conditioned upon a recipient's compromise, waiver or release (whether or not there is a determination or admission of liability). In short, payment in exchange for a Release, or satisfaction of judgment or award, triggers responsibility to reimburse.

Medicare is owed the money within a 60-day period which runs from the date of demand by Medicare. Thereafter, the matter is considered a debt, which may be referred to the U.S. Department of Treasury for Collection. Debt collection procedure is controlled by both the Medicare Secondary Payer Law and the Federal Debt Collection Procedure Act.[27]

Furthermore, payment by a Primary Plan to a Medicare beneficiary does not absolve it of responsibility under the law. Pursuant to 42 C.F.R. §411.24(i), Medicare may pursue the Primary Plan for recovery, even if it has already paid the Medicare beneficiary the settlement, judgment or award. The Primary Plan could pay twice for the same claim if the Medicare beneficiary does not complete the obligation owed Medicare. Should Medicare file a lawsuit, it can seek double damages. Ignoring this requirement could expose the Primary Plan to possibly paying three times for the same damages.

in addition, the Medicare beneficiary and his or her attorney is also responsible to reimburse Medicare. In order to complete this compliance bucket, the parties must lay out a process post settlement, judgment or award to ensure payment to Medicare. Of course, to identify what is owed to Medicare requires work early on in the case, and well before settlement. (See Chapter 2.)

1.2.2. Report to Medicare

After a settlement, judgment, award or other payment to a Medicare beneficiary, Medicare requires a Primary Plan to electronically report the information.[28] There are two types of information Medicare requires to complete this compliance bucket. The first situation occurs when a Primary Plan has an Ongoing Responsibility for Medicals (ORM). Medicare wants to avoid payments for medical items and services it should not have to pay for because it is covered by a claim. If there is Medical Payments coverage, or No-Fault is implicated, then Medicare requires information about the loss as soon as the determination to assume responsibility is made under law or by contract. The determination is a trigger for reporting and missing this window can result in significant penalties.

The second type of information involves lump sum payments for medicals that are alleged, claimed or otherwise released. Medicare calls this the Total Payment Obligation to the Claimant (TPOC).

---

[27] Federal Debt Collection Procedure Act 28 U.S.C. § 3001 *et seq.*
[28] 42 U.S.C. §1395y(b)(8).

direction is needed. There has been an absence of a liability industry voice in Washington D.C. to help shape its outcome. We may be too late to change the Act to be more user-friendly. However, we can possibly improve the Act to line up better with the liability claim process. CMS is given great deference because it is tasked to preserve the Medicare Trust Fund. The unfunded liability is ominous and only an overriding public policy concern will catch Congress' attention. Consequently, the mere fact that the Act will cost the liability industry more or upset our usual and customary practices pales against the mandate of CMS. Any pain felt by attorneys, insurance carriers or business entities will fall on deaf ears, and as such, change will be very slow, if it occurs at all.

Neither Congress, nor the Courts will allow Medicare to go bankrupt. Benefits must be available for beneficiaries who have qualified either through employment or disability and deference to CMS makes sense so long as the beneficiary's interest is protected. However, the Act's implementation has resulted in harm to the beneficiary. There are significant delays in delivering liability benefits to seniors and the disabled and it has had a chilling effect on their legal representation. This uncertainty will create problems for the liability industry unless clarified by the Courts or legislative changes are adopted by Congress.[39]

---

[39] The authors opine that the harm to Medicare beneficiaries has not yet been fully realized as the Act did not require Section 111 reporting until January 1, 2010. There are already delays, see Medicare won't let clients repay, lawyers say, July 10, 2009, McClatchy Newspapers. As liability cases are reported, the consequences of the Act will be felt and as the liability industry grapples with needed adjustments to the process, there will be significant delays suffered by the beneficiary. Furthermore, the volume of liability cases needed to be dealt with by the government will increase substantially and will further burden limited government resources adding to the delay.

2.1.1.   Options for the Plaintiff

Obviously, the plaintiff is in the best position to know whether he or she is a Medicare beneficiary. Upon acceptance into the Medicare program, a Medicare Card is issued. (See Appendix 6.) The card contains information that is important to complete when notifying Medicare, including the Health Identification Claim Number (HICN), the type of benefits to which the beneficiary is entitled, and the effective date of eligibility. A best practice for a liability practitioner representing a Medicare beneficiary is to inquire about this card and keep a copy on file.

If the plaintiff is not certain about his or her Medicare status, then the attorney should contact the Social Security Administration to determine status. The attorney may also want to collect a copy of the Social Security Card and obtain the appropriate consent forms (See Appendix 7) to confirm first-hand the eligibility status.[7] Again, because of the continuous obligation to identify Medicare beneficiary status, this process should be repeated frequently until the case is resolved through judgment, settlement, or award. The two most common ways to become a Medicare beneficiary are reaching the age of 65 and being on Social Security Disability Income (SSDI) for two consecutive years. If plaintiff will soon reach the age of 65 or is on SSDI then the practitioner is wise to keep an eye on beneficiary status.

If the plaintiff is aware that he or she is a Medicare beneficiary, it is appropriate to disclose that fact to the defendant or the plan handling the investigation of the liability claim. Whether private information is disclosed beyond Medicare beneficiary status, such as HICN or SSN, is a personal choice that would require adequate privacy protection for that information. However, keep in mind that if that information is not disclosed by the time of settlement, the defendant or the plan handling the investigation will not be able to complete the transaction, because the MMSEA requires the entity responsible for reporting to submit the SSN or HICN when submitting the electronic report. There is no exception to this rule.[8]

---

[7] See Social Security Administration Form OMB No. 0960-0566, at http://www.ssa.gov/ online/ssa-3288.pdf.

[8] See MMSEA Medicare Secondary Payer Mandatory Insurance Reporting User Guide Ver. 3.3, page 18.

2.1.2. Options for the Defendant

Best practice requires the liability practitioner representing the defendant to monitor the Medicare beneficiary status throughout the life of the claim. There is no good-faith exception from Section 111 penalties should there be a failure to electronically report a settlement, award, judgment, or other payment. Consequently, the liability practitioner must always be vigilant and continue to ask the Claimant about Medicare status. Of course, the best way to recognize a Medicare beneficiary is by age. If a claimant is 65 or older, then he or she is very likely to be receiving Medicare. However, 15% of the current Medicare population is under 65 and falls into one of the three following categories:

- Receipt of SSDI for 24 consecutive months;
- Receipt of SSDI for 1 month to pay for amyotrophic lateral sclerosis (ALS or Lou Gehrig's disease);
- Receipt of treatment for End-Stage renal disease (ESRD) or kidney failure.

Therefore, to be certain, a best practice would be to take advantage of Medicare's query process. This procedure is available to a plan registered as a Responsible Reporting Entity ("RRE"). The RRE may submit certain data fields about a potential Medicare beneficiary or beneficiaries once per calendar month. Medicare will return a response file to the RRE within 14 days. The response file advises if there is a match and in addition to updating any contact information will provide the HICN to the RRE. It is important to recognize that the HICN may only be used in connection with MMSEA Section 111 reporting and for no other reason, unless consent is provided by the Medicare beneficiary.[9]

---

[9] According to the Data Use Agreement, "Proper safeguards shall include the adoption of policies and procedures to ensure that the data obtained shall be used solely in accordance with Section 1106 of the Social Security Act [42 U.S.C. § 1306], Section 1874(b) of the Social Security Act [42 U.S.C. § 1395k(b)], Section 1862(b) of the Social Security Act [42 U.S.C. § 1395y(b)], and the Privacy Act of 1974, as amended [5 U.S.C. § 552a] MMSEA Section 111 Medicare Secondary Payer Mandatory Reporting Liability User Guide at p. 79.

contractor understand the process and regularly checks the contractor's website for further updates.[15]

The MSPRC has established a website that is helpful for the liability practitioner. A key feature of the site is the ability to schedule a call with the MSPRC to discuss a Medicare reimbursement claim. This feature will become more popular now that electronic reporting of ORM started on January 1, 2010 and settlement, awards, judgments, and other payments began on January 1, 2012. The added workload without increase in staff and budget will require greater organization. Scheduled calls will allow both the liability practitioner and the MSPRC service provider to better organize their time. The website is located at http://www.msprc.info.

The navigation page is a wealth of information. MSPRC issues a number of letters, and this site will help explain them to the liability practitioner. The site also provides help with regard to an overview of the process and FAQs. This improves communication and allows for smoother claims administration.

The MSPRC is located in Oklahoma City, Oklahoma and employs about 200 people. All written documentation sent into the MSPRC is received by their mail center located in Detroit. The mail center is responsible for imaging the written communication so it can be accessed by the MSPRC online at the call center in Oklahoma City. The MSPRC website also provides alerts to the liability practitioner to notify of any changes to policy and procedure. Additional helpful links,

---

[15] http://www.msprc.info.

tutorials, and other resources are provided to improve awareness of Medicare Secondary Payer requirements.

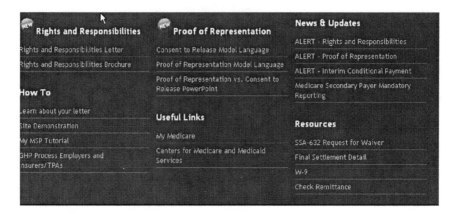

2.3.2.   Lifecycle of the Conditional Payment Letter

Approximately two business days after the COBC is aware of a potential liability claim, the information is transitioned to the MSPRC for reimbursement claim processing. This transition is a potential fail point in the process and needs to be monitored. To do so, call the COBC at 1.800.999.1118, a week after making it aware of the claim, to confirm a proper handoff to the MSPRC.

After three weeks of making the COBC aware of the claim, the MSPRC will issue a Rights & Responsibilities Letter to the Medicare beneficiary. (See Rights & Responsibilities Letter, Appendix 15.) This letter will always go to the beneficiary, and will be copied to the Beneficiary's attorney.[16] The Primary Plan or defendants will not receive a copy of this letter unless the Medicare beneficiary has provided consent and said form has been faxed into the MSPRC at 405.869.3309. (Medicare Consent Form, Appendix 16.) When faxing any information to the MSPRC always use the MSPRC Coversheet and check the

---

[16] The Medicare beneficiary's attorney is copied on the Rights & Responsibilities Letter if Medicare is aware of the representation through the COBC. For the attorney to receive further information from Medicare a Proof of Representation Letter must be submitted. (See Proof of Representation Letter, Appendix 18.)

applicable box. Using the MSPRC Coversheet directs information into the correct file. (See MSPRC Coversheet, Appendix 17.)

If the liability practitioner plans to discuss the Medicare beneficiary liability claim with the MSPRC (two-way communication), then an executed proof of representation document (See Appendix 18) is needed in addition to the consent form. In this document, the Medicare beneficiary has authorized the individual or entity (including an attorney) to act on the beneficiary's behalf, but the authorized representative has no independent standing. The representative may receive or submit information/requests, including responding to requests from the MSPRC, receiving a copy of recovery demand letter, and filing an appeal. A proper proof of representation must include:

- Name of Medicare beneficiary AS SHOWN ON Medicare card;
- HICN;
- Written appointment of the representative in writing;
- Specify the following information for the representative:
  - o Name,
  - o Type of representative (attorney, non-attorney, guardian, etc.),
  - o Firm/Company name if applicable,
  - o Address, and
  - o Telephone number
- Signature of the Medicare beneficiary; and
- Date of the appointment.

There are two important pieces of information on the Rights & Responsibilities Letter: 1) Date of Letter; and 2) MSPRC Case ID #. The assumption at this point is the Medicare beneficiary HICN is already available to the parties. The date is important because the MSPRC under its agreement with CMS has agreed to certain performance metrics. One of these metrics is to produce the Conditional Payment Letter within 65 days from the date of the Rights & Responsibilities Letter. If the Rights & Responsibilities Letter date is known, then the outside timeframe can be calculated as to when to expect the Conditional Payment Letter. Knowing the MSPRC Case ID# allows the parties to make a phone system inquiry regarding the status and amount of the CPL without speaking to a live operator. This process saves time.

2.3.2.1. ReMAS

Recovery Management and Accounting System (ReMAS) identifies mistaken Medicare primary payments. It replaced and merged several contractor and CMS systems into one centralized database. While ReMAS is researching the centralized database to identify those conditional payments, the case is completely outside the control of the MSPRC or the CMS Regional Office.

Medicare does not generally make a primary payment if it should be the secondary payer, and it is aware that the insurance obligated to pay before Medicare is available. If Medicare makes a mistaken primary payment in such a situation, Medicare pursues recovery of the mistaken primary payment from an appropriate party. ReMAS will identify these mistaken payments so that recovery can be initiated from the party that should have paid first. ReMAS will be replacing several contractor systems, as well as CMS systems, in order to integrate the identification of mistaken MSP overpayments into a centralized database. ReMAS depends on an interface with CWF to receive notification of beneficiaries that had insurance coverage primary to Medicare.

Once MSPRC receives an alert that ReMAS has pulled all related claims, the MSPRC staff will review the information, compare it to the actual claims, and prepare the Conditional Payment Letter. ReMAS works only if it receives notice of MSP situations, it will need to receive HUSC records from each CWF host on a daily basis. All CWF hosts will need to transmit HUSC records to ReMAS for every HUSP record that gets accepted in CWF. CWF will send these records to ReMAS using contractor number 11200. All files from each CWF host should be sent to the CMS Data Center through the CMS mainframe telecommunication information system (MTIS) process, to a data set name that will be defined at a later date.

2.3.3. Conditional Payment Letter

MSRPC will issue the Conditional Payment Letter (See Appendix 19) to the Medicare beneficiary and anyone else to whom the Beneficiary has issued Medicare Consent or other valid authorization (e.g., Proof of Representation). The Conditional Payment Letter is an estimate and parties should refrain from making any payment to Medicare based on it. The letter is stale after 90 days. There are a number of ways to secure an update of the Conditional Payment Letter prior to a settlement.

Attached to the conditional payment letter will be the Payment Summary Form (PSF). (See Appendix 20.) The fields contained on the PSF include:

- Type of Service (TOS)
- Internal Control Number (ICN)[17]
- Claim Line #
- Processing Contractor
- Provider Name
- Diagnosis Codes
- From Date
- To Date
- Total Charges
- Reimbursed Amounts; and
- Conditional Payment

---

[17] All Medicare claims are assigned a unique 14 digit ICN (sometimes known as claim control number (CCN)) to identify how, when, and where the claim was received. The ICN is used to track and monitor all claims submitted to Medicare. Depending on how the claim was submitted, electronically or on paper, the ICN indicates the region, method of claim submission, or if the claim was electronically transferred from another carrier, the year the claim was submitted, and the date Medicare received the claim. The first six digits reflect when the claim was received. The first digit is a century code ("2" indicates 2000 and after). The second two digits indicate the last two digits of the year the claim was received. The next three digits indicate the day of the year the claim was submitted, out of 365 days or 366 in a leap year. The last eight digits are a unique set of numbers representing internal batch and sequence numbers assigned to the claims received on a particular day by each Medicare contractor. Finally, the last digit of the ICN indicates whether the claim is an initial claim or an adjusted claim. If the last digit is 1 or higher, the claim has been adjusted. For example, a claim with ICN number 2 02 053 02000001 would have been received on February 22, 2002. It was an adjusted claim. With this information, providers can refer back to the claim submission summaries or confirmations to determine the source of the duplicate problem.

2.3.3.1. Using MyMedicare

After the Conditional Payment Letter is issued, it is also populated to MyMedicare.gov. To access this information, the Medicare beneficiary must first sign up at the website: http://www.mymedicare.gov.[18] The information contained on this site goes beyond reimbursement claim information, as it allows the Medicare beneficiary to manage their entire Medicare portfolio. However, if parties need to up-to-date conditional payment information for settlement purposes this may be a quick way to obtain it.

The MyMedicare website is structured into several areas. These areas are available by using the navigation menu located under the My Medicare banner. Additional buttons may appear, depending on the beneficiary.

The "My MSP" tab is only visible if/when the beneficiary has claims subject to recovery efforts. This area contains the conditional payment information about the specific case.

---

[18] To learn more about how to sign-up for mymedicare.gov, the Medicare beneficiary or their representative can visit http://www.msprc.info and click [tutorial].

seeking the adjustments. (See Appendix 22.) If done correctly, the MSPRC will respond within 30 to 45 days by issuing an adjusted Conditional Payment Letter. Again, do not attempt to pay the reimbursement claim. This will delay further processing. Rather, commence negotiations to resolve the case or seek out alternative dispute resolution programs to achieve resolution. The parties' best estimate of the exposure to Medicare is based on the last PSF received, but, as time passes, Medicare could incur additional charges for other medical items or services. As such, the conditional payment demand is a moving target. Call the MSPRC at 866.677.7220 after 45 days to follow-up if the corrected CPL has not issued. If the outcome is not acceptable, consider an appeal. (See Chapter 5.)

The Plan is not liable under the Act before settlement is reached between the settling parties or before a court renders a judgment, as there is no overpayment. Medicare's claim comes into existence by operation of law[22] when the plan makes payments for medical expenses for which Medicare has conditionally paid. Consequently, while Medicare may alert beneficiaries and their attorneys of Medicare's right to recover settlement proceeds in pre-settlement correspondence, no demand for recovery may be made until a settlement or other disposition of the liability claim has been reached.[23]

The CPL will automatically issue to the Medicare beneficiary and any authorized plan or entity (*i.e.*, executed Consent Form in place) within 65 days from the Rights and Responsibilities letter. There is no need to make a request for the conditional payment letter, as the separate requests for initial Conditional Payment Amounts will not make Conditional Payment information available sooner. However, keep in mind that the liability practitioner will not receive a copy of the conditional payment letter if no Consent Form has been submitted to Medicare.

Attached to the conditional payment letter will be the PSF. (See Appendix 20.) The fields contained on the PSF include:

---

[22] 42 U.S.C. §1395y(b)(2)(B)(ii).
[23] The authors are aware that this procedural requirement is counter-intuitive. Welcome to the Medicare bureaucracy!

- Type of Service (TOS)
- Internal Control Number (ICN)[24]
- Claim Line #
- Processing Contractor
- Provider Name
- Diagnosis Codes
- From Date
- To Date
- Total Charges
- Reimbursed Amounts ; and
- Conditional Payment

2.4.   The Medicare Demand Letter

Once relatedness issues are out of the way, the next step is to resolve the liability case. This is counterintuitive, but there is no method under the law to further dispute the conditional payments until a demand/ recovery letter is issued. (See Appendix 23.) Such letters will only be issued after the MSPRC is notified of the resolution of the liability case, usually within 14 days. The demand/recovery letter is considered an initial determination by Medicare that is subject to administrative review and appeal. The liability practitioner has 60 days to request a review or appeal; otherwise all further recourse is waived and the amount is final. Interest will be assessed at 11% 60 days after the letter

---

[24] All Medicare claims are assigned a unique 14 digit ICN (sometimes known as claim control number (CCN)) to identify how, when and where the claim was received. The ICN is used to track and monitor all claims submitted to Medicare. Depending on how the claim was submitted, electronically or on paper, the ICN indicates the region, method of claim submission or if the claim was electronically transferred from another carrier, the year the claim was submitted, and the date Medicare received the claim.

The first six digits reflect when the claim was received. The first digit is a century code ("2" indicates 2000 and after). The second two digits indicate the last two digits of the year the claim was received. The next three digits indicate the day of the year the claim was submitted, out of 365 days or 366 in a leap year. The last eight digits are a unique set of numbers representing internal batch and sequence numbers assigned to the claims received on a particular day by each Medicare contractor. Finally, the last digit of the ICN indicates whether the claim is an initial claim or an adjusted claim. If the last digit is 1 or higher, the claim has been adjusted. For example, a claim with ICN number 2 02 053 02000001 would have been received on February 22, 2002. It was an adjusted claim. With this information, providers can refer back to the claim submission summaries or confirmations to determine the source of the duplicate problem.

is issued. Furthermore, the MSPRC will begin the process to refer the matter over to the Department of Treasury for collection. A best practice for the liability practitioner is to pay the MSPRC the money it demands before the expiration of 60 days. If the liability practitioner is successful with the review or appeal, then Medicare will reimburse the beneficiary the disputed amount.

There is nothing final about the demand/recovery letter. Some Health care providers have up to 27 months to bill Medicare for services, and some may elect to not bill Medicare and pursue a recovery directly with the Medicare beneficiary or Primary Plan.[25] If Medicare receives additional billing related to the liability claim for items and services that pre-date the accident, it will attempt to recover those payments. Therefore, it is a best practice to carefully review all medical billing records related to the liability claim and, if there is a discrepancy between those records and what Medicare has issued in its demand/recovery letter, the parties should plan on protecting those funds. If not, Medicare may later make a subsequent demand that will need to be paid. More than likely, if the funds are not available, the Plan or entity may be asked to pay if the beneficiary cannot. As such, the risk of loss for this event should be covered within the settlement documents to minimize these unintended consequences.

The liability practitioner can continue to evaluate whether the demanded amount is accurate. Attached to the demand letter is a PSF, and relatedness issues should be raised and addressed in the same manner as discussed earlier. If the liability practitioner acts quickly, an updated demand/recovery letter could be issued before the 60 days expire. Obviously, if this process takes more than 60 days it is wise to pay the demanded amount to Medicare before pressing on with the dispute. If there are no issues of relatedness, the liability practitioner has several choices. He or she can either pay the demand amount and finalize the case or decide to file an appeal or request waiver under the Sections 1862(b) or 1870(c) of the Social Security Act. Additionally, he or she could simultaneously seek compromise under the Federal Claims Collection Act.[26]

---

[25] *See Medicare Secondary Payer Manual, Chapter 2, Section 40.2.*

[26] If Medicare's conditional payments are more than $100,000 and the Medicare beneficiary also wishes to compromise its recovery under the Federal Claims Collection

If the request for Demand Letter is made before any Conditional Payment Letter is issued, the MSPRC will issue a Conditional Payment Notice. (See Appendix 24.) The notice is like a Conditional Payment Letter, but different in that it will automatically convert to a Demand Letter in 30 days unless a party disputes or otherwise objects to it. If the parties agree to the Conditional Payment Notice they can reach out to the MSPRC and so advise to allow the immediate issuance of a Demand Letter. Medicare will consider the charges for items and services agreeable if accepted. Remember, it is more difficult to challenge unrelated charges after settlement than before, so a careful review is suggested.

2.5. Exceptional Situations

2.5.1.   Settlement Less than or Equal to $300

If no request for a Demand Amount Letter has been made and the liability claim is resolved for less than or equal to $300, no further action is required with regard to conditional payment reimbursement. This only applies to claims that do not involve implantation, ingestion, or exposure. See www.msprc.info.

2.5.2.   Fixed Payment Option Elected

Where Plaintiff has elected to accept the Fixed Payment Option, then no further action with regard to reimburse conditional payment compliance. Again, the claim cannot involve ingestion, implantation, or an exposure loss, and the settlement value cannot exceed $5,000. The Medicare beneficiary must elect and the money and election form is to be mailed to Medicare at:

MSPRC Fixed Percentage
PO Box 138880
Oklahoma City, OK 73113

Act provisions of 31 U.S.C. §3711, the case must be referred to CMS' Central Office who then forwards the matter to the Department of Justice.

liability industry was felt immediately, though actual reporting did not start until January 1, 2012. Hefty penalties for non-compliance renewed interest in overall industry compliance with the Medicare Secondary Payer Act. However, this particular aspect of compliance only applies to certain Primary Plans (insurance carriers and those that self insure). Furthermore, the Medicare beneficiary or their attorneys are not responsible for reporting, nor required to cooperate with the Primary Plan. Medicare is well aware of this issue and has attempted to help the Primary Plan to assist in collection of the required Social Security Number and or Medicare Number through Memoranda and development of forms. (See CMS Affidavit (Appendix 26) and CMS Memorandum Regarding Providing Social Security Numbers (Appendix 27)). Nonetheless, challenges remain in the process of determining whether a claimant is a Medicare beneficiary.

This reporting rule does not eliminate any existing statutory provisions for the Primary Plan.[5] It is a separate and distinct compliance bucket that the Primary Plan must meet. Only *certain* Primary Plans are required to electronically report information to Medicare. These Primary Plans are designated by Medicare as Responsible Reporting Entities (RRE). It is the Primary Plan's responsibility to determine if it is also an RRE. CMS has developed a website[6] to assist the RRE in making that evaluation, but there is not a safe harbor. Extra due diligence is required and where in doubt, it would be the author's recommendation to register.

The CMS website provides helpful information for compliance. The latest version of the Medicare & Medicaid SCHIP Extension Act Mandatory Insurance Reporting Manual is available at the website. The site also contains CMS Town Hall Transcripts which detail answers to commonly asked Industry compliance questions. Also available are CMS Alerts and requests for public comment, as Congress authorized Medicare to implement the mandatory reporting program through program directive and memorandum. No regulations are required; however, CMS will take constructive feedback about improvements for

---

[5] For example, CMS' process for self-identifying pending liability insurance claims to the Coordination of Benefits Contractor (42 C.F.R. §411.25(a)) remain applicable.

[6] http://www.cms.hhs.gov/MandatoryInsRep/

electronic reporting at: PL110-173SEC111-comments@cms.hhs.gov. No response will be provided, but CMS has advised that it will respond through improved process or during CMS Town Hall Conference Calls.

There are a couple of additional and important points to share on this topic. The query process made available by Medicare is a tool to help the Primary Plan identify Medicare beneficiary status. A successful match by this tool, identifying a claimant as a Medicare beneficiary, does not satisfy the Section 111 reporting obligation. Furthermore, identifying a claim to Medicare under Chapter 2 to secure a conditional payment letter does not relieve the Primary Plan of its electronic reporting obligation. Mistaken assumptions by the Primary Plan in either situation could lead to penalties for failure to report presently set at $1,000 per day for each claim. It is important to train claim staff on this important nuance.

3.1. Responsible Reporting Entity

Medicare initially designated all Primary Plans as Responsible Reporting Entities, but because of innumerable risk transfer arrangements that exist within the industry, processing the registration of each became overly burdensome. On February 24, 2010, Medicare scaled back its original definition by Memorandum.[7] Subsequent versions of the applicable User Guide have remained consistent, and it is the authors' opinion that it will not change in the near term. Nonetheless, Medicare has not covered every risk management program that may potentially cover the settlement, judgment, or award of a liability claim and gaps remain. Again, if in doubt, register. To summarize, the following are Primary Plans that should register as an RRE.

3.1.1. Insurance Carriers

An insurance carrier is the RRE under the Act. If the policy has a deductible, it is irrelevant whether the insured pays it. For electronic reporting, the insurance carrier reports and its insured do not. There are

---

[7] See alert issued February 24, 2010, ALERT for Liability Insurance (Including Self-Insurance), No-Fault Insurance, and Workers' Compensation: WHO MUST REPORT at page 6.

two exceptions: 1) where the insurance policy is what the industry terms a "fronting policy" and the insured pays the claim; or 2) where the insured resolves the liability case without recourse to its insurance. If either of those situations applies, the insurance carrier is not the RRE.

3.1.2. Self Insured

A self insured is a plan under which an individual, or a private or governmental entity, carries its own risk, whether by failure to obtain insurance or otherwise – in whole or by part.[8] If an individual carries a self insured retention, or goes without insurance coverage for a particular business, trade, or profession which may give rise to a liability claim, that entity is deemed to have self insurance and must register as an RRE. If a self insured should go bankrupt, it does not eliminate their responsibility as n RRE, where a settlement, judgment, or award is paid after approval by the court.[9] Should an insured act without recourse to its insurance, it is also deemed a self insured and, therefore, an RRE.[10]

Fronting policy situations does not equate to the level of insurance for purposes of being an RRE. Medicare believes the expectation of both the insured and insurer is that the insured will retain the ultimate risk. Where the insured pays the claim, the insured is the RRE. However, where the insurance carrier pays it, and is later reimbursed by the insured, the insurance carrier is the RRE.

If self insured claims are managed by a Captive insurance carrier, such carrier cannot be the RRE. Only the parent of the Captive carrier is allowed to be the RRE, which no doubt will cause debates amongst Captive carriers that carry risk beyond that of their parent. For example, what happens when a Captive provides personal lines coverage (e.g., home, life, auto) for employees of the parent? The Captive is the carrier on the risk, yet for reporting purposes the parent is responsible for electronic reporting. In some jurisdictions, the action involving the parent could be sufficient to breach the corporate veil to invoke

---

[8] *See* 42 C.F.R. §411.50.

[9] *See MMSEA Section 111 Medicare Secondary Payer Mandatory Reporting, Ver. 3.3, page 23.*

[10] *See MMSEA Section 111 Medicare Secondary Payer Mandatory Reporting Ver. 3.3, page 24.*

additional liability on the parent. As such, the current definition may have a "chilling effect" on what work captives may take on in the future.

Multi-Nationals Organizations, Foreign Nations, American Indian and Alaskan Native Tribes are self insured for RRE purposes, if they carry on liability insurance.[11]

3.1.3. Re-Insurance, Stop Loss Insurance, Excess Insurance, Umbrella Insurance, etc.

The test for RRE status in any of these situations is whether the payment is made direct to the claimant or if it is being reimbursed to the self insured. Where reimbursed the self insured remains the RRE.[12]

3.1.4. Self-Insured Pools

The RRE is the self-insured pool when all three characteristics are met: 1) The pool is a separate legal entity; 2) The pool has full responsibility to resolve and pay claims using pool funds; and 3) Claims are paid without review or approval authority by the participating self-insured entity. If any of these characteristics are not met, then the member of the self-insured pool is the RRE.[13] An important exception is where a statute authorizes the establishment of a self-insurance pool and requires such pool to be licensed and regulated in the same manner as a liability insurance carrier.

3.1.5. State Agency

Where a State Agency has review or approval authority, which has the ability to affect the payment or other terms of the settlement, judgment, award or other payment, then the State is the RRE, whether or not it has insurance.[14]

---

[11] *See MMSEA Section 111 Medicare Secondary Payer Mandatory Reporting Ver. 3.3, page 27.*

[12] *See MMSEA Section 111 Medicare Secondary Payer Mandatory Reporting Ver. 3.3, page 24.*

[13] *See MMSEA Section 111 Medicare Secondary Payer Mandatory Reporting Ver. 3.3, page 27.*

[14] *See MMSEA Section 111 Medicare Secondary Payer Mandatory Reporting Ver. 3.3, page 28.*

WHAT AND WHEN TO REPORT TO MEDICARE

3.2.   Section 111 Compliance

3.2.1.   Registration

If an entity determines it is an RRE, the first step to compliance is registration. It is recommended to first pencil-out the information required before logging into the Medicare contractor's website to begin registration. Here is a suggested checklist for a potential RRE to consider.

- ✓ What company in your organization is responsible for your claims? Many RREs have a number of subsidiaries. Will a subsidiary be the RRE or the parent? Are claims being handled by different subsidiaries and therefore is more than one RRE ID needed?
- ✓ Collect Company's Tax ID# to be assigned to the RRE;
- ✓ Identify the Account Representative, Account Manager and Account designees;
- ✓ Determine who will report – direct or by agent;
- ✓ Determine how files will be submitted; and
- ✓ Determine method of transmission

Once this information is collected, you can begin the process on the Internet by going to the following URL: *www.Section111cms.hhs.gov.* Once on this site you will be able to: 1) Complete the registration process; 2) Obtain login IDs and assign users; 3) Exchange files via HTTPS or SFTP; 4) View and update Section 111 reporting account profile info; 5) View status of current file processing; 6) View statistics related to previous file submission; and 7) View statistics related to compliance.

Before getting too far into this new website, you must complete the registration process which contains two steps: 1) Obtaining the RRE ID# and 2) Executing the profile report which includes execution of a voluntary data-sharing agreement. Once these two steps are complete you are ready to review CMS file specs, develop the software to produce Section 111 files, and be scheduled a date for quarterly submission. If you are using an agent to handle the data exchange to CMS, then the software development may not be an issue. If you are using a TPA then the TPA may already have this bridge in place with CMS and you will simply have to authorize the connection. If you self administer or have otherwise a stand-alone claims operation, and have not gone through this process, your claims administration software will require modification to produce the information being required by CMS; or you may have to retain a third party reporting vendor that will process the information with Medicare and upload it back into your system.

If fully prepared for registration then you should be able to obtain your profile report by following the registration steps outlined on the website. You will be mailed your profile report and it must be signed by the Account Representative, which is a person within the RRE that has the authority to bind the entity under contract. Pay careful attention to the profile report that will be submitted via mail, as it will include the voluntary data sharing agreement that will bind your company. You may want to review this sharing agreement with counsel to understand the implications of its execution for your Company. If you agree with the profile report, execute it and return it to the Medicare contractor. Upon receipt, the Account Representative designated by you will be given access to the website and can complete the registration process. Registration is complete only after the profile report is executed and received by the Medicare contractor. As of January 2012, the RRE's profile report will be e-mailed to the Authorized Representative annually, based upon the receipt date of the last signed profile report. The Account Manager will be copied on this e-mail. The Authorized Representative must return a signed copy of the report. If the profile is not returned in a timely manner, Medicare may deactivate the RRE ID.

Any changes because of cessation in company business or transition of reporting because of change in reporting structure, requires notification to Medicare. The transition of reporting responsibility from one RRE to another is the responsibility of the RREs involved. The new RRE may update and delete records previously submitted by the former RRE, under a different RRE ID, as long as the key fields for the records match.

3.2.2. Testing and Claim Data Submission Time Frames

Medicare has defined Section 111 Compliance as 1) Registration; 2) Testing; and 3) Ongoing claim submission. (See CMS Memorandum – NGHP RRE Compliance: Alert for Liability Insurance (Including Self-Insurance), No-Fault Insurance, and Workers' Compensation – dated February 24, 2010 (See Appendix 28). After registration, the next step concerns submitting certain claims information to Medicare. This process may be accomplished manually through input of individual claims into the COBSW Website (https://www.section111.cms.hhs.gov/MRA/LoginWarning.action); or electronically. If the latter is the desired method, the RRE may decide to program its claim system to communicate directly with Medicare or use a third party reporting vendor that specializes in this area.

Medicare assigns an Electronic Data Information Representative (EDI) to each RRE or its designated representative. The EDI is an employee of the Coordination Benefits Contractor (COBC). Medicare has designated the COBC to receive the data and upload it into a database known as the Common Working File. The Common Working File is the master record database that is used to coordinate benefits between Medicare and other plans. To determine whether Medicare is entitled to any recoveries related to the submitted information, the COBC will transmit information it receives to the Medicare Secondary Payer Recovery Contractor (MSPRC). The MSPRC will be responsible for generating any demand notices based on a judgment, settlement, or other payment.

Once the RRE claims system is able to communicate with Medicare, each RRE is assigned a quarterly Claim Input file submission time frame. Each three-month calendar quarter of the year is divided into 12 submission periods as shown in the chart below. For example, if the RRE is assigned to Group 7, the Claim Input file is due from the 15th through the 21st calendar day of the second month of each calendar year quarter; February 15th and February 21st for the first quarter, May 15th and May 21st for the second quarter, August 15th and August 21st for the third quarter, and November 15th and November 21st for the fourth quarter of each year.

Quarterly Claim Input File Submission Time Frames

Dates	1st Month	2nd Month	3rd Month
01 – 07	Group 1	Group 5	Group 9
08 – 14	Group 2	Group 6	Group 10
15 – 21	Group 3	Group 7	Group 11
22 – 28	Group 4	Group 8	Group 12

Quarterly Claim Input Files must include records for any new claims, where the injured party is a Medicare beneficiary, reflecting settlement, judgment, award, or other payment since the last file submission. The file submission date is based on the RRE assigned reporting window period. To avoid potential penalties, the submission date should be published to the liability adjuster. If a trigger event occurs, then information must be ready for reporting. The liability adjuster should be integrally involved with reporting because they have ready access and knowledge about critical pieces requested from Medicare.

Settlement, judgment, award, or other payment data must be ready within 45 days prior to the start of the 7-day file submission time frame. This allows the RRE a grace period to process the newly addressed/ resolved (partially addressed/resolved) claim information internally, prior to submission for Section 111. For example, if there is a reportable TPOC with a TPOC Date of May 1, 2011, and the file submission period for the second calendar quarter of 2011 is June 1-7, 2011, then the RRE may delay reporting that claim until the third calendar quarter file submission during September 1-7, 2011. However, if the TPOC Date is April 1, 2011, then the RRE must include this claim on the second calendar quarter file submission during June 1-7, 2011. Records not received in time will be processed, but marked as late and used for subsequent compliance tracking. A code indicating a late submission was received will be placed in the first available Compliance Flag (Fields 38 – 47) of the corresponding Claim Response File Detail Record.[15]

3.2.3.   What Type of Information to Report

Medicare requires two types of data for reporting under MSP – Ongoing Responsibility for Medical (ORM) and Total Payment Obligation to Claimant (TPOC). Both TPOC and ORM reporting allows Medicare to coordinate its benefits with the responsible Plan. When an RRE reports ORM it is advising Medicare that it is a Plan with primary responsibility for medical payments related to a particular claim. TPOC involves reporting to Medicare lump sum settlements, judgments or awards

---

[15] *See MMSEA Section 111 Medicare Secondary Payer Mandatory Reporting User Guide, Ver. 3.3, page 128* For additional information on compliance flags.

Specific fields to pay careful attention to are:

- TPOC Amount

  The general rule is the TPOC Amount is equal to the settlement amount. However, there are a few key exceptions: 1) If an annuity is part of the settlement, the TPOC Amount is any lump sum payment made to the Claimant plus the expected payout of the annuity; 2) If there are other settling parties, and the liability of such parties are joint and several, then the TPOC Amount is the total paid by all parties; 3) If there are layers of self insurance and insurance involved for a particular insured (assuming no other co-defendants with joint and several liability), then the TPOC Amount is what is paid by each paying entity. Recall that deductibles are included by the insurer as part of the TPOC Amount, unless the insured acted without recourse to his insurance. Furthermore, if a case is on appeal, whether there is a TPOC amount depends on whether a payment is or is not being made prior to the determination of the appeal.

- TPOC Date

  The date of the settlement agreement is generally the TPOC Date. If court approval is required then it is the date of the court approval or date set by the court to execute documents. If there is no settlement agreement or court involvement, the date of the check is the TPOC date. Reliance on the check date is risky in the authors' opinion as a general trigger for a RRE. The liability adjuster needs to record the settlement date or court approval date.

- CMS Date of Incident

  For liability claims not involving implantation (e.g., medical devices such as a pacemaker); ingestion (e.g., pharmaceuticals); or exposure (e.g., asbestos), then it is the industry date of loss. In its desire to preserve funding, Medicare requires a date of loss (whether or not the claimant is aware of the injury) to increase its recoveries.

- ICD-9 Codes

  These are International Classification of Disease Codes, version 9, issued by the World Health Organization. These are different from treating codes and it is best to match such codes with those reported on the Medicare Final Demand Letter, or accepted conditional payment letter, to mitigate future recovery letters from Medicare. Medicare has identified certain codes not to be used for reporting.[24] Where there is no injury, but medical specials are released (e.g., loss of consortium, wrongful termination, etc.) The RRE is to fill in the ICD-9 Code with the following: NOINJ. Medicare will eventually move to ICD-10 codes. Presently, such conversion is scheduled for October 1, 2014, but that date may not be firm, as it is a significant undertaking.

  The correct use of ICD-9 codes involves understanding the various classifications and sub-classes. This standard classification system guideline requires that the first code listed on the billing document should apply to the primary diagnosis or condition that was treated during the medical visit. The ICD-9 code structure is broken down into 18 categories, or codes, with a sub-classification contained within each structure to further specify diagnosis. Understand the code structures. They are 100-139 for infectious diseases, 140-239 for neoplasms, 240-279 for endocrine, metabolic and immunity disorders, 280-289 for blood-based diseases, 290-319 for mental disorders, 320-389 for nervous system, 390-459 for circulatory system, 460-519 for respiratory system, 520-579 for digestive system, 580-629 for genitourinary system, 630-677 for pregnancy, 680-709 for skin diseases, 710-739 for musculoskeletal systems, 740-759 for congenital conditions, 760-779 for prenatal conditions, 780-799 for miscellaneous otherwise undefined conditions and 800-999 for injury and poisoning.

---

[24] https://www.section111.cms.hhs.gov/MRA/help/nghp/icd9.htm

The ICD-9 diagnosis codes do not distinguish the left or right side of the body. This is an unfortunate drawback and a potential pitfall for the liability practitioner. As the reporting of ICD-9 diagnosis codes could impact the future Medicare benefits of the claimant, care should be exercised in being as accurate as possible. To the extent the ICD-9 diagnosis code is not sufficient to pinpoint the injury, add an additional narrative to identify specific body location. To be as complete as possible, the liability practitioner may want to review medical bills that may contain ICD-9 codes or retain a nurse to assist in proper identification. Acceptable ICD-9 diagnosis codes may be found at CMS website and is updated once per year.[25]

- Event Codes

  These codes are part of the ICD-9 codes. It describes the cause of the accident (e.g., slip and fall, product defect, auto accident).

- Claimant Attorney Info

  It is important that the attorney's information is accurate. Medicare usually directs recovery action letters to the Medicare beneficiary and will copy the attorney on record. Updating this information will make certain the intended communications are received.

3.2.4.   Special Circumstances

3.2.4.1.   Reporting Mass Torts

Medicare has, for the interim, elected to suspend the requirement by mass tort defendants to report information about settlements, judgments, awards or other payments to Medicare beneficiaries. Implementation of this reporting requirement has been a logistical headache for the agency because of the wording of the statute and the practical aspect of how such claims are resolved. The problem is that mass tort payers may never know who the ultimate recipients are.

---

[25] www.cms.hhs.gov/ICD9ProviderDiagnosticCodes/07_summarytables.asp#TopOfPage

Generally, settlements are paid into a fund managed by the class action's legal representative or a designated third party. Over time, several years, the funds are distributed based on injuries and as parties come forward. CMS's last attempt to require the RRE to report as soon as a Medicare beneficiary was identified was thought to be too burdensome, and Medicare's announcement that it would re-evaluate the process is the right step.

A possible solution the authors would suggest is to have the Court order the established Fund to be the RRE for purposes of Section 111 reporting. The Fund is in the best position to identify claimants and Medicare beneficiary status. At time of distribution it could electronically report this information as systems set up to track and make payment are as sophisticated as any claims system. This process would be like an RRE that has transitioned its reporting responsibility to another, albeit only partially. There is at least one U.S. Dist. Court case where the Court has taken upon itself to determine if a particular plan is an RRE. In *Oregon State Bar Professional Liability Fund vs. U.S. Department of Health and Human Services, 2012 U.S. Dist. LEXIS 43790,* the Court had to decide whether malpractice insurance was the type of liability insurance to be covered for reporting purposes under the MSP law. The court found that such insurance was for replacement of economic damages, not for medical items and services, and found against Medicare. The takeaway is that even though Congress authorized Medicare to implement Section 111 through program memo or directive, such power is not unlimited. A Court in the appropriate case has the authority to determine otherwise. It may be a case worth looking at by Medicare as a way to shape the mass tort reporting process. If the purpose of MSP reporting is to make Medicare aware of all settlements, judgments or awards, would not an order by a Court authorizing the fund to be an RRE achieve that result?

3.2.4.2. Third-Party Administrators

Finally, we would be remiss if we did not include a discussion about the RRE and the role of the Third Party Administrators (TPA). CMS will not allow a TPA to be the RRE. This decision has unfortunately added to the complexity of the process, as those entities that administer a significant portion of the universe of claims do not have control over the reporting. Medicare's decision in this regard has resulted in a lot of energy, effort, and time to educate the RRE that is not involved in the day-to-day process of liability claims. Some of these entities, usually smaller accounts, do not usually get involved with liability cases on a day-to-day basis, so there has been a great deal of surprise over the law. This is because the RRE must comply with the electronic process whether it has one case or many cases. Not allowing the TPA to be the RRE in certain situations has led to thousands of RRE IDs being registered with CMS. Not surprisingly, significant database sizing issues have been encountered.

In recognition of this problem, Medicare has updated its recent User Guide to allow for an improved flow of information to the TPA. If authorized by the RRE, the TPA will automatically receive any information previously directed by Medicare to the RRE. The change would occur with a minor adjustment of a data reporting file that allows the TPA to take the place for such communications in place of the RRE. This change would dispose of the requirement mentioned in Chapter 2 requiring a Letter of Agency from the RRE on each and every claim. No other change would occur, and the TPA would still require the cooperation of the Medicare beneficiary for it to complete MSP compliance on behalf of the RRE.

CHAPTER 4

PROTECTING MEDICARE'S INTEREST IN THE LIABILITY CLAIM –
The Liability Medicare
Set-Aside Arrangement

4.0.   The Liability Medicare Set-Aside – Myth or Reality?

Use of a Medicare Set-Aside (MSA) is an accepted practice in the resolution of a Worker's Compensation (WC) claim involving a Medicare beneficiary or potential Medicare beneficiary.[1] The Worker's Compensation Plan settling its obligation to pay for future injury-related care must allocate a certain amount of the proceeds to cover that care.[2] Medicare payments for such services are excluded until medical expenses related to the injury or disease equal the amount of the set-aside.[3] Should the settlement represent an attempt to shift to Medicare the responsibility for payment of medical expenses for the treatment of a work-related injury, Medicare will not recognize it and either suspend future payment of benefits or if it should pay by mistake, seek recovery.[4] To avoid this uncertainty by Medicare, WC plans follow Medicare recommended guidelines to establish and have approved a WC Medicare Set-Aside (WCMSA).[5] As a result, an entire industry has evolved to meet this need. Medicare, through the Centers for Medicare & Medicaid Services (CMS), updates regulations, and issues alerts and bulletins to better manage the workload. As a consequence of this developed process, WC Plans obtain approval from a special Medicare contractor for WCMSA it presents for review: the Workers Compensation Review Contractor

---

[1] Memorandum from Parashar B. Patel, Deputy Dire., Purchasing Policy Group, Ctr. For Medicare Mgmt. to All Assoc. Reg'l Adm'r (July 23, 2001) [hereinafter Patel Memo].

[2] 42 C.F.R. §411.46; Medicare Secondary Payer Manual, Chapter 7 §40.3.4.

[3] 42 C.F.R. §411.46(a).

[4] 42 C.F.R. §411.46(b)(2).

[5] See, http://www.cms.hhs.gov/WorkersCompAgencyServices/04_wcsetaside.asp#TopOfPage.

(WCRC). WC Plans may submit WCMSAs for approval through a portal maintained by the WCRC contractor.[6]

In contrast, CMS has published little[7] on how liability insurance, automobile insurance, no-fault as well as those that self insure for those exposures are to complete any obligation that may be owed when a judgment, award, or settlement is reached with a Medicare beneficiary.[8] The liability side of the Non-Group Plans does not have regulations, memos, or much guidance whatsoever like WC.[9] Yet, CMS takes the position that all parties to a liability settlement must "protect Medicare's interests" with regard to future medical, but admits that no formal procedures are in place on how this must be accomplished.[10]

Settling parties to a liability claim are left to their own devices as to the appropriate steps to take with respect to potential future medical care. [11] While at least one District Court has ruled that compliance can

---

[6] *See,* https://www.cms.gov/Medicare/Coordination-of-Benefits/WorkersCompAgency Services/WCMSAP.html

[7] CMS updated the Medicare Secondary Payer Manual, Chapter 1 on March 20, 2009. In Section 20 of that Manual, under definitions, the Liability Medicare Set-Aside is defined. CMS has issued only one memorandum – "Medicare Secondary Payer – Liability Insurance (Including Self-Insurance) Settlements, Judgments, Awards, or Other Payments and Future Medicals" – Information, dated September 29, 2011. The Medicare Secondary Payer Manuals, Bulletins, Alerts, or Regulations that have issued do not at all describe a process for liability as it does for the settling Workers' Compensation claim. There is some relief for a liability claim, but only where it arises from an industrial accident. *See* CMS Memoranda, 4/21/2003, Question 19. Otherwise, the parties to a resolving liability claim are left to their own devices, and Medicare is well aware of this issue.

[8] http://www.cms.hhs.gov/ThirdParty Liability/; *See also, The King Kong Contingent: Should the Medicare Secondary Payer Statute Reach to Future Medical Expenses in Personal Injury Settlements?* University Pittsburg Law Review (2007), volume 68, issue 2, p. 469 at p. 479.

[9] *See* 42 C.F.R. Subpart D – *Limitations on Medicare Payment for Services Covered under Liability or No-Fault Insurance,* compare to 42 C.F.R. Subpart C – *Limitations on Medicare Payment for Services Covered under Worker's Compensation.*

[10] http://www/cms.hhs.gov/MandatoryInsRep/Downloads/Jan28Transcript.pdf at p. 19.

[11] There is one exception. CMS has a documented procedure for the liability case that involves an underlying industrial injury case. Where the liability settlement relieves a Worker's Compensation plan from any future medical expense, a Workers Compensation Medicare Set-aside Arrangement (WCMSA) is appropriate. The WCMSA

occur from following the WC MSA requirements, this is a risky proposition; Medicare has made clear its intent to handle differently liability and WC. Title 42, Part 411 contains subparts, and there are separate categories for each line of business. To make the leap of logic that the workers' compensation regulations, set forth in subpart C, somehow were meant to be part of liability regulations in subpart D, may be a stretch under the *Chevron* deference. Even Medicare recognizes this potential issue as it has recently requested the Office of Management & Budget to review proposed new regulations in this regard.[12]

As it is more likely than not that no Regulations apply, then what are the appropriate steps parties should take when resolving a liability claim involving future incident-related treatment? If the purpose of Medicare Secondary Payer is to preserve Medicare's financial integrity and reverse payment order, [13] then how can that purpose be effectuated if, after a settlement, judgment, or award, a Medicare beneficiary can expect Medicare to pay for Medicare benefits related to the injury? The most logical response, and reasonable course of action to meet the MSP statutory purpose is for a fund to be established. Medicare is perfecting its awareness of settlements, judgments, and awards through electronic reporting and will not tolerate a shift of responsibility by the parties. If that outcome is certain, then how should the parties approach this issue?

There is no "threshold" figure that triggers a party's duty to allocate a part of the settlement or disposition proceeds to future medical. Prior to suggesting a possible solution, it is best to examine the Act to better understand why future medical specials should be of concern to parties. The liability industry is used to the concept of finality. If the

---

would need sufficient funds to cover future medical expenses incurred once the total third-party liability settlement is exhausted; however no WCMSA is required if it can be documented that the claimant does not require any further WC claim-related medical services or if the medical portion of the WC claim remains open. *See* CMS Memoranda, 4/21/2003, Question 19.

[12] As of date of publishing, such proposed regulations were not available for public review and comment. *See* http://www.gpo.gov/fdsys/browse/collection.action? collectionCode=FR

[13] *See Zinman v. Shalala* 67 F.3d 841, 845 (9th Cir.) (1993) at 1168.

conditional payments owed Medicare are satisfied then the liability practitioner is not likely to take on an exposure of insuring payment for future incident-related treatment. But there are a lot of catch phrases within the industry designed to scare liability practitioners into compliance. Frequently, the penalty applicable to electronic reporting is mischaracterized as a reason to require an LMSA, or simply that the MSP law "requires Medicare's interests to be protected." These tactics are not supported by the law. The basis for compliance must originate from the statute itself and not from a 2001 CMS Regional Office memo covering WC compromises and commutations.[14]

Therefore, the Act must be dissected to determine if it covers the future medical component.

4.0.1.   MSP Act and Future Medical Considerations for Liability

Congressional intent for the MSP Act is clear – preserve Medicare. The Act is intentionally prohibitory in design. "Payment [by Medicare] under this subchapter may not be made..." is the legislative text that the Act opens with.[15] There is no ambiguity here. Medicare is not required to pay, if another *plan* has responsibility to pay. Such responsibility is *demonstrated* by a judgment, a payment conditioned upon the recipient's compromise, waiver, or release (whether or not there is a determination of or admission of liability) of payment for items and services included in a claim against the plan.[16] Once responsibility is demonstrated, Medicare may not pay, but it may and often does on the

---

[14] Patel Memo at p. 1. This memo only applies to Worker's Compensation commutation of future benefits and is the first reference that Medicare's interests are to be considered when settling. It is an inference, drawn from the Act without supporting legal analysis, yet has been widely accepted as an axiom in evaluating the MSA requirement. Whether that is true or not, it is clear this memo has no applicability outside of Worker's Compensation and therefore, the reference cannot apply to the Liability Plan.

[15] 42 U.S.C. §1395y(b)(2)(A) states in part: "Payment under this subchapter may not be made, except as provided in subparagraph (B), with respect to any timer or service to the extent that - . . . (ii) payment has been made, or can reasonably be expected to be made under a workmen's compensation law or plan of the Unites States or a State our under an automobile or liability insurance policy or plan (including self insured plan) or no fault insurance." (Emphasis Added.).

[16] 42 U.S.C. §1395y(b)(2)(B)(ii) and 42 C.F.R. §411.22(b)(2).

condition it be reimbursed.[17] Reimbursement occurs whether or not the lump sum differentiates the sums between various elements of damages. So long as such medical specials were within the scope of the Medicare beneficiary's claim, Medicare is to be reimbursed.[18] The Act is not limited in time and characterizes a *Plan's responsibility* to pay where it "has or had a responsibility to make payment with respect to such item or service." *See* 42 U.S.C. §1395y(b)(2)(B)(ii). A plain reading of such language would implicate any general liability release and enforcement would be impractical, capricious, and arbitrary for Medicare to support without appropriate regulation. However, Medicare would not face similar obstacles where the resolution of the claim clearly involved issues of future treatment. If it is documented in a life care plan, treating physician reports, or in legal discovery – Medicare would have a good body of evidence to support a position that liability for such care was inappropriately shifted to the Medicare Trust Fund.

In the appropriate case, Medicare should be able to establish repayment responsibility for future medical. The authors are aware of at least one situation where Medicare has brought a claim seeking reimbursement after a settlement. In *U.S. v. Stricker*, the U.S. Attorney's office filed an action in 2009 to recover conditional payments arising from a settlement that took place in 2003. Medicare's claim in that case sought reimbursement for medical items and services it paid for both before and *after* the known settlement date.[19] *Stricker* was dismissed on procedural grounds. It is on appeal and it may be some period of time before this issue is reached by that court, assuming the case is remanded. But *U.S. v. Baxter International* is another situation where such medical specials were recovered which confirms the reality of the situation. This is not speculation or some myth. Medicare, in the right case, will seek reimbursement. In the absence of guidance from

---

[17] 42 U.S.C. §1395y(b)(2)(B)(i) states: "Authority to make conditional payment. The Secretary may make payment under this subchapter with respect to an item or service if a primary plan described in subparagraph (A)(ii) has not made or cannot reasonably be expected to make payment with respect to such item or service promptly (as determined in accordance with regulations)."

[18] *See Hadden v. U.S. 661 F.3d 298, 302 (6th Cir. 2011).*

[19] *See U.S. v. Stricker, U.S. Attorney's Motion for Summary Judgment,* Declaration of Betty Noble, pg. 19.

Medicare, the parties must act reasonably. See *Hosp. of the Univ. of PA v. Sebelius*, 2012 U.S. Dist. LEXIS 37027 (D.C.Cir.2012). "There is a relationship between the need for agencies to notify regulated parties of regulatory requirements and the text of the regulations that set out those requirements."...The Agency "must give regulated entities notice before enforcing requirements based on that interpretation."

CMS cannot defend their ultimate interpretation of a statute or regulation when there is no clearly defined policy statement. A regulated industry must be on notice of the intended consequences for non-compliance. No regulation exists that will invalidate a liability settlement, nor are there any policy statements to deal with situations involving the non-Medicare beneficiary, like there are in Worker's Compensation. In such situations, a regulated party may not be punished.[20] Therefore, unless CMS issues proper policy (which it can only do if it has a supporting regulation), the present statutory framework can be reasonably interpreted to not include a non-Medicare beneficiary. See *Miller v. US, 813 F. Supp 715 (1992)*. "Because no regulations had been promulgated, plaintiff could not possibly have been on notice of what he was required to do in order to exhaust his administrative remedies. In the absence of regulations, any action by plaintiff which reasonably could be said to have put the IRS on notice of the unenforceability of the liens on plaintiff's property may have been sufficient to satisfy the exhaustion requirement of section 7432(d)(1)."

4.0.2. Resolving Claims Involving Future Medical – No Future Medical Interests Involved

Every liability claim is unique and needs to be examined on its own merits when evaluating whether to protect Medicare's interest with regard to incident-related future medicals. The inquiry usually begins with: Who is responsible to meet this MSP obligation? But it is more practical to determine whether the particular claim even requires additional consideration by the parties. Not all liability cases do. The following are situations where there are no Medicare interests to protect. Prudence requires these situations to be adequately documented.

---

[20] *Gen. Elec. Co. v. U.S. Envtl Prot. Agency, 53 F.3e 1324, at 1333 – 1334 (D.C. Cir. 1995).*

Plan takes a holiday or credit with regard to the liability settlement and does not pay for future medical. For those situations, the parties to the liability settlement should take steps to protect Medicare's interest; otherwise, Medicare will expect the entire settlement to be available to pay for future medical care in light of the above regulation.

4.0.3.   Protecting Medicare – No Exception Applies

The concept of a WCMSA arose from a CMS Regional Office communication known as the Patel Memo.[32] (See Appendix 33.) This particular document laid out a basis for Workers' Compensation Plans to protect Medicare's interests. In doing so it identified two types of settlements – commutation and compromise. Commutation is akin to replacement of one for another. Where Workers' Compensation had a responsibility to pay for medical specials and there were no defenses to a claim, a settlement would simply mean the present value of the benefits available under the law for the injured worker. Except for an analysis of the medical treatment, not much is left. Compromise implied a discount of available benefits. Today, most workers' compensation settlements are compromises, but because Medicare has the authority to disregard such settlements, the WCMSA is more a review of the applicable medical treatment without regard to claim defenses or medical causation. Medicare does not have the same authority over a liability settlement. For Medicare's interests to be properly considered, the treatment will need to be adjusted to line up with the settlement value of the claim.

Medicare has no incentive to discount a Workers' Compensation MSA. If Medicare does not approve, Medicare is not exposed. Rather, the Workers' Compensation Plan continues to pay, which, from Medicare's perspective, prevents the transfer of risk to the Medicare Trust Fund. For liability matters, Medicare has to be much more flexible. There is no legal requirement, short of trial, to compel a Liability Plan to pay. In the interim, Medicare pays. Medicare can only recoup its cost once there is a settlement, judgment, or award. The Liability Plan will

---

[32] Parasher B. Patel, CMS Memorandum to All Regional Administrators, *Workers' Compensation Commutation of Future Benefits,* July 23, 2001.

not settle unless the amount is fair and equitable with regard to the issues presented by the claim. As such, compromise will be necessary.

Nonetheless, Medicare takes the position that the entire resolution amount is subject to recovery by Medicare. [33]   Further, it is irrelevant from Medicare's perspective how the parties have structured the terms.[34] Medicare will seek reimbursement to the extent of the settlement amount.[35] To ensure otherwise, the parties need to have more than a piece of paper outlining the proposed future medical treatment and a fund to support it – corroboration is also required. To confirm the validity of a future medical specials fund the parties should consider taking additional steps as outlined in Section 4.03.1. Allocation by Hearing on the Merits and Section 4.03.2. The Liability Medicare Set-Aside Arrangement.

4.0.3.1.   Allocation by Hearing on the Merits

Damages in a liability claim can fall under different categories such as pain and suffering, wage loss, property damage, medical, and so forth. Medicare will not distinguish between these damage types unless they are allocated by court order on the merits. If this is accomplished, Medicare will limit its claim to the portion of the resolution amount identified as medical. It will not go beyond that designated amount.

Absent a court order that is entered after a full hearing on the merits, the only number for Medicare to consider is the settlement, award, or judgment. What this means is that the Medicare beneficiary plaintiff cannot, with any confidence, use any portion of the settlement amount for non-Medicare purposes.[36] If they do, Medicare will not recognize it. The allocation allows the Medicare beneficiary plaintiff to know what they can or cannot spend from the settlement amount.

---

[33] Medicare Secondary Payer Manual, Chapter 7 §50.4.4.

[34] *See Hadden v. U.S.* 661 F.3d. 298 (6th Cir. 2011).

[35] *See Salvenson v. Sebelius*, 2012 U.S. Dist. LEXIS 66923 (U.S. Dist. of South Dakota, Southern Div.).

[36] The primary plan is exposed if the plaintiff does use the settlement, judgment, or award in a manner for purposes other than Medicare. If Medicare makes conditional payments, it can seek reimbursement from the primary plan even if it has already paid the plaintiff in resolving the claim. *See* 42 C.F.R. §411.24(i).

A good example to consider as a template for this process occurred in *Frank vs. Gateway Insurance Company*, 2012 U.S. Dist. LEXIS 33581 (U.S. Dist. for the Western Dis. of Louisiana). After settlement was reached, plaintiff brought a Motion for Court Determination of Need, and Amount of Medicare Set-Aside. A critical step to the process was an invitation to the U.S. Attorney's office to participate.[37] Evidence was then presented by the parties for Plaintiffs on the issues of present condition and expected future treatment related to the claim, including costs. The information provided was supported by Affidavit, and the court even requested additional documentation. Even though the U.S. Attorney's office indicated in a letter it would not participate, and CMS does not review a counsel's determination of future medical, the Court felt compelled to rule on the issues in order to effectuate the settlement. Finding the Medicare Secondary Payer Act applicable to future medical, it ruled in favor of establishing the Medicare Set-Aside amount. Other District Courts have ruled in a similar manner.[38]

Medicare has provided no guidance. Therefore, seeking a ruling from the Court is reasonable and protects Medicare's interests. Since it is appropriate for a court to rule on the requirement for the Medicare Set-Aside, it could clearly weigh in on the issues that may impact the amount available, such as plaintiff's own negligence or policy limits. As the *Frank* court expressed: "Since CMS provides no other procedure to determine the adequacy of protecting Medicare's interest for future medical needs and/or expenses in conjunction with the settlement of the third-party claims, and since there is a strong public interest in resolving lawsuits through settlement, the Court finds that Medicare's

---

[37] A direct action against the U.S. would simply draw a motion to dismiss as the U.S. is entitled to sovereign immunity, among other solid defenses, like failure to exhaust administrative remedies. *See Chapter One – Overview regarding Subject Matter Jurisdiction.*

[38] *See Schnexdayer v. Scottsdale Insurance Company*, 2011 U.S. Dist. LEXIS 83687 (US Dist. Crt. Western District of Louisiana, Lafayette Division). Since CMS provides no other procedure by which to determine the adequacy of protecting Medicare's interests for future medical needs and/or expenses in conjunction with the settlement of third party claims, and since there is a strong public interest in resolving lawsuits through settlement, *McDermott, Inc. v. AmClyde, 511 U.S. 202, 215, 114 S.Ct. 1461, 128 L.Ed.2d 148 (1994)*, the Court finds that Medicare's interests have been adequately protected in this settlement (See Appendix 22) within the meaning of the MSP.

interests have been adequately protected in this settlement with the meaning of MSP." *Infra*, at pg. 11.

Another interesting rule of law to consider concerns the fact that at least one federal court has held that a plaintiff attorney is entitled to his attorney's fees for the value of the LMSA established. *See Hinsinger v. Showboat Atlantic City, 18 A.ed 229 (2011).* In *Hinsinger*, the parties had agreed to the LMSA, but the court clearly accepted the idea surrounding the need to protect Medicare's interests, and even went so far as to carve out funds to be made payable to plaintiff's counsel.

This possible solution is gaining recognition by the courts.[39] But most claims are not litigated, and even those matters that reach litigation, the cost of motion practice is not worth it. An alternative method is to prepare a Liability Medicare Set-Aside Arrangement (LMSA) and submit to Medicare.

4.0.3.2.   The Liability Medicare Set-Aside Arrangement (LMSA)

Medicare's first use of the words "Liability Medicare Set-Aside Arrangement" can be traced to a definition section within a Medicare Manual in 2009. However, the first time these words appeared in a CMS Memo was on September 29, 2011.[40] (See Appendix 5.) Without any real guidance from CMS, parties settling claims involving Medicare beneficiaries who are extremely risk adverse have been known to include an LMSA in even the smallest of settlements. On the other end of the spectrum of risk are those liability practitioners who do nothing at all. It truly is an area rife with disinformation.

4.0.3.2.1.   The American Association for Justice (AAJ) Position

Let us dispel some of the common issues that serve as barriers to the use of the LMSA. On August 11, 2009, (See Appendix 34.) the AAJ communicated to its members that "Section 111 contains reporting requirements for responsible reporting entities (RREs) only. Section 111

---

[39] *Big R. Towing, Inc. v. David Wayne Benoit, et. al., 2011 U.S. Dist. LEXIS 1392.*

[40] See "Medicare Secondary Payer – Liability Insurance (Including Self-Insurance) Settlements, Judgments, Awards, or Other Payments and Future Medicals" – Information, dated September 29, 2011.

does not impact or change the requirement for plaintiff attorneys." Absolutely true! The MMSEA reporting requirements do not alter, amend or otherwise change what is already required by the MSP. The reporting obligation is simply an addition to those responsibilities.

Therefore, the AAJ message begs the question as to what is presently required by the MSP Act. The message attempts to state definitively that the LMSA is not appropriate because CMS made such statements on MMSEA Town Hall Conference calls.[41] However, a close examination of MMSEA Town Hall transcripts states otherwise.[42] To the contrary, CMS asserts that the LMSA is indeed appropriate.

4.0.3.2.2.   MSP Manual – No Liability beyond the Settlement Date

In one section of the MSP Manual, Medicare states there *should* be no recovery of benefits paid for services rendered after the date of a

---

[41] See AAJ Email Bulletin, dated August 11, 2009. (See Appendix 34.)

[42] (Bill Tominga): Hi. I'm with Global Aerospace in Short Hills, New Jersey. And we're curious about the applicability of Medicare set asides to liability claims?

Barbara Wright: If you've read transcripts from prior calls, that is not a Section 111 issue. And we are limiting these calls to Section 111 issues. There is not the same formal process for liability set asides that there is for Worker's Compensation set asides. However the underlying statutory obligation is the same. For liability set asides if you – for Worker's Comp the process is technically not required to have a CMS blessed set aside.

For liability situations as I said, the underlying obligation is the same if you wish to pursue CMS approval of a liability set aside, your avenue of approach is through the applicable regional office. Whether or not they agree to review, it does not provide – if they decline to review it, that doesn't provide any type of safe harbor. And the regions are making their determinations based on their workload. If their workload permits and they believe there are significant dollars at issue, regional offices are reviewing proposed set aside amounts but certainly not typically at the same small level that it's being reviewed through our Worker's Compensation review contractor or Worker's Comp set asides.

(Bill Tominga): Not sure, so is that a yes or a no? I'm not sure?

Barbara Wright: Well, I don't know what you mean by yes or no. There is not the same formal process. You have the same legal obligations. This has nothing to do with Section 111. 111 did not change any pre-existing obligations. It added a separate reporting requirement.

(Bill Tominga): Okay. Thank you.

MMSEA Town Hall Transcript, 9/30/2009, pages 25 – 26.

liability insurance settlement.[43] If the parties complete their obligations owed Medicare properly then there *should* be no reason for Medicare to pay after a settlement. However, what happens if the claimant seeks incident-related treatment, post-settlement, and the parties did not protect Medicare? The language contained in its Manual does not expressly prohibit Medicare from paying. Medicare is authorized to pay for items and services even after a liability settlement in the event of delayed compliance by primary plan.

The Manual offers no safe harbor for parties from compliance with the MSP, but simply reinforces that Medicare *should* not have to pay after a liability settlement. It does not mean that it is prohibited from doing so if the parties have not carefully considered Medicare's interests.

4.0.3.2.3.   Parties' Motivation to Adopt LMSA

Now that we have dispelled some of the barriers for the use of the LMSA in a liability settlement, what are the motivating factors for each party to secure the LMSA?

- Plaintiff

The key issue to consider, from a settling Plaintiff's perspective, is the potential for suspension of future Medicare benefits. Medicare is becoming aware of more liability claims each day[44] and it uses this information to coordinate future benefits. When Medicare is not properly informed of the claim settlement amount and allotment for future medical payments it will examine, and potentially take, the entire settlement amount.[45]

---

[43] Medicare Secondary Payer Manual, Chapter 7, §50.5.

[44] The liability industry is contacting the Coordination of Benefits Contractor (COBC) before settlement, judgment, award or other payment to start the process to secure the Conditional Payment Letter. When this information is received, the COBC populates its database, the Common Working File, to assist in coordinating future benefits. The COBC's primary mission is to prevent Medicare from making payment that is the responsibility of another plan.

[45] Medicare Secondary Payer Manual, §50.5. "However, the entire amount of a settlement is subject to recovery, whether the liability payment is made at the time of settlement, or over a period of time agreed by parties in a structured settlement."

CHAPTER 5

ADMINISTRATIVE DISPUTES AND APPEALS

5.0.   Initial Dispute to CMS

In the usual course of business, a Conditional Payment Letter ("CPL") is issued from CMS detailing the medical items and services Medicare claims it paid related to the loss in question. It is recommended that all CPLs are reviewed to ensure those charges contained in the CPL are, in fact, related to the loss in question. There are several reasons this review is essential to the proper handling of a claim involving a Medicare beneficiary. The first, and most obvious, is based upon the simple fact that Medicare should not be paid for charges not related to the underlying incident. Another reason is that if unrelated charges are not disputed, Medicare may take the position that such items and services are related to a tort settlement, and it may potentially deny claimant's medical benefits going forward. Other chapters in this book address the best practice and reasons for disputing unrelated charges contained in CPLs.

The practitioner should specifically reference all unrelated charges contained within a CPL and provide as much proof as possible for the exclusion of such charges. A brief letter should be drafted, including the position taken as to all unrelated charges, and sent onto the MSPRC for review. CMS may agree in part, or disagree in its entirety, but the practitioner can continue to dispute unrelated charges, as many times as necessary, until the claim is finalized by way of settlement, judgment, or award. Once the claim is finalized and the MSPRC issues the Final Demand Letter ("FDL"), if there are unrelated charges contained within the FDL the practitioner may dispute those charges with the MSPRC one last time. This dispute should be handled in the same manner as that for a CPL, however the MSPRC will label the dispute as an "Appeal" and the result of the dispute will be deemed "final."

5.1. Disputes to CMS, Post-settlement, Judgment, or Award: Maximus Federal Services

Relatedness disputes decided by CMS post-settlement, judgment, or award will be deemed "final" by Medicare. The practitioner who takes the position that Medicare has included unrelated charges within a final demand for payment letter must submit a request for "reconsideration" to a company called Maximus Federal Services within one hundred and twenty days from the date on the MSPRC FDL. It is recommended that the practitioner submit supporting medical documentation with the appeal; otherwise Maximus will request it, delaying its decision. If the desired result is not achieved after submitting a reconsideration request to Maximus then Maximus invites the practitioner to present the matter before an Administrative Law Judge ("ALJ"). If the request is denied before the ALJ, the practitioner may continue the appeals process to the Medicare Appeals Council, and then Federal District Court. As explained in various cases within this Chapter, this process takes years.

5.2. Jurisdiction over Medicare

Determinations by CMS are not subject to federal question jurisdiction under 28 U.S.C. § 1331. Congress expressly excluded such jurisdiction when it enacted 42 U.S.C. §§ 405 (g) and (h). Therefore, any appeal of CMS determinations, which include decisions made by its contractors, cannot be channeled into federal court unless administrative remedies provided by CMS are first exhausted.[1] The same requirement exists for constitutional violations.[2] Thus the first step in challenging CMS starts within the CMS through the process discussed above. Once the dispute turns into an appeal and becomes ripe for judicial review, the courts have jurisdiction, but it is rare for a case to reach this stage.

The *Cochran* court provides a brief overview of the administrative process that must be exhausted before federal jurisdiction is available. The Medicare beneficiary would have to exhaust her administrative remedies in the following manner:

---

[1] *See Cochran v. U.S. Health Care Fin. Admin.*, 291 F.3d 775 (11th Cir. 2002).

[2] In most cases, courts hold plaintiffs' constitutional claims to be "inextricably intertwined" with their claim for benefits. *Wilson v. U.S.*, 405 F.3d 1002 (Fed. Cir. 2005).

- Request that the agency exercise its discretion and waive its right to collect the medical expenses Medicare paid on her behalf from the proceeds of her tort suit.
- If the government denies the request for waiver, the Medicare beneficiary then must seek a review of that denial at a hearing before an administrative law judge ("ALJ").
- If the Medicare beneficiary is dissatisfied with the ALJ's decision, she may file a request for review with the Department of H&HS Appeals Board pursuant to 42 C.F.R. §§ 405.720, 405.724; At this time the Medicare beneficiary may raise any constitutional violations in addition to the underlying arguments.
- During that process, the Medicare beneficiary could raise any constitutional objections she has to CMS (formerly HCFA) subrogation practices.
- Finally, if the Medicare beneficiary is still displeased with the result, she may file a claim in federal court for review under 42 U.S.C. § 1395ff(b)(1).

As of the writing of this supplemental addition of our book, the *Cochran* case has been followed and cited no less than 61 times. It is clear that practitioners within the liability industry continue to prematurely commence suit against the Federal Government in an attempt to determine Medicare's interest in a given case. Since the passage of the SCHIP Extension Act in 2007, there has been an increase in such premature filings. The conclusion to be drawn from this increase is that liability practitioners are increasingly aware of the need to learn about the Medicare component of a given claim, but the administrative process is not being followed.

This is evident in yet another recent decision by the U.S. District Court for the Central District of Illinois: Springfield Division. Plaintiff Marjorie R. Braucher, individually, and as Special Administrator of the Estate of Georgia Braucher, commenced suit to adjudicate the Medicare reimbursement amount and approve Settlement Distribution between the Estate and surviving heirs. She argued that her authority to file suit against the United States was based on *Bradley v. Sebelius, 621 F.3d 1330 (11th Cir. 2010)*, but her claim was struck down because of one important difference. The Bradley case came to federal court in an action for judicial review after there was a final administrative decision, whereas, plaintiff Braucher did not request any administrative hearings from Medicare.   In light of this important distinction, the court in *Braucher v. Swagat Group, LLC, 2011 U.S. Dist. LEXIS 21190*, ruled that it could only review MSPRC's claim for reimbursement in a judicial review proceeding brought under 42 U.S.C. §§405(g) & 1395ff(b)(1)(A) because the Court otherwise lacks jurisdiction to make that determination 42 U.S.C. §§405(h) and 1395ii. The plaintiff must exhaust her administrative remedies before the Court can hear the matter under 42 U.S.C. §§ 405(g) and 1395fflb)(1)(A). Until those administrative remedies are exhausted the Court lacks jurisdiction.

A matrix is provided by the Office of Medicare Hearings and Appeals ("OMHA"): http://www.hhs.gov/omha/process/Appeals%20Process%20 by%20Medicare%20Type/parts_longdescrip.html. It is reprinted below and illustrates the five levels of review, which can take between three to four years. Any favorable decision for the Medicare beneficiary terminates further review. The liability practitioner should understand that the review process may be slightly different depending on what benefits are being reviewed.

Level of the Appeals Process	Medicare Part A & B	Medicare Part C	Medicare Part D
Level 1	Medicare Contractor [see note at end of table]	Medicare Advantage Plan	Medicare Prescription Drug Plan
Level 2	QIC	Independent Review Entity	Independent Review Entity
Level 3	Office of Medicare Hearings and Appeals	Office of Medicare Hearings and Appeals	Office of Medicare Hearings and Appeals
Level 4	Medicare Appeals Council	Medicare Appeals Council	Medicare Appeals Council
Level 5	Federal Court	Federal Court	Federal Court

5.3.   Due Process of Law

In each part of the Medicare program, the contractor administering the program makes a decision that impacts Medicare benefits. In most cases, the decision is whether a medical service or item is covered and how much Medicare will pay for the service or item. Under the Act, the contractor makes a decision about what it will collect from a settlement, judgment, award or other payment involving a tort claim. This is called a determination. Unless notice of that initial determination is provided to the Medicare beneficiary, there is no due process of law and the administrative review process does not commence.

CMS has satisfied the notice requirements for due process by providing for notice of appeal rights in the Recovery/Initial Determination Letter that is issued by the MSPRC. (See Appendix 36A.) The letter triggers the administrative appeal process, and the Medicare beneficiary has 60 days from its issuance to take advantage of the process or forever be bound by the initial determination. The manner in which the process is started is by a simple letter to the contractor. However, before writing that letter, it is necessary to understand the types of review available to the Medicare beneficiary.[3]

---

[3] At this point, it is abundantly clear that the RRE has very few rights within the MSP process. An interesting question arises whether the RRE can run directly to court. In *Bowen v. Michigan Academy of Family Physicians*, an exception to sections 405(g) & (h) was allowed when physicians were left with no meaningful administrative or federal review. *See Bowen*, 476 U.S. 667 (1986); *see also Protocols, LLC v. Leavitt,* (549 F.3d 1294(10th Cir. 2008), in which the Tenth Circuit reversed a lower court finding and held that plaintiff presented sufficient injury to confer standing. Protocols LLC provided consulting services for the settlement of workers' compensation claims. Its main expertise was structuring settlements that comply with Medicare regulations. Protocols commenced a declaratory judgment action against HHS and CMS, claiming that a 2005 memorandum issued by CMS misinterpreted the Medicare statute and regulations, exposing Protocols to unexpected liabilities arising out of settlements it structured on behalf of Medicare-eligible plaintiffs. The lower court dismissed for lack of standing, but the Tenth Circuit reversed, finding that the property interest affected in this case was Protocols' contingent liability as a result of the CMS Memo. Before reversing, the Tenth Circuit considered the regulatory scheme dictated by the MSP statute and the reason MSAs are utilized in the arena of workers' compensation. The court then found Protocols had the requisite standing to commence suit, but did not address the issue of jurisdiction.

An illustrative case is *Haro vs. Sebelius*.[4] In *Haro*, a group of plaintiffs challenged the U.S. Department of Health and Human Services collection practices used to recover reimbursement claims. The point to be taken from *Haro* is that the court granted jurisdiction to the plaintiffs, a very rare occurrence in this area of the law. The court found that plaintiff *Haro* had sustained an injury-in-fact based upon Medicare's collection procedures, thus meeting the standing requirement to commence suit against the government. Even more rare was the court's finding that plaintiff McNutt had satisfied the exhaustion of administrative remedies with respect to 42 U.S.C. § 405(h) as opposed to 42 U.S.C. § 405(g). This was a crucial distinction because it shows at least one court's willingness to entertain jurisdiction over the process versus the individual outcome of the claim.

The *Haro* case was appealed since the initial publication of our book. See *Haro v. Sebelius* 789 F. Supp 2d 1179. In the appeal the court held that Medicare beneficiaries are not required to reimburse Medicare within the prescribed 60-day period for the portion of conditional payment it disputes or otherwise seeks a waiver of. The Medicare beneficiary is encouraged to reimburse for that portion of the conditional payment obligation that is not in dispute or part of the request for waiver, but there is no requirement to do so. If designated amount is not reimbursed within the prescribed 60-day period then the portion that is not subject to dispute or waiver will be charged interest.

The plaintiff attorney representing the Medicare beneficiary is not obligated to withhold funds subject to dispute with Medicare. These funds can be promptly distributed to the Medicare beneficiary without incurring any MSP liability with Medicare. Although not clearly laid out in the Court's Order, it appears the plaintiff attorney is ethically bound to withhold the amount not in dispute with Medicare; to the extent that money is distributed to the claimant before the dispute with Medicare is finalized, the attorney could be exposed to MSP liability.

---

[4] *Haro v. Sebelius*, 2009 U.S.Dist. LEXIS 111053, CV 09-134-TUC-DCB (D. Ariz. November 30, 2009).

5.4.   Levels of Administrative Review

There are three administrative processes by which CMS may accept less than the full amount of its claim. They are not mutually exclusive, and the liability practitioner may employ all of them concurrently. These reviews are:

- Waiver or partial waiver for financial hardship;
- Waiver or partial waiver for equity and good conscience; and
- A request for compromise in the best interests of the Agency.

Each administrative procedure is different, and the liability practitioner needs to organize the appeal so as to not confuse those differences and unintentionally delay the process. Furthermore, the Agency's exercise of authority is limited to specific entities for each category of appeal. As is readily apparent, a full analysis of the CMS procedures demonstrates that the process is so dense as to essentially discourage claimants from requesting waivers of the MSP amount.

Medicare contractors have authority to consider beneficiary requests for waivers under Section 1870(c) of the Act. The authority to waive Medicare claims under Section 1862(b) and to compromise claims, or to suspend or terminate a recovery action under FCCA, is reserved exclusively to CMS. However, claims for compromise that exceed $100,000 are referred to the Department of Justice for negotiation and the Agency is divested of jurisdiction.[5]

5.4.1.   Waiver under Section 1870(c) of the Social Security Act

A Medicare beneficiary who is unable to repay the debt to Medicare may request a full or partial waiver. The request must be made in writing to the MSPRC.[6] The MSPRC has sole jurisdiction over waivers, without any threshold. To begin the appeal process, the requesting party must write to the MSPRC at the address contained within the Standard Recovery/Initial Determination Letter or visit www.msprc.info.

---

[5] 31 U.S.C. 3711 (b).

[6] If the beneficiary requests a waiver or an appeal of the overpayment determination, the beneficiary will be held responsible for the interest on the debt if the agency prevails and a refund is later collected. (*See* 45 C.F.R. 30.14(a)).

Who can request a waiver?

- The beneficiary;
- A surviving spouse or dependent child who is entitled to either:
- Social Security Disability Insurance payments (Title II); or Medicare

Once the waiver request has been received, the MSPRC sends the beneficiary the Standard Letter Acknowledging Waiver Request. (See Appendix 36B.) The letter provides the beneficiary with a Form SSA 632-BK Request for Waiver of Overpayment and acknowledges receipt of the waiver request. (See Appendix 36C.)[7]

The beneficiary need not complete Section 1 of the Form, "Without Fault," because CMS deems that beneficiaries are without fault.[8] The beneficiary or his representative must complete all other aspects of the form and submit supporting documentation that includes (i) procurement costs; (ii) accident-related, out-of-pocket medical expenses incurred; and (iii) expenses and income information that demonstrate financial hardship. The form must be submitted within 60 days from the date it is received.

A successful request for waiver will detail the impact to the beneficiary, who is being deprived of income required for ordinary and necessary living expenses. A tipping point is whether the beneficiary has income or financial resources sufficient for more than ordinary and necessary expenses or is dependent upon all of his or her current benefits for such needs. A beneficiary's ordinary and necessary expenses include:

- Fixed living expenses, such as food and clothing, rent, mortgage payments, utilities, maintenance, insurance (*e.g.*, life, accident, and health insurance, including premiums for supplementary medical insurance benefits under Title XVIII), taxes, installment payments, etc.;
- Medical, hospitalization, and other similar expenses not covered by Medicare or any other insurer;

---

[7] This form can also be found at: http://www.ssa.gov/online/ssa-632.pdf. or at http://www.msprc.info/forms/Request_for_Waiver_Form_ssa632.pdf.

[8] *See* 20 C.F.R. § 404.507.

- Expenses for the support of others for whom the beneficiary is legally responsible; and
- Other miscellaneous expenses that may reasonably be considered necessary to maintain the beneficiary's current standard of living.

Examples of factors to consider when determining financial hardship with respect to a Medicare beneficiary are:

- The beneficiary has spent the settlement proceeds and the only remaining income from which the beneficiary could attempt to satisfy Medicare's claim would be from the money that is needed for his or her monthly living expenses. Waiver may be appropriate under this aspect of the waiver criteria. If documented and appropriate monthly expenses consume the entire amount of money available, a full waiver may be warranted. A partial waiver may be appropriate if the beneficiary retains at least some discretionary income (for example, $25) each month;
- The beneficiary's demonstrated income and resources are at a poverty level standard, such as being in an SSI pay status. A beneficiary may demonstrate proof of SSI pay status by requesting the Form SSA-2458, Benefit Verification, from an SSA office. If Medicare's claim would have to be satisfied from income and resources that meet an established level of poverty, waiver may be appropriate. However, preexisting financial hardship alone may be an insufficient basis for granting a waiver. All factors, not just the existence of poverty, must be weighed before a waiver decision can be made; or
- An unforeseen severe financial circumstance existing at the time Medicare's claim comes into existence can also constitute financial hardship. If a beneficiary has become legally financially responsible for an unforeseen obligation, has acted in good faith at all times with respect to Medicare's claim, and has no other financial resources to meet this legal obligation, waiver may be warranted. For example, waiver would be appropriate if a beneficiary's grandchildren became the beneficiary's legal

responsibility under a will or trust that came into existence upon the sudden death of the beneficiary's child (the parent of the grandchildren).

The manner in which this evidence is presented to the MSPRC is also important. The liability practitioner should consider providing where appropriate:

- A notarized/sworn statement attesting to the validity of the expenses;
- Canceled checks (that correlate to bills received);
- Receipts for services furnished;
- Copies of bills demonstrating services furnished; and
- Evidence of medical goods and services not covered by Medicare or other insurance (out of pocket).[9]

Upon receipt of the completed form and supporting documents, the MSPRC will then determine whether the beneficiary meets the criteria for waiver determinations under Section 1870(c) of the Act (42 C.F.R. § 405.355 and 20 C.F.R. § 404.506-512). There is no hearing, and based upon the submitted information the MSPRC will issue a Standard Letter for Granting Full Waiver or Partial Waivers. (See Appendix 36D and 36E.)

5.4.2.   Waiver under Section 1862(b) of the Social Security Act

A request for waiver or partial waiver under this provision is made by application to the Regional CMS office.[10] (See Appendix 37.) The standard applied is "equity and good conscience" and factors to consider include, but are not limited to, the following:

---

[9] The MSPRC contractor will not automatically assume that out-of-pocket expenses should be considered in determining if a full or partial waiver is warranted. Out-of-pocket expenses are defined as those medical expenses for which a beneficiary has paid, or is responsible to pay, for injuries directly related to the accident and that are not covered by insurance (including Medicare), settlement proceeds, or court-awarded damages. In determining the amount of out-of-pocket expenses to be waived, each case must be considered on its own merits.

[10] See the CMS office locations referred to previously.

- The degree to which the beneficiary contributed to causing the overpayment;
- The degree to which Medicare and/or its contractors contributed to causing the overpayment;
- The degree to which recovery or adjustment would cause undue hardship for the beneficiary;
- Whether the beneficiary would be unjustly enriched by a waiver or adjustment of recovery; and
- Whether the beneficiary changed his or her position to his or her material detriment as a result of receiving the overpayment or as a result of relying on erroneous information supplied to the beneficiary by Medicare.

5.4.3.   Waiver Request Based upon Non-Relatedness

Application of "equity and good conscience" may result in a waiver of adjustment and recovery. For example, there are times when the MSPRC includes medical treatment costs in its Conditional Payoff Summary Form that are not related to the tort at issue. Such inclusion is in error, and the practitioner must strike each medical expense that was included in error. The stricken portions must be sent to the MSPRC office that issued the Conditional Payoff Summary Form. The cover letter enclosing the challenged expenses should explain, point for point, why each medical treatment should be excluded from the case.

The case must be settled for a waiver request to be valid. Waiver determinations should be completed within 120 days from the date a waiver request is received (and date stamped) in the contractor mailroom.[11] If a contractor receives a request for a waiver of a Medicare overpayment that meets the cited criteria, the attorney's written request must be forwarded to the Lead Contractor.

Medicare may deny the request for waiver outright. (See Appendix 36F.) If the beneficiary disagrees with the decision to only grant a partial

---

[11] In cases of joint and several liability among two or more debtors, federal regulations at 42 C.F.R. § 401.623 prohibit CMS from allocating the burden of claims payment among the debtors. CMS will proceed with a collection action against one debtor even if other liable debtors have not paid their proportionate shares. Therefore, if one of the joint debtors owes Medicare, contractors may assess interest on the debt.

waiver, or no waiver at all, then the beneficiary must request reconsideration within 60 days from the date he or she receives the letter. The request for reconsideration will be sent to the address on the letterhead of the entity issuing the decision.

5.4.4.   Compromise

The Federal Claims Collection Act governs a beneficiary's request to compromise on a reimbursement amount.[12] This statutory provision gives federal agencies the authority to compromise where:

- The cost of collection does not justify the enforced collection of the full amount of the claim;
- The individual against whom the claim is made is unable to pay within a reasonable time; or
- The chances of successful litigation are questionable, making it advisable to seek a compromise settlement.

Medicare contractors are not permitted to compromise Medicare claims; instead, CMS handles a compromise internally. If a beneficiary offers to pay Medicare less than the full amount of its claim, the contractor informs the inquiring party of his or her rights to request waiver, appeal, or compromise of the claim. It advises him or her that, while contractors may assist in securing a waiver or appeal, they are not permitted to compromise claims on behalf of the United States government.

When a beneficiary agrees to a compromise settlement under the FCCA, the beneficiary also agrees not to appeal the matter further. The beneficiary, a spouse, an immediate family member, or an attorney may request a compromise. A compromise can be pre-settlement or post-settlement. It should be noted that prompt repayment to Medicare will avoid accruing interest charges. Payment does not cost the beneficiary the right to dispute, appeal, or request waiver of the debt.

To request a compromise, the requesting party must submit in writing the reason for the compromise, specify an amount that he or she wishes to pay, and how this amount was determined. Parties cannot request a full reduction.

---

[12] *See* 31 U.S.C. § 3711.

What to Send:

- The Medicare beneficiary's full name, Medicare number, date of incident/ingestion/exposure;
- Settlement specifics: a copy of the settlement agreement from the third party showing the total amount of the settlement, signed and dated by the Medicare beneficiary, and a closing statement reflecting the actual amount of attorney's fees and case expenses;
- Valid privacy release or a copy of the representation contract signed by the Medicare beneficiary;
- Incident/case-related facts that support a favorable decision; and
- The Medicare beneficiary's financial information, such as monthly income and expenses; assets and debts; documentation of loss of income due to what was claimed and/or released in the settlement judgment, or award; and expenses for widened doorways, ramps, absence of Medigap insurance, and/or other medical out-of-pocket expenses, etc.

All compromise requests are referred to the Centers for Medicare & Medicaid Services Regional Office in Kansas City, Missouri for determination. This process may take up to 120 days. If CMS decides to compromise a debt of $100,000 or more, then the matter must be referred to the Department of Justice. Negotiation of a compromise, or suspension or termination of collection action under the Federal Claims Collection Act, is not an initial determination, and therefore generates no appeal rights.[13]

The liability practitioner must become familiar with the processes involved with the above review types to successfully challenge a determination of the Agency. Even so, an administrative victory has no precedential value beyond the law of the case. If the issue should arise in a subsequent matter, the administrative process starts over. Only when a case reaches federal court and a decision is reached is there precedent.

---

[13] *See* 42 C.F.R. § 405.705(d).

In *Merrifield v. U.S.*,[14] the plaintiffs, all New Jersey residents, commenced an action against the U.S. government and HHS on a theory that defendants wrongfully, and in violation of plaintiffs' constitutional due process rights, demanded reimbursement for those medical expenses pursuant to the MSP. Plaintiffs argued that CMS was not entitled to reimbursement under the MSP provision because their medical expenses were not by law an element of recovery against a tortfeasor.[15] The plaintiffs did not prevail, despite the fact they made no recovery for medical expenses. They were required to pay Medicare its reimbursement claim and to further dispute the issue would require years of appeals within CMS.

5.5.   Appealing CMS/MSPRC Denials for Request for Waiver

Initial determinations generate appeal rights. There are three types of initial determinations made within the context of the MSP program that generate appeal rights. The beneficiary may appeal:

- The existence of the overpayment;
- The amount of the overpayment; and
- A less than fully favorable determination of §1870(c) waiver request.

The beneficiary must be given notice of appeal rights within the document reflecting the initial determination. If the beneficiary continues to follow through with the appeal process, notice of the next sequential appeal right must be given with each new determination. (See Appendix 36G.) It should be noted that in the context of a potential Medicare secondary payer recovery, the overpayment is created not with the Medicare payment to a provider of medical services or equipment, but instead with a beneficiary's failure to repay Medicare from the proceeds of an insurance recovery or settlement. "If the beneficiary or other party receives a third party payment, the beneficiary or other party must reimburse Medicare within 60 days."[16]

---

[14] 2009 U.S. Dist. LEXIS 55377 (D.N.J. 2009).
[15] *See* N.J. Stat. Ann. § 2A:15-97.
[16] 42 C.F.R. § 411.24(h).

A person other than the one who made the initial determination must decide an appeal. The objective is to decide whether the initial determination was correct. As part of the appeal determination, staff may need to conduct medical review of the services in question. Therefore, it is important to obtain all related documentation (*i.e.*, emergency room reports, admission history, physician orders, nursing notes, and discharge summary) so that the person reviewing the file may make an informed evaluation. Other steps that should be followed include:

- Checking all mathematical computations for accuracy;
- Determining whether any new evidence has been produced since the time the initial determination was made; if so, that information must be considered;
- If the beneficiary is appealing a denial of a waiver request, using the criteria discussed above in the Waiver section to determine whether the initial determination is correct;
- Once the determination has been made, sending the beneficiary/attorney the standard letter, depending upon whether the beneficiary is appealing the overpayment or a waiver determination. The contractor's letter must include a clear rationale for its determination; and
- Making sure the determination contains notification of the second appeal right. This appeal right automatically comes into effect when the beneficiary is dissatisfied with the reconsideration or review determination, and makes a written request for such an appeal.

Reconsideration letters from Medicare contain important language with respect to the appeal process. If the beneficiary disagrees with the reconsidered determination, involving more than $100.00, then there is a right to request a hearing before an Administrative Law Judge (ALJ) in the Office of Hearing and Appeals of the Social Security Administration. The following timeline is critical at this point in the case:[17]

---

[17] See Medicare Secondary Payer Manual at Chapter 7.

1. 60 days to request an ALJ hearing;
2. The 60 days starts upon receipt of the reconsideration determination;
3. Even one day past the 60th day from receipt of the reconsidered determination, the appeal will be dismissed, unless a good explanation is offered as to why the request was late; and,
4. A hearing must be specifically requested in writing, and sent to the office that issued the reconsidered determination or a local Social Security office which will provide the necessary forms.
5. After the ALJ hearing, an appeal must be brought within 60 days to the Medicare Appeals Council.
6. The Medicare Appeals Council can decline review of and summarily affirm the ALJ's decision, making the ALJ decision final and binding 60 days from service of the Medicare Appeals Council decision.[18]
7. Judicial review is available in an appropriate United States District Court if a civil action is filed within 60 days after service of the decision.[19]
8. If the Medicare Appeals Council grants review of the ALJ decision and issues a decision of its own, then judicial review is available if an appeal is filed within 60 days of receiving the decision.

5.6.   Judicial Review of an Agency Determination

When an agency interprets its own regulation, that interpretation is given a great deal of weight by the courts.[20] However, the way in which a given regulation applies may be challenged if it does not give fair warning that the allegedly violative conduct was prohibited.[21]

When a court reviews an agency's construction of a statute, it must first decide whether Congress has directly spoken to the precise question at issue.[22] "If the intent of Congress is clear, that is the end of

---

[18] *See* 42 C.F.R. § 1005.21(j).
[19] *See* §§ 1128(f)(1) and 205(g) of the Social Security Act and 42 C.F.R. § 1005.21(k)(1).
[20] *Udall v. Tallman*, 380 U.S. 1 (1965).
[21] *See Daily v. Bond*, 623 F.2d 624 (9th Cir. 1980) (*per curiam*).
[22] *Furlong v. Shalala*, 156 F.3d 384 (2d Cir. 1998).

the matter; for the court, as well as the agency, must give effect to the unambiguously expressed intent of Congress."[23] "If the statute is silent or ambiguous with respect to the specific issue, the question for the court is whether the agency's answer is based on a permissible construction of the statute."[24]

The APA provides that "[a] person suffering legal wrong because of agency action, or adversely affected or aggrieved by agency action within the meaning of a relevant statute, is entitled to judicial review thereof."[25] This provision permits review of "final agency action for which there is no other adequate remedy in a court."[26] However, review under the APA may be excepted where: (i) "statutes preclude judicial review;" or (ii) "agency action is committed to agency discretion by law."[27] These exceptions are construed narrowly and apply only if there is "clear and convincing evidence of legislative intention to preclude review."[28]

"Whether and to what extent a particular statute precludes judicial review is determined not only from its express language, but also from the structure of the statutory scheme, its objectives, its legislative history, and the nature of the administrative action involved."[29] Indeed, the "clear and convincing evidence" standard is met, "and the presumption favoring judicial review overcome, whenever the congressional intent to preclude judicial review is fairly discernible in the statutory scheme."[30] However, the clear and convincing evidence standard is "a useful reminder to the courts that, where substantial

---

[23] *Chevron, U.S.A., Inc. v. Natural Resources Defense Council, Inc.*, 467 U.S. 837 (1984).

[24] *Chevron*, 467 U.S. at 843.

[25] 5 U.S.C. § 702.

[26] *Id.*, at § 704.

[27] *Id.* at § 701(a).

[28] *Japan Whaling Ass'n v. Am. Cetacean Soc'y*, 478 U.S. 221, 230 (1986); *see also Abbott Labs. v. Gardner*, 387 U.S. 136 (1967), *abrogated on other grounds by Califano v. Sanders*, 430 U.S. 99 (1977).

[29] *Block v. Cmty. Nutrition Inst.*, 467 U.S. 340, 345 (1984); *see also Bowen v. Michigan Acad. of Family Physicians*, 476 U.S. 667, (1986) (holding that the presumption favoring judicial review may be overcome by "specific language" or "inferences of intent drawn from the statutory scheme as a whole").

[30] *Block*, 467 U.S. at 350-51 (citation and internal quotation marks omitted).

doubt about the congressional intent exists, the general presumption favoring judicial review of administrative action is controlling."[31]

Under 42 U.S.C. § 405(h) — made applicable to the Medicare Act by 42 U.S.C. § 395ii — 42 U.S.C. § 405(g) is the sole avenue for judicial review for all claims arising under the Act. To the exclusion of 28 U.S.C. § 1331, and to be true to the language of the statute, the inquiry in determining whether 405(h) bars federal question jurisdiction is whether the claim "arises under" the Medicare Act, not whether it lends itself to a substantive rather than a procedural label.

The Court extended the bar to federal review of Social Security claims to include Medicare claims in *Heckler v. Ringer*.[32] In *Ringer,* four Medicare recipients brought an action in federal court based on federal question jurisdiction challenging the disallowance of benefits to cover a surgical procedure to relieve respiratory distress.[33] Medicare patients seeking reimbursement for the procedure were awarded money to cover their surgery costs until 1980, when the Department of Health and Human Services issued a formal administrative ruling prohibiting reimbursement for the surgery. Three of the four claimants had already had the surgery before 1980 and were seeking reimbursement, while Ringer, the fourth claimant, was seeking money to undergo surgery. Each claimant was at a different stage in the appeal process, but none of the claimants had received a final ruling from the Secretary. The Court dismissed the three cases where the claimants had had surgery before the Secretary issued the administrative ruling and were not barred from reimbursement by the ruling. The only remaining claimant, Ringer, had requested payment from HHS, but the Secretary was unwilling to issue a ruling in his case until he underwent the surgery. Ringer had not undergone the surgery because he was indigent and was seeking a judgment to obtain the money necessary for the surgery.

The Court ruled that section 405(h) applied to Ringer's claim because although he maintained that the administrative ruling was unconstitutional, he was still seeking reimbursement of the award of

---

[31] *Id.* at 351.

[32] *See* 466 U.S. 602 (1984).

[33] *See A Right to No Meaningful Review under the Due Process Clause: The Aftermath of Judicial Deference to the Federal Administrative Agencies,* by Ruqaiijah A. Yearby, HEALTH MATRIX: JOURNAL OF LAW-MEDICINE (Summer 2006).

benefits under the Medicare Act. Thus, his claims arose under the Medicare Act. According to the Court, regardless of whether his claim challenged the procedures of HHS or the substance of HHS's actions, Ringer's claims arose under 42 U.S.C. § 405(h), which barred federal review on the claims until a final action from the Secretary. The Court barred review even though there was an exception to the 405(h) bar that would have allowed a federal court to review Ringer's case. Specifically, the Secretary had drafted an exception to the subject matter jurisdiction requirement to allow cases to go to federal court after the reconsideration stage "when the only factor precluding an award of benefits is a statutory provision which the claimant challenges as unconstitutional." [34] The Court ruled that the exception did not apply in this case because the constitutional claims were inextricably linked with Ringer's benefits claims. Furthermore, the Court ruled that the claimant seeking money to have the surgery still had an avenue of review even if there was a presumption against reimbursement. Thus, Ringer's case was dismissed for lack of subject matter jurisdiction. Effectively, this left Ringer with no avenue for review because he had no right to agency review until after he underwent the surgery, which he could not afford.

Although the Court's decision in *Ringer* left the claimant with no meaningful administrative or federal review, the Court did not allow this as an exception. The Court's decision was particularly disturbing because in *Bowen v. Michigan Academy of Family Physicians*, an exception to sections 405(g) & (h) was allowed when physicians were left with no meaningful administrative or federal review, a direct contradiction to the *Ringer* decision. [35]

In *Bowen*, the Court allowed Medicare providers to forgo presentment to HHS and a final decision because there was no right to agency review. The Supreme Court also created an exception to the subject matter jurisdiction bar in *Matthews v. Eldridge*. [36] In *Eldridge*, the Court allowed a Social Security beneficiary to obtain federal review without a final ruling because his constitutional claim was *collateral* to his claims arising under the Social Security Act. In a similar fashion, the

---

[34] 42 C.F.R. §§ 4-05.718-718e (1982); 20 C.F.R. §§ 404.923-404.928 (1983). *Heckler v. Ringer*, 104 S. Ct. 2013, 2017 (1984).

[35] *See Bowen*, 476 U.S. 667 (1986).

[36] 424 U.S. 319 (1976).

nursing home association in *Shalala v. Ill. Council on Long Term Health Care, Inc.*[37] argued that its case met both of these exceptions; the Court, however, classified the nursing homes' claims as similar to those filed in *Weinberger v. Salfi*[38] and *Ringer* and dismissed the claims for lack of subject matter jurisdiction.

An important practical point before starting the administrative appeal process is deciding whether to hold on to the disputed funds or pay them over to the agency. Given that interest at 11% accrues on the unpaid amount 60 days from the date of the agency's demand for payment by the MSPRC, it would be a best practice to pay it. Furthermore, as non-payment during the dispute could lead to collection action by the Department of Treasury, not only could the Medicare beneficiary face possible suspension of his or her Social Security or Medicare benefits, but a plan could be implicated as well and assets such as tax refunds or payroll taxes could be levied. These issues could unnecessarily complicate the appeal and therefore, it would be best to reimburse the agency before the 60-day time frame to avoid these unintended consequences.

42 C.F.R. § 411.37(c) states that Medicare will recognize a proportionate share of the necessary procurement costs incurred through obtaining a settlement. In order for Medicare to calculate the net refund that is due, it is a best practice for the plaintiff's counsel to prepare and submit a Final Settlement Detail Document contemporaneously with the settlement agreement and release. (See Appendix 36H.) In fact, the authors have found that there is a practical benefit to submitting the Final Settlement Detail Document with the release upon the settlement of a case. The MSPRC places a value on this practice.

Practice Tip: Plaintiffs' attorneys should fill out the 1-page document known as the Final Settlement Detail Document. This document was drafted by CMS and will assist in expediting the final demand for payment from the MSPRC. Be sure to handwrite plaintiff's HIC# on the document because the MSPRC tracks each piece of correspondence by using this number.

---

[37] 127 F.3d 496 (6th Cir. 1997).
[38] 422 U.S. 749 (1975).

CHAPTER 6

WHAT'S ON THE MSP HORIZON

Implementation of new electronic reporting requirements has resulted in renewed interest in Medicare Secondary Payer Compliance. In the past, Medicare "liens" were left for the Claimant or Claimant's attorney to resolve. This no longer works for the Primary Plan; it can be exposed to Medicare claims years after settlement and there is little comfort that the hold harmless agreement will be of any relief at that time. To manage this obligation today, Primary Plans must be involved as soon as possible and take a proactive approach. Funds should not be disbursed until adequate assurances of MSP compliance have been met. This involves cooperation by all parties involved.

Congress did not equip Primary Plans with any enforcement tools to assist in protecting against their exposure. Medicare has clarified the responsibility, but has provided little to no guidance on how to achieve compliance. Primary Plans have therefore looked elsewhere to seek insulation from contingent liabilities. In doing so, the authors have discovered some alternatives that help fill the void.

6.0. Involving Medicare in the Case

Generally, courts have disfavored any action by the Primary Plan to act unilaterally and add Medicare as a payee.[1] However, there is no appellate decision on point. If Medicare is added to the check, it is the authors' recommendation that both sides agree to this prior to settlement. If done without the other side's agreement, the Primary Plan may be adding unnecessary cost to the defense of the case. CMS has made it clear that adding Medicare to the disbursement check would protect its interest.[2] However, the plaintiff's bar is dead set

---

[1] *Tomilson v. Landers*, 2009 U.S. Dist. LEXIS 38683.
[2] *See* CMS Town Hall Conference Call, 02/25/2010, pg. 49-50, http://www.cms.gov/Medicare/Coordination-of-Benefits/MandatoryInsRep/downloads/Feb2510NGHPTranscript.pdf.

against this practice.[3] Thus, while adding Medicare as a payee to a check is an excellent solution for the Primary Plan to resolve MSP compliance, it may be difficult for the plaintiffs' bar to play along. However, it is a possible remedy the authors have seen used.

In situations where the funds available for settlement are limited, the Court has been asked to get involved in allocating the funds between competing interests. The authors had once taken the position that Medicare's involvement is necessary for such an allocation. However, in recent matters involving allocations for future medical, having Medicare at the table was not necessary. (See Chapter 5). It would, at a minimum, require an invitation to Medicare and for the Court to be satisfied that Medicare had declined to participate, before the Court would act. It is in the best interests of the Court to promote settlements, so Courts are taking evidence and making determinations on this topic. It is important that where Medicare's conditional payments exceed the settlement amount, the parties are aware that various Circuit Courts interpret differently whether Medicare can collect 100% of its reimbursement claim. Thus far, the 11th Circuit, in *Bradley*, is contrary to the decision of the 9th Circuit (*Zinman*) and 6th Circuit. (*Hadden*). *Hadden* is presently on writ to the U.S. Supreme Court, so there remains a possibility the conflict may be resolved soon.

Another method of obtaining a procedure to assist in complying with the Medicare Secondary Payer Act is to educate the Court. As mentioned above, the Primary Plan has no enforcement tools available to ensure compliance with the Act. The court can help to streamline data that is necessary to obtain information from Medicare, in order to increase the likelihood of settlement, and decrease the waste of precious judicial resources. The liability practitioner must start early to educate the court about the impact of the Act and request assistance. (See Appendix 38.) Pre-trial assistance can come in the form of a scheduling order that will manage what each party is doing to obtain conditional payment information. A simple case management order from the court will significantly increase the likelihood that information will be available to the parties at the time the case is resolved through settlement or trial.

---

[3] *Lienholders on Settlement Checks, When Hell Freezes Over*, by Raizman, Frischman & Matzus, 2010.

A proper scheduling order (See Appendix 39) should consider the following elements:

- Continuous obligation on the part of the plaintiff to identify himself or herself as a Medicare beneficiary;
- Assignment of one party as lead to seek the appropriate information from the Medicare contractor;
- Specified time period before contact is made with the Medicare contractor for the parties to agree on the appropriate ICD-9 codes related to the claim;
- Specified time period in which the lead will notify the Medicare contractor and provide updates to the parties as to the progress;
- Opportunity for the parties to discuss the initial Payment Summary Form and determine whether it is appropriate to enter into relatedness discussions with Medicare;
- Ruling that the plaintiff should sign up for MyMedicare.gov so that he or she can manage online the conditional payments information under the My MSP tab;
- A provision that any information shared or discussed is for settlement purposes only and not admissible at trial;
- Notification to the court when conditional payment information is available so the court may start the procedural processes to set the case for trial or alternative dispute resolution, or employ other methods to move the case along toward resolution; and
- Requirement that the plaintiff provide a properly executed Consent to Release Form to the defense.

6.1. Post-Trial

The courts also have an important role post-trial. The plan is required to report judgments electronically. If not properly allocated through the use of special verdict forms, jury sheets or the like, the plaintiff beneficiary will face similar problems as discussed above. Although the plan has lost the case, it still has a vested interest in making certain Medicare is properly handled. If not, the plan may be subject to pay the judgment again under 42 C.F.R. § 411.24(i). Therefore, it may be appropriate in a post trial motion to have the court require that the Medicare issue be resolved in a manner satisfactory to all parties involved.

We know CMS will respect a judicial determination. The question is whether that determination requires a trial or can be accomplished through a hearing with evidence presented. A good insight into this question is to look at Chapter 7 of the MSP Manual at §50.4.4 which sets forth the following:

> The only situation in which Medicare recognizes allocations of liability payments to non-medical losses is when payments is based on a *court order* on the merits of the case. If the court or other adjudicator of the merits specifically designates [*sic*] amounts that are for not related to medical services, Medicare will accept the Court's designation. Medicare does not seek recovery from portions of court awards that are designated as payment for losses other than medical services. (Emphasis added).

Several court decisions involving Act issues support this reference in the manual.[4] The following passage is particularly illuminating: "Medicare will relent, however, and exercise its right of reimbursement only against damages found for medical expenses where the medical and non-medical damages items are determined by judgment or arbitration."[5] The import of this reference is that the courts do have a role that can be used to achieve finality of a settlement. If there is no allocation, the plaintiff who is a Medicare beneficiary is forever looking over his or her shoulder, concerned about what portion of the settlement can be spent beyond medical expenses. The plan also has a similar concern because if the Medicare beneficiary exhausts the settlement proceeds on non-medical expenses, Medicare may suspend benefits in the future until the plaintiff beneficiary can demonstrate, through an audit process and review of receipts, that the settlement proceeds were exhausted for medical expenses. This could trigger the private cause of action under the Act and re-open litigation.

---

[4] *See Zinman v. Shalala*, 67 F.3d 841 (9th Cir. 1995); *and Denekas v. Shalala*, 943 F. Supp. 1073 (S.D. Iowa 1996).

[5] *See Denekas*, 943 F. Supp. 1073, at 1079, citing *Zinman*.

6.2. Discovery

The authors have had ongoing conversations with courts in Erie County, New York, and Cook County, Illinois, to impress upon state court judges the need to require liability litigants to provide basic information concerning the Medicare component of their claims. Without question, one of the more frustrating situations for state court judges is to encounter concerns at settlement that both parties are willing to settle the case, but for the unknown Medicare component.

To avoid such frustration — at trial, settlement or mediation — it would behoove all state court jurisdictions to utilize and implement a scheduling order that addresses the disclosure of Medicare information, where applicable. The proposed scheduling order, set forth in the Appendix, should produce basic information, such as (i) Health Identification Card Number; (ii) the beneficiary's address; (iii) the beneficiary's date of birth; (iv) a properly executed Consent to Release Form entitling counsel for defendants to communicate with the federal government and its contractors (MSPRC and COBC); (v) and a properly executed Medicare Section 111 form.[6] (See Appendix 40.) This will go a long way to ease the administrative concerns created by the Act and eliminate any confusion by the parties as to why the information is required. We have also provided proposed discovery demands that should be utilized in the absence of the scheduling order. (See Appendix 41.)

Another discovery tool to utilize is a pleading we call Notice of Medicare Involvement. If a case is destined for trial, then it would be prudent for the defendant Primary Plan to serve notice upon the court and plaintiff's counsel of the challenges posed by the Medicare Secondary Payer Act. The pleading we use regularly cites to the specific facts of a given case to lay out for the court and plaintiff's counsel a number of factors:

1. The defendant is serving the "Notice of Medicare Involvement" with the court to ensure compliance with the Medicare Secondary Payer Act, 42 U.S.C. 1395y.

---

[6] This form can be found at the Centers for Medicare and Medicaid Services website: http://www.cms.hhs.gov/MandatoryInsRep/Downloads/NGHHICNSSNNGHPForm.pdf.

2. In this matter, plaintiff alleges that defendant was negligent and therefore responsible for, among other elements of damages, the retail medical expenses associated with injuries alleged sustained and medical treatment and medicines related to the incident giving rise to the litigation.

3. The liability in this matter is disputed. Plaintiff is over the age of 65 or otherwise qualifies for Medicare on other grounds. The retail medical costs and expenses are alleged to have reached and exceeded $_____. It is currently unknown what Medicare is claiming it paid in expenses related to the incident. Given the extremely questionable liability, there is very little possibility that the claim will be resolved short of trial.

4. Defendant is taking very seriously its obligations under the Medicare Secondary Payer Act found at 42 U.S.C. 1395y (b)(2)(B) (ii) *et seq.* (hereinafter "MSPA"). For example, defendant utilizes the services of a Medicare Consultant to assist with traversing the MSPA and is of the opinion that this court should be aware of Medicare's interests and guidance as it pertains to the above-captioned matter.

5. While the ability to settle this matter short of trial is unlikely, there are ways the court and counsel can utilize a jury verdict form to ensure that past and future medical expenses, if awarded, are properly accounted for by the court and/or jury in order to satisfy Medicare's requirements. This is important because the Government has made it clear that, while a Medicare reimbursement amount ("Lien") cannot be reduced by fault-based allocations, there is explicit language in the Medicare Secondary Payer Manual making it clear that a court's designation will be honored by the Government, after a full hearing on the merits. In the event of an adverse judgment, Primary Plan could then satisfy its Medicare obligations by tendering payment to Medicare for the medical related damages set forth in the special verdict.

6. Stated specifically, "The only situation in which Medicare recognizes allocations of liability payments to non-medical

losses is when payment is based on a court order on the merits of the case. If the court or other adjudicator of the merits specifically designates amounts that are for payment of pain and suffering or other amounts not related to medical services, *Medicare will accept the Court's designation. Medicare does not seek recovery from portions of court awards that are designated as payment for losses other than medical services."* (Emphasis added). See Chapter 7, Section 50.4.4 of the MSP Manual.

7.   The costs and expenses Medicare has paid as a result of the incident being litigated stand in the way of any cost-to-defend settlement that might be offered in a case without a Medicare component. If the court does not control the way in which past and future medical costs are awarded at trial, if at all, then there is a distinct likelihood that whatever award is entered will be completely consumed by Medicare and that defendant, to protect itself, will be forced to tender payment to Medicare in the full amount of Medicare's lien.

The above is example language only, and the liability practitioner should mold the facts to the pleading. The authors have first-hand experience with the effect filing such a pleading has on the court and plaintiff's counsel. It is an attention-getter.

6.3.   Legislative Reform

The Medicare Advocacy Recovery Coalition (MARC) has supported the efforts of Congress to introduce legislation to bring needed implementation reforms. The coalition's membership is as varied as the liability industry itself. Whether it be the plaintiff attorney, defense attorney, insurance carrier, Medicare beneficiary plaintiff, self insured or Medicare Secondary Payer vendor, each have asked Congress to pass legislation to help improve compliance. In March, 2011, The Strengthening Medicare and Reimbursing Taxpayers Act (SMART) was introduced by Representatives Tim Murphy of Pittsburg, PA and Tom Wyden of Wisconsin. The proposed legislation, H.R. #1063, would cause the following reforms to the present MSP law:

1) Eliminate the requirement forcing Primary Plans to collect Social Security Numbers to identify Medicare Secondary Payer cases for reporting purposes;

2) Allow Primary Plans the right to appeal Medicare determinations regarding conditional payments that may be owed related to a liability claim;

3) Allow for parties to self calculate what is owed Medicare and have that binding on Medicare before a settlement, judgment, or award for a certain period of time;

4) Adjust electronic reporting penalties discretion by CMS to cover good faith and other situations where it would be unfair and unjust to issue it;

5) Implement a clear limitations period when Medicare must act to protect its interest; and

6) Exempt certain claims from MSP compliance that cost more for Medicare to pursue recovery, than the recovery itself.

The proposed legislation has received favorable support by well over 110 Representatives as of the time this book went to print. It also enjoys the support of the Senate, as S. 1718 was introduced last fall (2011), a mirror image of H.R. #1063, with over 17 sponsors.

The SMART Act cannot fix all of the issues with MSP. The most glaring issue not covered by the Bill is the Medicare Set Aside Arrangement. This was purposeful because of the nature of Congress and its requirement that legislation have a zero cost to the budget. As Medicare presently approves certain Medicare Set Asides, any attempt to adjust the program would be deemed to have an adverse impact on the budget. The Congressional Budget Office (CBO) would have to issue a score under its methodology. As legislation requires a CBO score, MSAs were left out for the short term. In the long term, the MSA is proper subject of Regulatory reform, not legislation.

6.4.   CMS Upcoming Actions

CMS issued an interim draft Statement of Work to integrate the Coordination of Benefits Contractor (COBC) and Medicare Secondary Payer Recovery Contractor (MSPRC) into one contractor. The new contractor, Medicare Secondary Payer Integrated Contractor (MSPIC), in addition to responsibility for both functions, would also have involvement with potential Recovery Audit Contractors (RAC). CMS initially piloted the use of RAC for Group Health Plans to review medical billings. The RAC was paid 12% of any errors it found. If implemented for the Non-Group Health Plans, the authors suspect the RAC would be paid similarly. The RAC would be authorized to audit RREs based on RRE agreements signed with Medicare that allow for such. Target areas for such RAC audits would be:

1. Notification to Medicare under 42 C.F.R. 411.25
2. Timely reporting of claim based on TPOC Date versus Report Date under Section 111
3. Payment of Conditional Payments.

The implications for the very existence of such contractors should not be lost on the reader. Essentially, Medicare is likely to employ bounty hunters to audit large claims operations and perhaps law firms and such bounty hunters will be paid more for the lack of compliance uncovered. The need to have a protocol in place to manage the issues springing from Medicare Secondary Payer compliance is very essential, indeed.

Medicare is also implementing recovery against Social Security Payments made to Medicare beneficiaries. As Section 111 data is received, CMS is looking to recoup that recovery, if any conditional payments are outstanding, by attaching such benefits. The challenge for CMS in implementing this process will be whether the injury code data submitted by the RRE is accurate with regard to the injury related to the claim. If not, a number of potential appeals may be triggered.

The alternative would be for Medicare to suspend benefits which could occur in one of two ways:

First, the payment demand issued by the Medicare contractor is not a *final* payment demand. This does not exist, and a careful reading of the payment demand letter on this point will quickly articulate this fact.

While it is true that Medicare does not seek payments subsequent to the settlement date[7] (assuming proper notification of settlement) it does intend to fully recover any goods and services that it has paid before the settlement. Health care providers have up to 27 months to bill Medicare. That being the case, the parties need to be certain that all related bills are covered when resolving the case, not only those that Medicare may have received. When upon receipt of such bills, Medicare will issue subsequent payment demand letters and expect reimbursement. Medicare has the right to seek reimbursement up to the entire amount of the settlement. Unless the settlement is properly apportioned, a plaintiff cannot have certainty as to what is allowed to be spent for other purposes. At a minimum, such uncertainty will cause a great number of questions to be raised post settlement — sometimes two years after a case is resolved. If an allocation is established, the amount that Medicare can reach is limited.

Second, the issue of future medical liability (covered in Chapter 4) needs to be addressed. Such liability could certainly consume the settlement and any plaintiff beneficiary would be foolish to settle without certainty of what he or she can or cannot spend.

While MSP allows Medicare such authority, the disruption in delivering benefits could be catastrophic to the Medicare beneficiary, and have negative implications to Medicare with Congress. Reducing Social Security may be the lesser of two evils, if Medicare intends to go only after the Medicare beneficiary and not the Primary Plan and Claimant's Attorney.

Medicare has an $89 trillion problem. MSP is designed to protect the Medicare Trust Fund. CMS has been careful not to tread much on the RRE, and focus on the Medicare beneficiary. However, over the long term, the Medicare beneficiary is not as sophisticated to deliver consistent reimbursement to Medicare and, over time, the authors believe that Medicare will need to go direct to the Primary Plan. It has already exhibited this propensity when it sought electronic reporting. It would not surprise the authors that after a short period of failing to collect what it requires to meet the Trust Fund's needs further reimbursement rules are implemented against the primary plan.

---

[7] See the discussion of future medical considerations in Chapter 4.

6.5   Advanced Notice of Proposed Rulemaking (ANPRM)

CMS has published an "Advanced Notice of Proposed Rulemaking" on the issue of "Liability Medicare Set Asides." The final document has been sent to the Federal Register, and can be identified as CMS-6047-ANPRM.

In this document, the Agency proposes seven different options for treating the reimbursement of future medical expenses in NGHP (Non-Group Health Plan) settlements.

First there are exceptions to when CMS would consider an LMSA to not be necessary. We are pleased to see that CMS is proposing a position that the authors have taken with the issue of when Medicare's interests do **not** need to be protected. They are:

- $300 Exemption. (See ANPRM Option 5).
- Fixed Payment Option in cases settling for $5,000 or less. (See ANPRM Option 5).
- Self Calculated Conditional Payment Option in cases settling for $25,000 or less. (See ANPRM Option 5).
- Existence of another primary payer, like Workers' Compensation or No-Fault.(See ANPRM Option 2).

CMS is presently looking for comments. Our thoughts regarding the ANPRM follows, but the authors encourage its readers to submit their own comments to help shape the final rule.

- Pay careful attention to the proposed definitions section, at pages 8 and 9. How terms are defined can lead to significant confusion in the liability industry where liability and relatedness of injury to tort are not as precise as CMS envisions;
- Option 1 really is not an option. A Medicare beneficiary will not settle the claim, and agree to pay for all future-related care and treatment from the settlement, until all settlement funds are exhausted. This option has the effect of a claimant commencing suit to achieve exactly what the beneficiary already has: Medicare benefits, or some entity to pay for treatment. We commonly refer to this option as the Poor Man's MSA;

- Option 2 includes the language "expectation of a Medicare beneficiary within 30 months." This language does not fit the liability claim. The most glaring reason concerns the fact that there is no reporting requirement, under Section 111 or under the existing Medicare regulations, for the "almost Medicare beneficiary." It is already difficult to obtain Social Security Numbers from someone who already is a Medicare beneficiary — It will be next to impossible to obtain SSNs from someone who is "almost a Medicare beneficiary;"
- Option 6 a, Up Front Payment to Medicare, appears to bring Workers' Compensation plans into the scope of this proposed rulemaking;
- This proposed rulemaking document is using the term "conditional payments" to mean past and future incident-related payments made by Medicare. This statement needs further clarification to define who is responsible for such payments. The Medicare beneficiary may be responsible for this, but primary plans are statutorily obligated for conditional payments, so if Medicare is taking an official position that post-settlement payments made by Medicare, related to the loss, are also "conditional" then primary plans would also be obligated to manage the future component;
- There are no timelines offered for submission, review, and appeal.
- Medicare Advantage Private Cause of Action Claims — The ANPRM does not cover the impact of the recant ruling by the Third Circuit Court of Appeals in Avandia. Medicare Advantage Plans typically provide greater coverage than traditional Medicare. A concern is whether MSAs based on Medicare covered events foreclose any future claim for damages by an MA plan which may go beyond traditional Medicare coverage. Medicare should put boundaries around MA plans to avoid confusion by the industry on whether an approved MSA is the final word that forecloses any possible private cause of action claim.

Overall, the document is attempting to offer a level of precision on a topic that is not precise. For example, the severity of injury formulas and concepts do not translate in a liability claim atmosphere where fault is usually at least somewhat in dispute. We like to say that CMS is using a scalpel to arrive at MSP solutions when the liability industry is using a chainsaw. Such precision is nearly impossible to reach consensus amongst traditionally adverse parties.

This is where success of the *Hadden* appeal is critical. Recall that *Hadden* (now on a writ before the US Supreme Court seeking *certiorari*) deals with the concept that if a claimant takes less in a settlement, based upon factors of fault, then Medicare should also take less. This will be an important case to monitor. Without a fault-based analysis, Medicare will continue to take full value.

APPENDIX CONTENTS

APPENDIX 1

Medicare Secondary Payer Act
Title 42, Chapter 7, Subchapter XVIII, Part E § 1395y –
Exclusions from Coverage and Medicare
as Secondary Payer

42 USC §1395y(b)

(b) Medicare as secondary payer

Intentionally omitted 42 USC §1395y(b)(1) "Requirements of group health plans"

(2) Medicare secondary payer
(A) In general
Payment under this subchapter may not be made, except as provided in subparagraph (B), with respect to any item or service to the extent that—
(i) payment has been made, or can reasonably be expected to be made, with respect to the item or service as required under paragraph (1), or
(ii) payment has been made, or can reasonably be expected to be made under a workmen's compensation law or plan of the United States or a State or under an automobile or liability insurance policy or plan (including a self-insured plan) or under no fault insurance.
In this subsection, the term "primary plan" means a group health plan or large group health plan, to the extent that clause (i) applies, and a workmen's compensation law or plan, an automobile or liability insurance policy or plan (including a self-insured plan) or no fault insurance, to the extent that clause (ii) applies. An entity that engages in a business, trade, or profession shall be deemed to have a self-insured plan if it carries its own risk (whether by a failure to obtain insurance, or otherwise) in whole or in part.

(B) Conditional payment

(i) Authority to make conditional payment The Secretary may make payment under this subchapter with respect to an item or service if a primary plan described in subparagraph (A)(ii) has not made or cannot reasonably be expected to make payment with respect to such item or service promptly (as determined in accordance with regulations). Any such payment by the Secretary shall be conditioned on reimbursement to the appropriate Trust Fund in accordance with the succeeding provisions of this subsection.

(ii) Repayment required A primary plan, and an entity that receives payment from a primary plan, shall reimburse the appropriate Trust Fund for any payment made by the Secretary under this subchapter with respect to an item or service if it is demonstrated that such primary plan has or had a responsibility to make payment with respect to such item or service. A primary plan's responsibility for such payment may be demonstrated by a judgment, a payment conditioned upon the recipient's compromise, waiver, or release (whether or not there is a determination or admission of liability) of payment for items or services included in a claim against the primary plan or the primary plan's insured, or by other means. If reimbursement is not made to the appropriate Trust Fund before the expiration of the 60-day period that begins on the date notice of, or information related to, a primary plan's responsibility for such payment or other information is received, the Secretary may charge interest (beginning with the date on which the notice or other information is received) on the amount of the reimbursement until reimbursement is made (at a rate determined by the Secretary in accordance with regulations of the Secretary of the Treasury applicable to charges for late payments).

(iii) Action by United States In order to recover payment made under this subchapter for an item or service, the United States may bring an action against any or all entities that are or were required or responsible (directly, as an insurer or self-insurer, as a third-party administrator, as an employer that sponsors or contributes to a group health plan, or large group health plan, or otherwise) to make payment with respect to the same item or service (or any portion thereof) under a primary plan. The United States may, in accordance with paragraph (3)(A) collect double damages against any such entity. In addition, the United States may recover under this clause from any entity that has received payment from a primary plan or from the proceeds of a primary plan's payment to any entity. The United States may not recover from a third-party administrator under this clause in cases where the third-party administrator would not be able to recover the amount at issue from the employer or group health plan and is not employed by or under contract with the employer or group health plan at the time the action for recovery is initiated by the United States or for whom it provides administrative services due to the insolvency or bankruptcy of the employer or plan.

(iv) Subrogation rights The United States shall be subrogated (to the extent of payment made under this subchapter for such an item or service) to any right under this subsection of an individual or any other entity to payment with respect to such item or service under a primary plan.

(v) Waiver of rights The Secretary may waive (in whole or in part) the provisions of this subparagraph in the case of an individual claim if the Secretary determines that the waiver is in the best interests of the program established under this subchapter.

(vi) Claims-filing period Notwithstanding any other time limits that may exist for filing a claim under an employer group health plan, the United States may seek to recover conditional payments in accordance with this subparagraph where the request for payment is submitted to the entity required or responsible under this subsection to pay with respect to the item or service (or any portion thereof) under a primary plan within the 3-year period beginning on the date on which the item or service was furnished.

(C) Treatment of questionnaires

The Secretary may not fail to make payment under subparagraph (A) solely on the ground that an individual failed to complete a questionnaire concerning the existence of a primary plan.

(3) Enforcement
(A) Private cause of action
There is established a private cause of action for damages (which shall be in an amount double the amount otherwise provided) in the case of a primary plan which fails to provide for primary payment (or appropriate reimbursement) in accordance with paragraphs (1) and (2)(A).
(B) Reference to excise tax with respect to nonconforming group health plans
For provision imposing an excise tax with respect to nonconforming group health plans, see section 5000 of the Internal Revenue Code of 1986.
(C) Prohibition of financial incentives not to enroll in a group health plan or a large group health plan
It is unlawful for an employer or other entity to offer any financial or other incentive for an individual entitled to benefits under this subchapter not to enroll (or to terminate enrollment) under a group health plan or a large group health plan which would (in the case of such enrollment) be a primary plan (as defined in paragraph (2)(A)). Any entity that violates the previous sentence is subject to a civil money penalty of not to exceed $5,000 for each such violation. The provisions of section 1320a–7a of this title (other than subsections (a) and (b)) shall apply to a civil money penalty under the previous sentence in the same manner as such provisions apply to a penalty or proceeding under section 1320a–7a (a) of this title.

Intentionally omitted 42 USC §1395y(b)(4) "Coordination of benefits"

Intentionally omitted 42 USC §1395y(b)(5) "Identification of secondary payer situations"

Intentionally omitted 42 USC §1395y(b)(6) "Screening requirements for providers and suppliers

Intentionally omitted 42 USC §1395y(b)(7) "Required submission of information by group health plans"

(8) "Required submission of information by or on behalf of liability insurance (including self-insurance), no fault insurance, and workers' compensation laws and plans"

(A) Requirement

On and after the first day of the first calendar quarter beginning after the date that is 18 months after December 29, 2007, an applicable plan shall—

(i) determine whether a claimant (including an individual whose claim is unresolved) is entitled to benefits under the program under this subchapter on any basis; and

(ii) if the claimant is determined to be so entitled, submit the information described in subparagraph (B) with respect to the claimant to the Secretary in a form and manner (including frequency) specified by the Secretary.

(B) Required information

The information described in this subparagraph is—

(i) the identity of the claimant for which the determination under subparagraph (A) was made; and

(ii) such other information as the Secretary shall specify in order to enable the Secretary to make an appropriate determination concerning coordination of benefits, including any applicable recovery claim.

(C) Timing

Information shall be submitted under subparagraph (A)(ii) within a time specified by the Secretary after the claim is resolved through a settlement, judgment, award, or other payment (regardless of whether or not there is a determination or admission of liability).

(D) Claimant

For purposes of subparagraph (A), the term "claimant" includes—

(i) an individual filing a claim directly against the applicable plan; and

(ii) an individual filing a claim against an individual or entity insured or covered by the applicable plan.

(E) Enforcement

(i) In general An applicable plan that fails to comply with the requirements under subparagraph (A) with respect to any claimant shall be subject to a civil money penalty of $1,000 for each day of noncompliance with respect to each claimant. The provisions of subsections (e) and (k) of section 1320a–7a of this title shall apply to a civil money penalty under the previous sentence in the same manner as such provisions apply to a penalty or proceeding under section 1320a–7a (a) of this title. A civil money penalty under this clause shall be in addition to any other penalties prescribed by law and in addition to any Medicare secondary payer claim under this subchapter with respect to an individual.

(ii) Deposit of amounts collected Any amounts collected pursuant to clause (i) shall be deposited in the Federal Hospital Insurance Trust Fund.

(F) Applicable plan

In this paragraph, the term "applicable plan" means the following laws, plans, or other arrangements, including the fiduciary or administrator for such law, plan, or arrangement:

(i) Liability insurance (including self-insurance).

(ii) No fault insurance.

(iii) Workers' compensation laws or plans.

(G) Sharing of information

The Secretary may share information collected under this paragraph as necessary for purposes of the proper coordination of benefits.

(H) Implementation

Notwithstanding any other provision of law, the Secretary may implement this paragraph by program instruction or otherwise.

Intentionally omitted 42 USC §1395y(c) "Drug Products"

Intentionally omitted 42 USC §1395y(d)) "Items or services provided for emergency medical conditions"

Intentionally omitted 42 USC §1395y(e) "Item or service by excluded individual or entity or at direction of excluded physician; limitation of liability of beneficiaries with respect to services furnished by excluded individuals and entities"

Intentionally omitted 42 USC §1395y(f) "Utilization guidelines for provision of home health services"

Intentionally omitted 42 USC §1395y(g) "Contracts with utilization and quality control peer review organizations"

Intentionally omitted 42 USC §1395y(h) "Waiver of electronic form requirement"

Intentionally omitted 42 USC §1395y(i) "Awards and contracts for original research and experimentation of new and existing medical procedures; conditions"

Intentionally omitted 42 USC §1395y(j) "Nonvoting members and experts"

Intentionally omitted 42 USC §1395y(k) "Dental benefits under group health plans"

Intentionally omitted 42 USC §1395y(l) "National and local coverage determination process"

Intentionally omitted 42 USC §1395y(m) "Coverage of routine costs associated with certain clinical trials of category A devices"

APPENDIX 2

U.S. v. James Stricker, et al., Civil Action No. 1:09-cv-02423-KOB Complaint

IN THE UNITED STATES DISTRICT COURT
FOR THE NORTHERN DISTRICT OF ALABAMA
EASTERN DIVISION

UNITED STATES OF AMERICA, Plaintiff,	|	
v.	|	CV 09-BE-2423-E
JAMES J. STRICKER; et al, Defendants.	|	

MEMORANDUM OPINION
GRANTING CERTAIN DEFENDANTS' MOTIONS TO DISMISS

In this case, the United States seeks from attorneys and corporations reimbursement of Medicare benefits the Government paid to individuals who participated in a 2003 class tort settlement with Monsanto and other chemical companies involving PCB contamination in Anniston, Alabama. This matter comes before the court on the Plaintiff's "The United States' Motion for Partial Summary Judgment on Liability" (doc. 23) and six motions to dismiss by certain Defendants filed as follows: "Defendant Monsanto Company's Motion to Dismiss" (doc. 31); "Motion to Dismiss on Behalf of Defendant of Solutia Inc." (doc. 35); "Motion to Dismiss" (doc. 37) filed by Defendant Pharmacia Corporation; "Motion of Defendants James J. Stricker, Daniel R. Benson, Donald W. Stewart, and Kasowitz, Benson, Torres and Friedman LLP to Dismiss the Complaint" (doc. 40); "Motion to Dismiss" (doc. 46) filed by Defendants Don Barrett, The Barrett Law Firm, PA, Charles E. Fell, Jr., Charles Cunningham, Jr., and Cunningham & Fell, PLLC; and "Defendants American International Group, Inc.'s and the Travelers Companies, Inc.'s Motion to Dismiss Counts III and IV" (doc. 66). The motions to dismiss argue primarily that the Plaintiff's claims should be time-barred by the applicable statute of limitations, among other defenses.

The court held an extensive hearing on Monday, September 13, 2010, which addressed the issues and arguments presented in the motions to dismiss. For the reasons stated on the Record and elaborated below, the court finds that the longest applicable statute of limitations of six years has expired prior to December 1, 2009, when the Government filed this suit; therefore, the claims against these Defendants are barred by the statute of limitations. Accordingly, the court simultaneously will enter an Order dismissing the Plaintiff's claims as to the Defendants who filed motions to dismiss.[1]

I. Factual Background

This case stems from a famous set of facts. From 1929 to 1971, Monsanto Company and its predecessors—including Solutia, Inc. and Pharmacia Corporation—produced polychlorinated biphenyls ("PCBs") at a chemical manufacturing plant about one mile west of downtown Anniston, Alabama. In addition to environmental hazards identified from PCB emissions, the United States Environmental Protection Agency has found PCB exposure to cause health dangers such as cancer, decreased fertility, still births, and potential birth defects.

As a result, tort litigation erupted across Alabama. Thousands of plaintiffs filed toxic-tort actions against Monsanto Company and its corporate predecessors, alleging a range of harms caused by the release of PCBs near Anniston. Multiple cases were filed in state and federal court, beginning in 1996. Plaintiffs sought compensatory and punitive damages for personal injury and property damage. Because of the mass scale of litigation, many cases were consolidated in their respective state or federal courts. Significant to this present litigation is the "global settlement" of $300 million

---

[1] Not all Defendants filed motions to dismiss. The court does not presume to know why, but without information before it concerning the precise nature of the claims against those Defendants, the court cannot determine when those claims may have accrued for application of the statute of limitations. Accordingly, the decision set forth in this Memorandum Opinion and accompanying Order does not apply to those Defendants.

that was reached and announced in a historic joint session of federal district court and state circuit court on August 20, 2003, resolving the consolidated cases *Tolbert v. Monsanto Co.*, CV-01-C-1407-S (N.D. Ala.) and *Abernathy v. Monsanto Co.*, No. CV-01-832 (Circuit Court of Etowah County, Ala.). As explained by then-Chief Judge Clemons during the settlement hearing, the named plaintiffs in those cases represented a combined total of more than 20,500 people. *See* Tr. of Proceedings, CV-01-C-1407-S, Doc. 58-1. Professor Eric Green guided negotiations to reach the $300 million settlement, which has become known and referred to as the "*Abernathy* Settlement."

On August 26, 2003, one week following the public announcement of the *Abernathy* Settlement, Solutia, Pharmacia, and Monsanto transferred by wire the initial $75 million settlement payment into a settlement account established by the Circuit Court of Calhoun County. *See* Settlement Agmt., Doc. 77-1. On September 9, 2003, the parties formalized and executed a twenty-page Settlement Agreement. The next day, on September 10, 2003, Judge Laird of the Calhoun County Circuit Court entered an order approving the terms of the Settlement Agreement. A week later, on September 17, 2003, $200 million was transferred to the court-established settlement account under the terms of the Settlement Agreement. The terms of the Settlement Agreement provide for the remainder of the settlement funds to be paid in annual $2,500,000 installments from 2004 through 2013. Settlement Agmt. ¶ 1.b & 1.c.

While $275 million of the $300 million settlement was deposited into the court registry by mid-September 2003, the Settlement Agreement provided specific terms concerning distribution of those funds as allocated to the individual plaintiffs. On October 28, 2003, the *Abernathy* plaintiffs' counsel filed a certification that seventy-five percent of the adult plaintiffs had signed releases required by the terms of the Settlement Agreement, and requested transfer of the $275 million to the court-approved trust account held by the law firm of Kasowitz, Benson, Torres & Friedman LLP.

Further, on December 2, 2003 the *Abernathy* plaintiffs' counsel filed a certification that the last

remaining condition for distribution had been met; namely, that they had obtained court approval of

settlement of the claims involving minors and that at least ninety-seven percent of the total plaintiffs

had signed releases. *See* Doc. 77-2. For ease of reference, the court will refer to these certifications

as the "75% Certificate" and the "97% Certificate," respectively.

With articles spanning pages across widely disseminated publications such as *The

Washington Post*,[2] *The New York Times*,[3] *The Wall Street Journal*,[4] the *San Francisco Chronicle*,[5]

the *Atlanta Journal and Constitution*,[6] the *St. Louis Post-Dispatch*,[7] *The National Law Journal*,[8]

---

[2] *E.g.*, Michael Grunwald, *Monsanto Hid Decades of Pollution; PCBs Drenched Ala. Town, But No One Was Ever Told*, Wash. Post, Jan. 1, 2002, at A1.

[3] *E.g.*, David Firestone, *Alabama Jury Says Monsanto Polluted Town*, N.Y. Times, Feb. 23, 2002 at A11; *$700 Million Settlement in Alabama PCB Lawsuit*, N.Y. Times, Aug. 21, 2003, *available at* http://www.nytimes.com/2003/08/21/business/700-million-settlement-in-alabama-pcb-lawsuit.html?ref=monsanto_company.

[4] *E.g.*, Thaddeus Herrick & Scott Kilman, *Solutia, Monsanto Agree to Pay $600 Million to Settle PCB Claims*, Wall St. J., Aug. 21, 2003.

[5] *E.g.*, Michael Grunwald, *Jury finds Monsanto liable for releasing tons of PCB–Firm covered up pollution for more than 40 years*, San Fran. Chron., Feb. 23, 2002, at A7.

[6] *E.g.*, Charles Seabrook, *$700 Million Deal on Anniston PCBs*, Atlanta J. & Const., Aug. 21, 2003, at A1.

[7] *E.g.*, Rachel Melcer, *New Claims Come Out of PCB Case: Lawyers Sue Monsanto, Solutia for Millions in Alabama Contamination*, Nov. 13, 2003, at B1.

[8] Elizabeth Amon, *Monsanto's PCB Woes: Thousands Take Company to Court*, Nat'l L. J., Feb. 11, 2002, at A1, Col. 2.

People Magazine,[9] and multiple reports airing on NPR,[10] no one could characterize *Abernathy* mass

tort litigation and the multi-million dollar settlement as "quiet." Even the Alabama Supreme Court

referenced the media frenzy in its 2001 ruling on a writ of mandamus requesting change of venue

in the consolidated state court proceedings against Monsanto, stating "we are concerned about the

potential bias created by the numerous newspaper articles and the extensive television news coverage

of this case . . . ." *Ex parte Monsanto Co.*, 794 So. 2d 350, 355 (Ala. 2001). Still today, the PCB-

related legal drama continues to liven the courtroom.

In this case, the Government alleges that some unnamed 907 recipients of settlement funds

from the *Abernathy* litigation also received Medicare payments for unidentified medical expenses

related to the injuries or illnesses caused by the PCB contamination. More than fourteen years since

litigation was initiated against Monsanto, the Government filed this lawsuit on December 1, 2009,

seeking to recover reimbursement for its Medicare payments from the corporate tortfeasors named

in the *Abernathy* litigation, their insurance carriers and subsidiaries, and certain attorneys who

represented the *Abernathy* plaintiffs and allegedly received the settlement funds. The Government

did not sue any of the alleged Medicare beneficiaries as defendants to this recovery action or identify

them in pleadings.

Certain issues raised by the motions to dismiss require the court to conduct a separate legal

analysis as to the different types of defendants sued in this case. The court identifies at least two

---

[9] Bill Hewitt, *Living on Poisoned Ground*, People, Mar. 25, 2002, *available at* http://www.people.com/people/archive/article/0,,20136662,00.html.

[10] *E.g.*, *Profile: Alabama Community that claims PCBs manufactured by Monsanto years ago has caused serious damage to personal health and property values*, NPR *Morning Edition* (Jan. 11, 2002); *Analysis: Federal regulators reach deal for the cleanup of a site contaminated by PCBs in Alabama*, NPR *All Things Considered* (Mar. 25, 2002).

distinct categories of defendants: (1) the attorneys who were involved in some capacity as representing the *Abernathy* plaintiffs; and (2) the chemical companies sued in *Abernathy* as the alleged tortfeasor defendants, including their liability insurance carriers (and their subsidiaries) who are joined as Defendants in this case.[11] For ease of reference, the court will refer to the two categories as the "Attorney Defendants" and the "Corporate Defendants," or sometimes "tortfeasor defendants," respectively.

II. Issues Before the Court

Though not unanimous in the details, Defendants have filed multiple motions to dismiss asserting various theories. A defense common to all asserts that the case is barred by the statute of limitations. Because the court's ruling on this issue effectively resolves the case, the court does not address the alternative and supplementary dismissal theories presented.

As raised in the briefs of the parties regarding the motions to dismiss pursuant to Fed. R. Civ. P. 12(b)(6), the court must resolve several key issues. First, the court must determine the applicable statute of limitations to the Government's causes of action. Second, the court must determine the appropriate time of accrual concerning the causes of action. To resolve these issues, the court finds it must analyze these questions separately as to the two categories of defendants defined above—the Attorney Defendants and the Corporate Defendants.

---

[11] The Government's Amended Complaint, filed May 26, 2010 added certain subsidiaries of the insurance company Defendants. (Doc. 77.) The court entered an Order on June 9, 2010 finding that the motion to dismiss and briefing previously filed by Defendants American International Group, Inc. and The Travelers Companies, Inc. are deemed applicable to the Newly Added Defendants and relieved those parties from filing additional individual motions to dismiss in response to the Amended Complaint. (Doc. 86.)

III. Standard of Review

A Rule 12(b)(6) motion to dismiss attacks the legal sufficiency of the complaint. Generally, the Federal Rules of Civil Procedure require only that the complaint provide "'a short and plain statement of the claim' that will give the defendant fair notice of what the plaintiff's claim is and the grounds upon which it rests." *Conley v. Gibson*, 355 U.S. 41, 47 (1957) (quoting Fed. R. Civ. P. 8(a)(2)). A plaintiff must provide the grounds of his entitlement, but Rule 8 generally does not require "detailed factual allegations." *Bell Atl. Corp. v. Twombly*, 550 U.S. 544, 555 (2007) (quoting *Conley*, 355 U.S. at 47).

Rule 12(b)(6) can also provide the appropriate vessel for evaluating a motion to dismiss based on running of the statute of limitations. *Quiller v. Barclays American/Credit, Inc.*, 727 F.2d 1067, 1069 (11th Cir. 1984) ("[A] complaint may be dismissed under Rule 12(b)(6) when its own allegations indicate the existence of an affirmative defense, so long as the defense clearly appears on the face of the complaint."); *see, e.g., Mann v. Adams Realty Co.*, 556 F.2d 293 (5th Cir. 1977).

In evaluating a motion to dismiss, the court assumes that all factual allegations set forth in the complaint are true, *United States v. Gaubert*, 499 U.S. 315, 327 (1991), and construes all factual allegations in the light most favorable to the plaintiff. *Brower v. County of Inyo*, 489 U.S. 593, 598 (1989). In other words, "[o]n a motion to dismiss, the facts stated in the . . . complaint and all reasonable inferences therefrom are taken as true." *Bickley v. Caremark RX, Inc.*, 461 F.3d 1325, 1328 (11th Cir. 2006) (quoting *Stephens v. Dep't of Health & Human Servs.*, 901 F.2d 1571, 1573 (11th Cir. 1990)).

IV. Legal Background

A. MSPA Generally

The law and statutes implicated by this case involve the common situation of a personal injury or illness giving rise to the need for payment of medical expenses. Medicare provides a government payment scheme to fund medical expenses for qualified individuals. *See* 42 U.S.C. §§ 1395-1395ggg. In general terms, Medicare will not pay for medical expenses where a reasonable certainty exists that an insurance company, or another liable third party, will cover the costs. *See generally Rybicki v. Hartley*, 792 F.2d 260, 262 (1st Cir. 1986). In cases of uncertainty, however, or where the injured or ill person is not likely to receive prompt payment for medical expenses, Medicare may make payment for the expenses conditioned upon later reimbursement.

Though it has been called "convoluted and complex" by some courts and labeled a "model of un-clarity," *Estate of Urso v. Thompson*, 309 F. Supp. 2d 253, 259 (D. Conn. 2004), the Medicare Secondary Payer Act ("MSPA" or the "MSP statute"), put simply, is a statutory reimbursement mechanism for the Government to recover expenses conditionally paid by Medicare. *See* 42 U.S.C. § 1395y. The history and purpose of the MSPA "plainly indicate that Congress wanted Medicare's payments to be secondary and subject to recoupment in all situations where one of the statutorily enumerated sources of primary coverage [termed 'primary payers'] could pay instead." *United States v. Baxter Int'l, Inc.*, 345 F.3d 866, 888 (11th Cir. 2003). As the Eleventh Circuit noted,

> In a nutshell, the MSP declares that, under certain conditions, Medicare will be the secondary rather than primary payer for its insureds. Consequently, Medicare is empowered to recoup from the rightful primary payer (or from the recipient of such payment) if Medicare pays for a service that was, or should have been, covered by the primary insurer. Although the statute is structurally complex—a complexity that has produced considerable confusion among courts attempting to construe it—the MSP's function is straightforward.

Id. at 875. Those "certain conditions" that must be met for the Government to file a claim against

a "primary payer" for reimbursement under the MSPA are fleshed out by the statute's implementing

regulations at 42 C.F.R. § 411.20 *et seq.*

   As relevant here, any recipient of a payment that qualifies as reimbursable to Medicare under

the MSPA must reimburse Medicare within sixty days. 42 C.F.R. § 411.22(a), 411.24(h) (2006).

If Medicare does not receive timely reimbursement, the Government, as it has done here, may file

a lawsuit for recovery against any entity that qualifies as a "primary payer." 42 C.F.R. § 411.24(e)

("[The Government] has a direct right of action to recover from any primary payer."). Though the

MSPA does not reference "primary payer" within the text of the statute itself, the term is defined in

the regulations as follows:

> Primary payer means, when used in the context in which Medicare is the secondary
> payer, *any entity that is or was required or responsible to make payment* with respect
> to an item or service (or any portion thereof) *under a primary plan.* These entities
> include, but are not limited to, insurers or self-insurers, third party administrators,
> and all employers that sponsor or contribute to group health plans or large group
> health plans.

42 C.F.R. § 411.21 (emphasis added). Responsibility to pay under a "primary plan," therefore, is

an integral part of the analysis as to whether an entity qualifies as a "primary payer."

   The MSPA defines "primary plan" as follows: "A primary plan, and an entity that receives

payment from a primary plan, shall reimburse [Medicare] for any payment made . . . with respect to

an item or service if it is demonstrated that such primary plan has or had a responsibility to make

payment with respect to such item or service." 42 U.S.C. § 1395y(b)(2)(B)(ii). The 2004

amendments to the MSPA clarified the scope of third-party liability in the context of a "self-insured

plan": "An entity that engages in a business, trade, or profession shall be deemed to have a self-insured plan if it carries its own risk (whether by failure to obtain insurance, or otherwise) in whole or in part." *Id.* Thus, a "primary payer" with responsibility to make payments under a "primary plan," is ultimately responsible to reimburse Medicare for its payments toward the same item or service rendered.

The MSPA regulations also clarify the Government's direct right of action to recover "from parties that *receive* primary payments," including "any entity, including a beneficiary, provider, supplier, physician, *attorney*, State agency or private insurer that has received a third party payment." 42 C.F.R. § 411.24(g) (emphases added). This provision and others indicate how the MSPA contemplates that a settlement scenario—in this case, arising from tort litigation—could qualify as a primary payment falling within the scope of liability for Medicare reimbursement. Section 411.22(b) specifically lists a "judgment," "settlement," or an "award" as examples of the nonexhausive means which may demonstrate "responsibility for payment" by a primary payer, ultimately triggering the obligation to reimburse Medicare.

Important to accrual analysis of the statute of limitations discussed below, the regulations define the Government's right to initiate recovery as beginning "as soon as it learns that payment has been made or could be made under workers' compensation, any liability or no-fault insurance, or an employer group health plan." 42 C.F.R. § 411.24(b).

For the sole purpose of analysis on the statute of limitations at issue, the court will assume that all Corporate Defendants qualify as "primary plans" under the 2004 amended definition of "primary plan" in the MSPA and will further assume no issue concerning retroactive application of these amendments. The court will also assume that the Attorney Defendants are entities that have "received payment from a primary plan or from the proceeds of a primary plan's payment to any entity" under the MSPA, notwithstanding the argument of certain Attorney Defendants that they received only attorneys fees for their early involvement and were not involved in the settlement process.

B. *Statute of Limitations*

Because the MSPA is silent as to a deadline for filing a claim for recovery, the parties agree that the relevant statute of limitations for the Government's claims, if any, is governed by the Federal Claims Collection Act ("FCCA"). 28 U.S.C. § 2415 (2008); *see also In re Dow Corning*, 250 B.R. 298, 350-51 (Bktrpcy. E.D. Mich. 2000) (stating the universal recognition of FCCA's applicability to the Government's MSPA claims). The parties disagree, however, as to whether the FCAA's six-year or three-year statute of limitations applies.

Subsection (a) of the FCAA provides that "every action for money damages brought by the United States . . . *which is founded upon any contract* express or implied in law or fact, shall be barred unless the complaint is filed within six years after the right of action first accrues . . . ." 28 U.S.C. § 2415(a) (emphasis added). Subsection (b) states that "every action for money damages brought by the United States . . . *which is founded upon a tort* shall be barred unless the complaint is filed within three years after the right of action first accrues . . . ." 28 U.S.C. § 2415(b) (emphasis added). The issue in the present case then becomes whether the Government's MSPA action is founded upon contract or tort. While courts have not developed any bright line test or rote rule to govern interpretation of these sections, the court recognizes that analysis should be guided by "logic and reason." *Cockerham v. Garvin*, 768 F.2d 784, 787 (6th Cir. 1985) (analyzing the applicability of 28 U.S.C. § 2415(a) or (b)).

Because the nature and origin of the purported relationship between the Government and the two categories of defendants differ, the court will conduct a separate analysis for each.

1. The Corporate Defendants

At the outset, the court notes that no precedent in the Eleventh Circuit analyzes whether the three- or six-year statute of limitations applies where the Government files MSPA claims against entities who were defendants in private mass tort litigation; neither could the parties point to a relevant case from any circuit court of appeals. The only identified reported case that analyzes closely analogous facts in application to the statute of limitations controlling MSPA claims is *In re Dow Corning*, 250 B.R. 298 (Bktrpcy. E.D. Mich. 2000).

The Government in *Dow Corning* sought reimbursement under the MSPA from a bankrupt tort defendant involved in ongoing breast implant litigation. To determine whether the Government's MSPA claim was founded upon a tort or a contract for the purposes of statute of limitations analysis under the FCCA, the court, using principles of logic and reason, labeled the analysis "truly elementary." *Id.* at 352. Finding significance in the fact the Government could identify "no contractual provision binding Dow Corning to pay for medical benefits to an implant recipient who also received medical benefits from the Government," among other reasons, the court held that the MSPA action was "founded upon tort" and thus the three-year statute of limitations applied. *Id.* at 352-53.

Similarly here, the defendant's reimbursement duties to the Government are based solely on the MSP statute because *no express contract exists* between the Defendants and the Government. The defendant's relationship with the Government prompting liability for reimbursement under the MSPA arises only, if at all, from the defendant's tortious relationship with any potential Medicare beneficiaries arising from allegations of reckless and negligent behavior, which prompted the $300 million settlement agreement. Thus, under a "but for" analysis, the Corporate Defendants argue that the Government's claim against them for Medicare reimbursement is founded upon tort and the three-year bar should apply.

The Government, however, strongly argues an implied contract at law theory to establish a contractual relationship between itself and the Corporate Defendants, which can be characterized as tenuous at best. Conceding the lack of an express contract, the Government, quoting *United States v. Weinberg*, 2002 U.S. Dist. LEXIS 12289 (E.D. Penn. 2002), argues that its claim is "*more akin to a suit for restitution than tort.*" *Id.* at *15 (emphasis added). While the Government emphasizes that its claim against the Corporate Defendants is not a common-law tort action and will not require direct proof of any tort elements, the language of 28 U.S.C. § 2415(b) contemplates that the three-year bar applies to any action *founded upon* a tort—not that the action itself is a tort claim or necessarily involves proof of tort elements.

To avoid the FCCA's three-year tort bar, the Government also asserts that its right of action "stems from [its] statutory right to recover monies conditionally paid by Medicare." Pl's Omnibus Resp., Doc. 55 at 22. Contrary to this argument, however, the court in *Dow Corning* , applying the three-year statute of limitations, explained that "[t]he fact that the Government's rights are created by statute is not a defining or even relevant factor." 250 B.R. at 351.

The Government also cites a number of non-binding authorities that apply the six-year statute of limitations to MSPA claims on a restitution theory. These cases are distinguishable from the present fact scenario, however, because the defendants by nature possessed some type of express contractual relationship with the Medicare beneficiary that conceivably gave the Government rights as a third-party beneficiary. *United States v. Weinberg*, 2002 U.S. Dist. LEXIS 12289, *7-*9 (E.D. Penn. 2002) (suing attorney of Medicare beneficiary); *Brooks v. Blue Cross/Blue Shield of Fla., Inc.*, 1995 U.S. Dist. LEXIS 22124, *5-*10 (suing several insurance companies as "group health plans" under MSPA and Blue Cross "as the fiscal intermediary or administrator for the Medicare program"); *Provident Life & Accident Ins. Co. v. United States*, 740 F. Supp. 492, 496 (E.D. Tenn. 1990) (action for MSPA recovery against private insurance carrier who acted as administrator of an employer's group health care plan); *United States v. Blue Cross Blue Shield*, 726 F. Supp. 1517, 1518 (suing insurance carrier as "fiscal agent" of hospitals and physicians administering Medicare benefits).

The Government also cites to "overwhelming authority" holding that courts, in general, consistently apply the six-year statute of limitations to government suits involving cost-recovery statutes. *E.g., United States v. P/B STCO 213*, 756 F.2d 364 (5th Cir. 1985) (involving the Federal Water Pollution Control Act); *United States v. Limbs*, 524 F.2d 799 (9th Cir. 1975) (Federal Employees' Compensation Act); *United States v. Sunoco, Inc.*, 501 F. Supp. 2d 641 (E.D. Pa. 2007) (Pennsylvania Storage Tank and Spill Prevention Act). This court is not convinced of the relevance of these cases to the MSPA. That Act presents a unique statutory framework that extends jurisdiction beyond the Government's direct right of action against Medicare beneficiaries and entities in contractual privity to Medicare beneficiaries, such as health insurance carriers. Instead, the jurisdictional tentacles of the MSPA reach out to remote third-party payers whose MSPA liability arises solely on the basis of independent tort liability or some other situation not involving an intentional, preexisting contract with the Government or Medicare beneficiaries. This scenario heightens the complexity of the MSPA.

The Government has not cited to a single case where a court has applied the six-year statute

of limitations in the situation where the defendant's responsibility for Medicare reimbursement under

the MSPA claim arises solely because of that entity's liability in a tort settlement to pay plaintiffs

who received a Medicare payment for items or services necessitated by the defendant's alleged

tortious conduct. This court declines the opportunity to be the first to do so using the Government's

implied-at-law contract theory.[12] While creative, it stretches too far beyond the bounds of logic and

reason to adopt absent precedent.

The only purported contractual relationship in this scenario lies *not* between the tortfeasor

defendants and the Government, but between the tortfeasor defendants and the alleged Medicare

beneficiaries because of a settlement resolving allegations of tort liability. The Government

concedes that the relationship between the Corporate Defendants and the alleged Medicare

beneficiaries arises solely because of tort allegations (Hearing Tr. at 34), and that "but for" the

settlement of the tort claims, the Government would have no MSPA claim (*id.* at 30-31). The court

finds in this scenario that logic and reason compel the application of the three-year statute of

limitations founded upon tort, because the Government's MSPA claims are founded upon allegations

of the Corporate Defendant's tortious activity and the resulting tort settlement. In the alternative,

even if the six-year statute were to apply to the Corporate Defendants, the court finds the cause of

action accrued more than six years before the suit was filed, as discussed below. Regardless of

which statute of limitations applies, the Government's claims against the Corporate Defendants were

filed too late.

---

[12] The Government raises no alternative contract theory for why the six-year statute of limitations should apply and the court will not invent any.

2. The Attorney Defendants

As counsel for Attorney Defendants based their statute of limitations argument on the six-year statute founded upon contract and did not argue applicability of the three-year limitations period founded upon tort, the court need not engage in a lengthy analysis as to which statute of limitations applies to the Attorney Defendants. The court does, however, note several points of reasoning that may distinguish these Defendants from the Corporate Defendants.

Logic suggests that the Attorney Defendants who represented the tort plaintiffs in the *Abernathy* case, the alleged Medicare beneficiaries in the instant case, essentially acted as agents pursuant to the contractual relationship between the Government and the Medicare beneficiaries. More specifically, the Attorney Defendants' obligation to pay their clients any monies allegedly owed to the Government for Medicare reimbursement, unlike that of the Corporate Defendants, arose not from any tortious conduct on behalf of the Attorney Defendants themselves but from an express contractual relationship with the Medicare beneficiaries—namely, any fee agreement or attorney-client agreement between them. From that perspective, the Attorney Defendants' MSPA obligation is essentially founded upon a contractual obligation.

For these reasons, the grounds for statute of limitations determination as applied to the Attorney Defendants is more reasonably founded upon contract rather than tort. The contractual nexus is clearer in this instance than as alleged against the Corporate Defendants, whose MSPA obligations ultimately arose from, and cannot be divorced from, allegations of tortious conduct. The court, therefore, concurs that the six-year statute of limitations applies as to the Attorney Defendants.

C. *Accrual of Government's MSPA Action*

To determine when the Government's MSPA cause of action first accrued for purposes of the statute of limitations, the court considers the point of time when the Government could have brought an independent action for Medicare reimbursement related to the *Abernathy* settlement. *See* 42 C.F.R. § 411.24(b) ("[The Government] may initiate recovery as soon as it learns that payment has been made or could be made under . . . any liability or no-fault insurance, or an employer group health plan."). Again, the court separates its analysis as to the two categories of defendants because the Government's asserts a different basis for liability for each.

1. Corporate Defendants

Read together, the MSPA and its implementing regulations provide that an entity's liability for Medicare reimbursement arises upon demonstration of its *responsibility to pay* under a primary plan, including a self-insured plan. *See* 42 U.S.C. § 1395y(b)(2)(B)(ii) (imposing an obligation to reimburse Government upon demonstration of "a responsibility to make payment with respect to" an item or service supplied by Medicare); (iii) (enabling the Government to bring an action under the MSPA against a primary payer that is or was "required or responsible . . . to make payment" for a primary benefit). A primary payer's responsibility to pay may be demonstrated by a variety of means, "including but not limited to a *settlement*, award, or contractual obligation." 42 C.F.R. § 411.22(b)(3) (emphasis added). The key fact for analyzing accrual of the Government's cause of action as against the Corporate Defendants, therefore, is at what point their "responsibility to pay" arose in relation to the *Abernathy* Settlement.

In light of the facts, the court finds that the Corporate Defendants' responsibility to pay arose no later than the point of execution and court approval of the *Abernathy* Settlement Agreement. The parties negotiated the $300 million settlement during the summer of 2003 and announced it to the world pursuant to the public joint hearing on August 20, 2003. The *Abernathy* defendants transferred the initial $75 million payment into the court registry on August 26, 2003. All parties signed the finalized 20-page Settlement Agreement on September 9, 2003, which the state court approved by order the very next day. Alabama law, which governs the Settlement Agreement, dictates that court-approved settlements are fully enforceable by law. *See* Ala. Code § 34-3-21 ("An attorney has authority to bind his client, in any action or proceeding, by an agreement in relation to such case, made in writing, or by an entry to be made on the minutes of the court."); *Beverly v. Chandler*, 564 So. 2d 922, 923 (Ala. 1990) (stating that "agreements made in settlement of litigation" are "binding on the parties"); *Contractor Success Grp., Inc. v. Serv. Thrust Org.*, 681 So. 2d 212, 215 (Ala. Civ. App. 1996) ("[O]nce a settlement agreement has been entered into, it is binding and will be summarily enforced."). On September 17, 2003, the *Abernathy* defendants transferred $200 million to the court registry pursuant to the terms of the Settlement Agreement.

Even apart from the court-enforceable executed Settlement Agreement, the court finds that the August 26 and September 17 payments reflect a demonstrated responsibility to pay. Despite these dates reflecting the accrual of its cause of action, the Government did not bring its MSPA claims until December 1, 2009.

To analyze the accrual date of its cause of action, the Government adds a curious twist to the language of the MSPA statute, arguing that the Corporate Defendants' "responsibility to pay" did not actually arise until payment was *distributed* to the *Abernathy* plaintiffs in exchange for the signed releases. Because payment was "conditioned" on certification to the state court that at least ninety-seven percent of the plaintiffs had signed release waivers, the Government argues that the "responsibility to pay" was not ultimately established until the 97% Certificate was filed on December 2, 2003—in other words, until the condition was met. This argument directly contradicts the plain reading of the language in the MSP statute, which provides that responsibility to pay "may be demonstrated by a judgment, *a payment conditioned upon* the recipient's compromise, *waiver*, or *release* (whether or not there is a determination or admission of liability) . . . or by other means." 42 U.S.C. § 1395y(b)(2)(B)(ii) (emphasis added).

The Corporate Defendants did in fact effectuate $275 million in settlement payments in August 2003 and in September 2003. The fact these payments were "conditioned upon release" did not absolve the Corporate Defendants from their "responsibility to pay" pursuant to the language of the MSPA; to the contrary, the statute expressly contemplates these types of conditional payments as demonstrative of responsibility to pay.[13] The Government's reading of the statute, that "responsibility to pay" does not arise until all conditions are met and distribution is achieved, requires adding language to the statute that does not appear and directly contradicts its plain meaning. The court will not so expand the clear intent of Congress by adding language to the MSPA statute.

Once responsibility to pay is demonstrated, the MSPA unambiguously establishes the earliest point at which the Government could have asserted its claims for reimbursement against Monsanto and the other Corporate Defendants, as third party payers: as soon as it learned that "payment has

---

[13] The court also finds merit in the Defendants' contention that the 97% Certificate condition is akin to a condition subsequent in a contract, which would not, and did not, affect the overall enforceability of the Settlement Agreement. In this regard, the 97% Certificate was merely "a post-execution contractual condition" relating to the administrative task of *distribution*, not negating Defendants' ultimate responsibility to pay. Pharmacia Reply, Doc. 58, at 6.

been made *or could be made* under . . . any liability or no-fault insurance." 42 C.F.R. § 411.24(b)

(emphasis added). The Government does not argue that it did not learn of the *Abernathy* Settlement

until December 2, 2003, which is the latest possible accrual date that would enable its claims filed

on December 1, 2009 to survive under the longest applicable statute of limitations.[14] Instead, the

Government argues that "[t]he statute of limitations could not have accrued prior to December 2,

2003, for the simple reason that the government did not have a cause of action prior to that point."

Pl's Omnibus Resp., Doc. 55 at 32.

The basis for the Government's reasoning is that "*[d]istribution of settlement monies* to the

Abernathy plaintiffs was contingent on certification to the state court that 97 percent of the

Abernathy plaintiffs had signed releases, which certification occurred on December 2, 2003." *Id.*

(emphasis added). However, the express terms of the MSPA unambiguously state that, in context,

"responsibility to make payment," which then triggers the statutory obligation to reimburse

Medicare, "may be demonstrated by a judgment, *a payment conditioned upon the recipient's*

compromise, waiver, or *release* (whether or not there is a determination or admission of liability)

. . . or by other means," 42 U.S.C. § 1395y(b)(2)(B)(ii) (emphasis added). The statute does *not*

reference an "unrestricted payment" or a "fully distributed payment" or even a "final payment."

None of the regulations hinge a defendant's obligation to pay upon distribution. Despite the

Government's attempts to twist the reading of the statute, its terms squarely contemplate that a

---

[14] Considering the widely publicized nature of the *Abernathy* Settlement Agreement—a comprehensive 20-page document detailing the logistics of the settlement payments, including dates, times, and specific accounts—the court finds it hard to conceive a reasonable argument as to the Government's lack of knowledge about its MSPA claims at the time the settlement was executed.

payment conditioned upon release triggers a responsibility to reimburse Medicare under the MSPA, which is exactly the situation presented here.

Consequently, as to the Corporate Defendants, the court finds that the Government's cause of action accrued, *at the latest*, on September 10, 2003, when the state court approved the executed *Abernathy* Settlement Agreement and at which point Defendants' responsibility to pay was clearly established. The Government reasonably could have intervened in the *Abernathy* litigation to initiate its MSPA-related claims against the Corporate Defendants at least by September 10, 2003, if not earlier. Applying either the three- or six-year statute of limitations, the Government's right of action expired long before it filed suit on December 1, 2009.

2. Attorney Defendants

As to the Attorney Defendants, the court employs a different standard for analyzing the point of accrual for statute of limitations purposes because they have a different basis for liability under the MSPA as alleged "recipients" of payments owed to the Government for Medicare reimbursement. Still, the court finds the Attorney Defendants "received payment" from a primary payer, *i.e.*, the Corporate Defendants, at the latest on October 29, 2003. On that date, the court governing the *Abernathy* litigation ordered the transfer of $275 million in settlement monies from the court registry to the attorneys' escrow account.

The court finds no merit in the Government's contention that the Attorney Defendants did not actually "receive" the payment on October 29, 2003 because of the nature of the escrow account and the attorneys' inability to immediately distribute the funds. The Government argues that it could not have intervened with its MSPA claim until the filing of the 97% Certificate on December 2, 2003, which released the funds for distribution. To the contrary, the most logical and appropriate time for the Government's right of reimbursement under the MSPA to be honored would have been at the time of initial transfer of the settlement funds into the attorneys' escrow account, if not earlier. At that time, a court could have determined proper distribution of those funds as allocated to the plaintiffs, to vendors, to attorneys for legal fees, and to any parties with subrogation claims, including the Government's claim here for Medicare reimbursement.

The Government most certainly could, and should, have intervened *before* the *Abernathy* settlement monies were actually distributed to the thousands of plaintiffs. The Government's MSPA claims were, therefore, ripe for accrual *no later than* October 29, 2003, the date the Attorney Defendants received payment of the $275 million settlement monies in escrow. The court notes that in practical terms, the Government likely could have intervened at any time during the pendency of the *Abernathy* litigation, and certainly at the time the Settlement Agreement was executed and judicially approved in September 2003. To afford every possible benefit to the Government, however, the court reaches its generous conclusion that accrual of its MSPA claim occurred no later than October 29, 2003.[15]

D. *Tolling*

The Government argued in brief that its MSPA claims "likely did not accrue until much later [than December 2, 2003] due to the federal tolling statute." Pl's Omnibus Resp., Doc. 55 at 33. The tolling statute on which the Government relies provides that the FCCA statute of limitations period

---

[15] The court briefly notes that at the close of the hearing on the motions to dismiss, the Government raised for the first time a theory of continuing accrual, vaguely proposing that a new MSPA cause of action accrues every year when the Corporate Defendants make additional payments to the Attorney Defendants. Because this theory was admittedly not raised in any briefs before the court and not pled in the Amended Complaint, it is not properly before the court and the court does not reach this issue.

is stopped during periods when "facts material to the right of action are not known and *reasonably could not be known* by an official of the United States charged with the responsibility to act in the circumstances." 28 U.S.C. § 2146(c) (emphasis added). In the Eleventh Circuit, "once the facts making up the 'very essence of the right of action' are reasonably knowable, the § 2146 bar is dropped." *United States v. Kass*, 740 F.2d 1493, 1497 (11th Cir. 1984). The Eleventh Circuit in *Kass* explains the history and purpose of the FCCA: "The limitation period was designed to promote diligence by the government in bringing claims to trial and also to make the position of the government more nearly equal to that of a private litigant." *Id.* at 1496 (citations omitted). The court further explained:

> Although one motivation behind enacting a time limit on government-prosecuted civil actions was the desire to inspire diligence in discovering claims, Congress also intended that the government should not be penalized for excusable ignorance of such claims. Foremost in the enactment of § 2416(c) was the thought that the government should not be penalized if the *fraud* of an adverse party restricted its ability to discover a valid cause of action until long after its accrual. Cong. News at 2507 ("The committee understands that the principal application of this exclusion will probably be in connection with fraud situations.").

Id. at 1497 (emphasis in original).

The facts of this case do not implicate any fraudulent concealment of any related MSPA claim. Moreover, the Government has not alleged that it did not or *reasonably could not have known* the facts giving rise to its MSPA causes of action prior to December 2, 2003. While the Eleventh Circuit has not designated which party bears the burden of proving the elements of this particular federal tolling statute, "federal courts have repeatedly held that plaintiffs seeking to toll the statute of limitations on various grounds must have included the allegation in their pleadings." *Wasco Prods. v. Southwall Techs., Inc.*, 435 F.3d 989, 991 (9th Cir. 2006) (citing cases from the Ninth, Tenth, Eighth, and D.C. Circuit Courts of Appeals). Indeed, the Government would be hard pressed to show that it reasonably could not have known of the widely reported *Abernathy* litigation, initiated in 1996, and the ensuing settlement reached in August 2003. Rather, the Government argues the "obvious fact" that it "could not have had knowledge of its claim before that claim arose, which . . . was on December 2, 2003." Doc. 55 at 34. Because the court ultimately disagrees with the Government as to the accrual date of its claim, it finds no merit in this particular argument.

The Government does not suggest a time frame during which the court should consider its lack of knowledge of material facts sufficient to toll the statute of limitations, and the court declines to speculate as to such a period. Because the court finds no reasonable or compelling argument that the Government "could not have known" of its rights to collect reimbursement related to the *Abernathy* settlement before December 2, 2003, the tolling provision does not apply to extend the Government's time period to file its MSPA claims.

CONCLUSION

For these reasons, the court holds that the three-year statute of limitations began running against the Corporate Defendants no later than September 10, 2003, the date the executed Settlement Agreement was approved by order of the state court. The statute of limitations, therefore, expired no later than September 10, 2006, and bars the Government's claims filed against the Corporate Defendants on December 1, 2009 as untimely. Alternatively, under the six-year statute of limitations, the court finds that the Government's claims against the Corporate Defendants expired no later than September 10, 2009, still barring the Government's MSPA claims as untimely.

As to the Attorney Defendants, the court holds that the six-year statute of limitations began running no later than October 29, 2003, when they received the $275 million payment from the *Abernathy* settlement. The statute of limitations, therefore, expired no later than October 17, 2009 and also bars the Government's claims filed against the Attorney Defendants on December 1, 2009.

Because the court reaches a resolution of the motions to dismiss on statute of limitations grounds, it does not reach the additional grounds for dismissal asserted by various Defendants. The Government's claims as to the Defendants who filed the motions to dismiss listed in this Opinion will be dismissed; accordingly, the Plaintiff's motion for summary judgment on the question of liability will be denied. A separate Order to this effect will be filed simultaneously.

DONE and ORDERED this 30th day of September, 2010.

KARON OWEN BOWDRE
UNITED STATES DISTRICT JUDGE

APPENDIX 3

Sally Stalcup E-mail to CMS Regional Office

DEPARTMENT OF HEALTH & HUMAN SERVICES
Centers for Medicare & Medicaid Services
Division of Financial Management and Fee for Service Operations, Region VI

May 25, 2011

1301 Young Street, Room 833
Dallas, Texas 75202
Phone (214) 767-6441
Fax (214) 767-4440

This specific handout was prepared as a service to the public and is not intended to grant rights or impose obligations. It may contain certain references or links to statutes, regulations, or other policy materials. The information provided is only intended to be a general summary. It is not intended to take the place of either the written law or regulations. Readers are encouraged to review the specific statutes, regulations and other interpretive materials for a full and accurate statement of their contents. It is intended to provide consolidated guidance to those attorneys, insurers, etc., working liability, no-fault and general third party liability cases for any Medicare beneficiary residing in Oklahoma, Texas, New Mexico, Louisiana and Arkansas and is not to be considered a CMS official statement of policy.

If the Medicare beneficiary involved in your case is not a resident of one of these states, please contact the appropriate Centers for Medicare & Medicaid Services' (CMS) Medicare Secondary Payer Regional Office (MSP RO). If you do not have that information please contact Sally Stalcup (contact information below) for that information.

Medicare's interests must be protected; however, CMS does not mandate a specific mechanism to protect those interests. The law does not require a "set-aside" in any situation. The law requires that the Medicare Trust Funds be protected from payment for future services whether it is a Workers' Compensation or liability case. There is no distinction in the law.

Set-aside is our method of choice and the agency feels it provides the best protection for the program and the Medicare beneficiary.

Section 1862(b)(2)(A)(ii) of the Social Security, Act [42 USC 1395 y(b)(2)], precludes Medicare payment for services to the extent that payment has been made or can reasonably be expected to be made promptly under liability insurance. This also governs Workers' Compensation. 42 CFR 411.50 defines the term "liability insurance". Anytime a settlement, judgment or award provides funds for future medical services, it can reasonably be expected that those monies are available to pay for future services related to what was claimed and/or released in the settlement, judgment, or award. Thus, Medicare should not be billed for future services until those funds are exhausted by payments to providers for services that would otherwise be covered and reimbursable by Medicare. If the settlement, judgment, award .y are not funded there is no reasonable expectation that third party funds are available to pay for those services.

The new provisions for Liability Insurance (including Self-Insurance), No-Fault Insurance, and Workers' Compensation found at 42 U.S.C. 1395y(b)(8) add reporting rules and do not eliminate any existing statutory provisions or regulations. The new provisions do not eliminate CMS' existing processes if a Medicare beneficiary (or his/her representative) wishes to obtain interim conditional payment amount information prior to a settlement, judgment, award, or other payment. The new provisions do NOT require a set-aside when there is a recovery for future medicals, in fact this legislation does not address that subject. This legislation is unofficially known as "Mandatory Insurer

Reporting" because it does just and only that. It specifies the entity mandated to report a settlement/judgment/award/recovery to Medicare and addresses specifics of that issue.

There is no formal CMS review process in the liability arena as there is for Worker' Compensation. However, CMS does expect the funds to be exhausted on otherwise Medicare covered and otherwise reimbursable services related to what was claimed and/or released before Medicare is ever billed. CMS review is decided on a case by case basis.

The fact that a settlement/judgment/award does not specify payment for future medical services does not mean that they are not funded. The fact that the agreement designates the entire amount for pain and suffering does not mean that future medicals are not funded. The only situation in which Medicare recognizes allocations of liability payments to nonmedical losses is when payment is based on a court of competent jurisdiction's order after their review on the merits of the case. A review of the merits of the case is a review of the facts of the case to determine whether there are future medicals - not to determine the proper allocation of funds. If the court of competent jurisdiction has reviewed the facts of the case and determined that there are no future medical services Medicare will accept the Court's designation.

While it is Medicare's position that counsel should know whether or not their recovery provides for future medicals, simply recovers policy limits, etc, we are frequently asked how one would 'know'. Consider the following examples as a guide for determining whether or not settlement funds must be used to protect Medicare's interest on any Medicare covered otherwise reimbursable, case related, future medical services. Does the case involve a catastrophic injury or illness? Is there a Life Care Plan or similar document? Does the case involve any aspect of Workers' Compensation? This list is by no means all inclusive.

We use the phrase "case related" because we consider more than just services related to the actual injury/illness which is the basis of the case. Because the law precludes Medicare payment for services to the extent that payment has been made or can reasonably be expected to be made promptly under liability insurance, Medicare's right of recovery, and the prohibition from billing Medicare for future services, extends to all those services related to what was claimed and/or released in the settlement, judgment, or award. Medicare's payment for those same past services is recoverable and payment for those future services is precluded by Section 1862(b)(2)(A)(ii) of the Social Security Act.

"Otherwise covered" means that the funds must be used to pay for only those services Medicare would cover so there is a savings to the Medicare trust funds. For example, Medicare does not pay for bathroom grab bars, handicapped vans, garage door openers or spas so use of the funds for those items is inappropriate. We include the designation of "otherwise reimbursable" because Medicare does not pay for services that are not medically necessary even if the specific service is designated as a covered service and Medicare does not pay primary when Group Health Plan insurance has been determined to be the primary payer.

At this time, the CMS is not soliciting cases solely because of the language provided in a general release. CMS does not review or sign off on counsel's determination of the amount to be held to protect the Trust Fund in most cases. We do however urge counsel to consider this issue when settling a case and recommend that their determination as to whether or not their case provided recovery funds for future medicals be documented in their records. Should they determine that future services are funded, those dollars must be used to pay for future otherwise Medicare covered case related services.

CMS does not review or sign off on counsel's determination of whether or not there is recovery for future medical services and thus the need to protect the Medicare Trust Funds and only in limited cases do they review or sign off on counsel's determination of the amount to be held to protect the Trust Funds.

There is no formal CMS review process in the liability arena as there is for Worker' Compensation, however Regional Offices do review a number of submitted set-aside proposals. On occasions, when the recovery is large enough, or other unusual facts exist within the case, this CMS Regional Office will review the settlement and help make a determination on the amount to be available for future services.

We are still asked for written confirmation that a Medicare set-aside is, or is not, required. As we have already covered the "set-aside" aspect of that request we only need to state that IF there was/is funding for otherwise covered and reimbursable future medical services related to what was claimed/released, the Medicare Trust Funds must be protected. If there was/is no such funding, there is no expectation of 3rd party funds with which to protect the Trust Funds. <u>Each attorney is going to have to decide, based on the specific facts of each of their cases, whether or not there is funding for future medicals and if so, a need to protect the Trust Funds.</u> They must decide whether or not there is funding for future medicals. If the answer for plaintiff's counsel is yes, they should to see to it that those funds are used to pay for otherwise Medicare covered services related to what is claimed/released in the settlement judgment award. If the answer for defense counsel or the insurer, is yes they should make sure their records contain documentation of their notification to plaintiff's counsel and the Medicare beneficiary that the settlement does fund future medicals which obligates them to protect the Medicare Trust Funds. It will also be part of their report to Medicare in compliance with Section 111, Mandatory Insurer Reporting requirements.

Medicare educates about laws/statutes/policies so that individuals can make the best decision possible based on their situation. This is not new or isolated to the MSP provisions. Probably the best example I can give is the 2008 final rule adopting payment and policy changes for inpatient hospital services paid under the Inpatient Prospective Payment System. That final rule also adopted a number of important changes and clarifications to the physician self-referral rules sometimes known as the Stark provisions. The physician self-referral law prohibits physicians from referring Medicare and Medicaid patients to certain entities with which the physician or a member of their immediate family has a financial relationship. Exceptions apply. Requests for determinations as to whether or not the physician met the exception criteria, or whether or not their situation was covered by this prohibition poured in. CMS/Medicare did not and continues to make no such determinations. It is the responsibility of the provider to know the specifics of their situation and determine their appropriate course of action.

Sally Stalcup
MSP Regional Coordinator
CMS
Medicare Fee for Service Branch
Division of Financial Management
  and Fee for Service Operations
1301 Young Street, Room 833
Dallas, Texas 75202
(214) 767-6415
(214) 767-4440 fax

APPENDIX 4

Title 42, Part 411 – Selected Regulations Applicable to Liability Cases

§ 411.22 Reimbursement obligations of primary payers and entities that received payment from primary payers.

(a) A primary payer, and an entity that receives payment from a primary payer, must reimburse CMS for any payment if it is demonstrated that the primary payer has or had a responsibility to make payment.

(b) A primary payer's responsibility for payment may be demonstrated by—

(1) A judgment;

(2) A payment conditioned upon the recipient's compromise, waiver, or release (whether or not there is a determination or admission of liability) of payment for items or services included in a claim against the primary payer or the primary payer's insured; or

(3) By other means, including but not limited to a settlement, award, or contractual obligation.

(c) The primary payer must make payment to either of the following:

(1) To the entity designated to receive repayments if the demonstration of primary payer responsibilities is other than receipt of a recovery demand letter from CMS or designated contractor.

(2) As directed in a recovery demand letter.

§ 411.23 Beneficiary's cooperation.

(a) If CMS takes action to recover conditional payments, the beneficiary must cooperate in the action.

(b) If CMS's recovery action is unsuccessful because the beneficiary does not cooperate, CMS may recover from the beneficiary.

§ 411.24   Recovery of conditional payments.

If a Medicare conditional payment is made, the following rules apply:

(a) *Release of information.* The filing of a Medicare claim by on or behalf of the beneficiary constitutes an express authorization for any entity, including State Medicaid and workers' compensation agencies, and data depositories, that possesses information pertinent to the Medicare claim to release that information to CMS. This information will be used only for Medicare claims processing and for coordination of benefits purposes.

(b) *Right to initiate recovery.* CMS may initiate recovery as soon as it learns that payment has been made or could be made under workers' compensation, any liability or no-fault insurance, or an employer group health plan.

(c) *Amount of recovery.* (1) If it is not necessary for CMS to take legal action to recover, CMS recovers the lesser of the following:

(i) The amount of the Medicare primary payment.

(ii) The full primary payment amount that the primary payer is obligated to pay under this part without regard to any payment, other than a full primary payment that the primary payer has paid or will make, or, in the case of a primary payment recipient, the amount of the primary payment.

(2) If it is necessary for CMS to take legal action to recover from the primary payer, CMS may recover twice the amount specified in paragraph (c)(1)(i) of this section.

(d) *Methods of recovery.* CMS may recover by direct collection or by offset against any monies CMS owes the entity responsible for refunding the conditional payment.

(e) *Recovery from primary payers.* CMS has a direct right of action to recover from any primary payer.

(f) *Claims filing requirements.* (1) CMS may recover without regard to any claims filing requirements that the insurance program or plan imposes on the beneficiary or other claimant such as a time limit for filing a claim or a time limit for notifying the plan or program about the need for or receipt of services.

(2) However, CMS will not recover its payment for particular services in the face of a claims filing requirement unless it has filed a claim for

recovery by the end of the year following the year in which the Medicare intermediary or carrier that paid the claim has notice that the third party is a primary plan to Medicare for those particular services. (A notice received during the last three months of a year is considered received during the following year.)

(g) *Recovery from parties that receive primary payments.* CMS has a right of action to recover its payments from any entity, including a beneficiary, provider, supplier, physician, attorney, State agency or private insurer that has received a primary payment.

(h) *Reimbursement to Medicare.* If the beneficiary or other party receives a primary payment, the beneficiary or other party must reimburse Medicare within 60 days.

(i) *Special rules.* (1) In the case of liability insurance settlements and disputed claims under employer group health plans, workers' compensation insurance or plan, and no-fault insurance, the following rule applies: If Medicare is not reimbursed as required by paragraph (h) of this section, the primary payer must reimburse Medicare even though it has already reimbursed the beneficiary or other party.

(2) The provisions of paragraph (i)(1) of this section also apply if a primary payer makes its payment to an entity other than Medicare when it is, or should be, aware that Medicare has made a conditional primary payment.

(3) In situations that involve procurement costs, the rule of §411.37(b) applies.

(j) *Recovery against Medicaid agency.* If a primary payment is made to a State Medicaid agency and that agency does not reimburse Medicare, CMS may reduce any Federal funds due the Medicaid agency (under title XIX of the Act) by an amount equal to the Medicare payment or the primary payment, whichever is less.

(k) *Recovery against Medicare contractor.* If a Medicare contractor, including an intermediary or carrier, also insures, underwrites, or administers as a third party administrator, a program or plan that is primary to Medicare, and does not reimburse Medicare, CMS may offset the amount owed against any funds due the intermediary or carrier under title XVIII of the Act or due the contractor under the contract.

(l) *Recovery when there is failure to file a proper claim* —(1) *Basic rule.* If Medicare makes a conditional payment with respect to services for which the beneficiary or provider or supplier has not filed a proper claim with a primary payer, and Medicare is unable to recover from the primary payer, Medicare may recover from the beneficiary or provider or supplier that was responsible for the failure to file a proper claim.

(2) *Exceptions:* (i) This rule does not apply in the case of liability insurance nor when failure to file a proper claim is due to mental or physical incapacity of the beneficiary.

(ii) CMS will not recover from providers or suppliers that are in compliance with the requirements of §489.20 of this chapter and can show that the reason they failed to file a proper claim is that the beneficiary, or someone acting on his or her behalf, failed to give, or gave erroneous, information regarding coverage that is primary to Medicare.

(m) *Interest charges.* (1) With respect to recovery of payments for items and services furnished before October 31, 1994, CMS charges interest, exercising common law authority in accordance with 45 CFR 30.13, consistent with the Federal Claims Collection Act (31 U.S.C. 3711).

(2) In addition to its common law authority with respect to recovery of payments for items and services furnished on or after October 31, 1994, CMS charges interest in accordance with section 1862(b)(2)(B)(i) of the Act. Under that provision—

(i) CMS may charge interest if reimbursement is not made to the appropriate trust fund before the expiration of the 60-day period that begins on the date on which notice or other information is received by CMS that payment has been or could be made under a primary plan;

(ii) Interest may accrue from the date when that notice or other information is received by CMS, is charged until reimbursement is made, and is applied for full 30-day periods; and

(iii) The rate of interest is that provided at §405.378(d) of this chapter.

§ 411.25 Primary payer's notice of primary payment responsibility.

(a) If it is demonstrated to a primary payer that CMS has made a Medicare primary payment for services for which the primary payer has made or should have made primary payment, it must provide notice about primary payment responsibility and information about the underlying MSP situation to the entity or entities designated by CMS to receive and process that information.

(b) The notice must describe the specific situation and the circumstances (including the particular type of insurance coverage as specified in §411.20(a)) and, if appropriate, the time period during which the insurer is primary to Medicare.

(c) The primary payer must provide additional information to the designated entity or entities as the designated entity or entities may require this information to update CMS' system of records.

§ 411.28   Waiver of recovery and compromise of claims.

(a) CMS may waive recovery, in whole or in part, if the probability of recovery, or the amount involved, does not warrant pursuit of the claim.

(b) General rules applicable to compromise of claims are set forth in subpart F of part 401 and §405.376 of this chapter.

(c) Other rules pertinent to recovery are contained in subpart C of part 405 of this chapter.

§ 411.37   Amount of Medicare recovery when a primary payment is made as a result of a judgment or settlement.

(a) *Recovery against the party that received payment* —(1) *General rule.* Medicare reduces its recovery to take account of the cost of procuring the judgment or settlement, as provided in this section, if—

(i) Procurement costs are incurred because the claim is disputed; and

(ii) Those costs are borne by the party against which CMS seeks to recover.

(2) *Special rule.* If CMS must file suit because the party that received payment opposes CMS's recovery, the recovery amount is as set forth in paragraph (e) of this section.

(b) *Recovery against the primary payer.* If CMS seeks recovery from the primary payer, in accordance with §411.24(i), the recovery amount will be no greater than the amount determined under paragraph (c) or (d) or (e) of this section.

(c) *Medicare payments are less than the judgment or settlement amount.* If Medicare payments are less than the judgment or settlement amount, the recovery is computed as follows:

(1) Determine the ratio of the procurement costs to the total judgment or settlement payment.

(2) Apply the ratio to the Medicare payment. The product is the Medicare share of procurement costs.

(3) Subtract the Medicare share of procurement costs from the Medicare payments. The remainder is the Medicare recovery amount.

(d) *Medicare payments equal or exceed the judgment or settlement amount.* If Medicare payments equal or exceed the judgment or settlement amount, the recovery amount is the total judgment or settlement payment minus the total procurement costs.

(e) *CMS incurs procurement costs because of opposition to its recovery.* If CMS must bring suit against the party that received payment because that party opposes CMS's recovery, the recovery amount is the lower of the following:

(1) Medicare payment.

(2) The total judgment or settlement amount, minus the party's total procurement cost.

§ 411.52 Basis for conditional Medicare payment in liability cases.

(a) A conditional Medicare payment may be made in liability cases under either of the following circumstances:

(1) The beneficiary has filed a proper claim for liability insurance benefits but the intermediary or carrier determines that the liability insurer will not pay promptly for any reason other than the circumstances described in §411.32(a)(1). This includes cases in which the liability insurance carrier has denied the claim.

(2) The beneficiary has not filed a claim for liability insurance benefits.

(b) Any conditional payment that CMS makes is conditioned on reimbursement to CMS in accordance with subpart B of this part.

APPENDIX 5

CMS Memorandum — Medicare Secondary Payer — Liability Insurance (Including Self Insurance) Settlements, Judgments, Awards, or Other Payments and Future Medicals — INFORMATION, dated September 29, 2011

DEPARTMENT OF HEALTH & HUMAN SERVICES
Centers for Medicare & Medicaid Services
7500 Security Boulevard, Mail Stop C3-14-00
Baltimore, Maryland 21244-1850

MEMORANDUM

DATE: September 29, 2011

FROM: Acting Director
               Financial Services Group
               Office of Financial Management

SUBJECT: Medicare Secondary Payer—Liability Insurance (Including Self-Insurance)
               Settlements, Judgments, Awards, or Other Payments and Future Medicals --
               INFORMATION

TO: Consortium Administrator for Financial Management and Fee-for-Service
               Operations

The purpose of this memorandum is to provide information regarding proposed Liability
Medicare Set-Aside Arrangement (LMSA) amounts related to liability insurance (including self-
insurance) settlements, judgments, awards, or other payments ("settlements").

Where the beneficiary's treating physician certifies in writing that treatment for the alleged
injury related to the liability insurance (including self-insurance) "settlement" has been
completed as of the date of the "settlement", and that future medical items and/or services for
that injury will not be required, Medicare considers its interest, with respect to future medicals
for that particular "settlement", satisfied. If the beneficiary receives additional "settlements"
related to the underlying injury or illness, he/she must obtain a separate physician certification
for those additional "settlements."

When the treating physician makes such a certification, there is no need for the beneficiary to
submit the certification or a proposed LMSA amount for review. CMS will not provide the
settling parties with confirmation that Medicare's interest with respect to future medicals for that
"settlement" has been satisfied. Instead, the beneficiary and/or their representative are
encouraged to maintain the physician's certification.

The above referenced guidance and procedure is effective upon publication of this memorandum.

Charlotte Benson

Charlotte Benson

APPENDIX 6

Health Insurance Card – *Example*

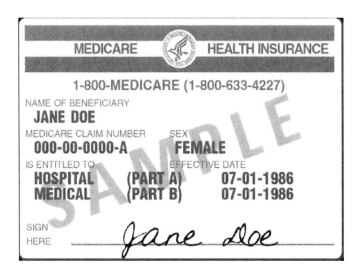

1. Carry your card with you when you are away from home.
2. Let your hospital or doctor see your card when you require hospital, medical, or health services under **Medicare**.
3. Your card is good wherever you live in the United States.

WARNING: Issued only for use of the named beneficiary. Intentional misuse of this card is unlawful and will make the offender liable to penalty. If found, drop in nearest U.S. Mail box.

CMS/
CENTERS for MEDICARE & MEDICAID SERVICES

Centers for Medicare & Medicaid Services
Baltimore, MD 21244-1850
Form CMS-1966 (01/2002)

If you have questions about Medicare, call 1-800-MEDICARE (1-800-633-4227; TTY/TDD: 1-877-486-2048) or visit us at www.medicare.gov.

APPENDIX 7

Social Security Administration Consent for Release of Information Form

Form Approved
OMB No. 0960-0566

Social Security Administration
Consent for Release of Information

Please read these instructions carefully before completing this form.

When to Use **This Form**	**Complete this form only if you want the Social Security Administration to give information or records about you to an individual or group (for example, a doctor or an insurance company).**

Natural or adoptive parents or a legal guardian, acting on behalf of a minor, who want us to release the minor's:
' **nonmedical** records, should use this form.
' medical records, should not use this form, but should contact us.

Note: Do not use this form to request information about your earnings or employment history. To do this, complete Form SSA-7050-F4. You can get this form at any Social Security office.

This consent form must be completed and signed only by:
' the person to whom the information or record applies, or

How to
Complete
This Form

' the parent or legal guardian of a minor to whom the **nonmedical** information applies, or
the legal guardian of a legally incompetent adult to whom the information applies.

To complete this form:
' Fill in the name, date of birth, and Social Security Number of the person to whom the information applies.
' Fill in the name and address of the individual or group to which we will send the information.
' Fill in the reason you are requesting the information.
' Check the type(s) of information you want us to release.
' Sign and date the form. If you are not the person whose record   we will release, please state your relationship to that person.

PRIVACY ACT NOTICE: The Privacy Act Notice requires us to notify you that we are authorized to collect this information by section 3 of the Privacy Act. You do not have to provide the information requested. However, we cannot release information or records about you to another person or organization without your consent for release of information. Your records are confidential. We will release only records that you authorize, and only to persons or organizations who you authorize to receive that information.

PAPERWORK REDUCTION ACT STATEMENT: This information collection meets the clearance requirements of 44 U.S.C. §3507, as amended by section 2 of the Paperwork Reduction Act of 1995. You do not need to answer these questions unless we display a valid Office of Management and Budget control number. We estimate that it will take about 3 minutes to read the instructions, gather the facts, and answer the questions. **SEND OR BRING THE COMPLETED FORM TO YOUR LOCAL SOCIAL SECURITY OFFICE. The office is listed under U.S. Government agencies in your telephone directory or you may call Social Security at 1-800-772-1213.** *You may send comments on our time estimate above to: SSA, 6401 Security Blvd., Baltimore, MD 212345-6401. Send only comments relating to our time estimate to this address, not the completed form.*

Form **SSA-3288** (5-2007) EF (5-2007)

Form Approved
OMB No. 0960-0566

Social Security Administration
Consent for Release of Information

TO: Social Security Administration

Name	Date of Birth	Social Security Number

I authorize the Social Security Administration to release information or records about me to:

NAME	ADDRESS

I want this information released because:

(There may be a charge for releasing information.)

Please release the following information:

_____ Social Security Number
_____ Identifying information (includes date and place of birth, parents' names)
_____ Monthly Social Security benefit amount
_____ Monthly Supplemental Security Income payment amount
_____ Information about benefits/payments I received from_____ to _____
_____ Information about my Medicare claim/coverage from_____ to _____
       (specify) _____
_____ Medical records
_____ Record(s) from my file (specify) _____

_____ Other (specify) _____

I am the individual to whom the information/record applies or that person's parent (if a minor) or legal guardian. I know that if I make any representation which I know is false to obtain information from Social Security records, I could be punished by a fine or imprisonment or both.

Signature:_____
(Show signatures, names, and addresses of two people if signed by mark.)
Date: _____ Relationship: _____

Form **SSA-3288** (5-2007) EF (5-2007)

APPENDIX 8

**CMS Alert on Collection of
Social Security Numbers and Affidavit –
Beneficiaries to Cooperate (June 23, 2008)**

Office of Financial Management/Financial Services Group

DATE: June 23, 2008

SUBJECT: Collection of Social Security Numbers (SSNs), Medicare Health Insurance Claim Numbers
               (HICNs) and Employer Identification Numbers (EINs) (Tax Identification Numbers) –
               ALERT

This ALERT is to advise that collection of SSNs, HICNs, or EINs for purposes of compliance with the
reporting requirements under Section 111 of Public Law 100-173 is appropriate.

SSNs and EINs:

- The SSN is used as the basis for the Medicare HICN. The Medicare program uses the HICN to
  identify Medicare beneficiaries receiving health care services, and to otherwise meet its administrative
  responsibilities to pay for health care and operate the Medicare program. In performance of these
  duties, Medicare is required to protect individual privacy and confidentiality in accordance with
  applicable laws, including the Privacy Act of 1974 and the Health Insurance Portability and
  Accountability Act Privacy Rule. Please note that The Centers for Medicare & Medicaid Services
  (CMS) has a longstanding practice of requesting SSNs or HICNs for coordination of benefit purposes.

- The EIN is the standard unique employer identifier. It appears on the employee's federal Internal
  Revenue Service Form W-2, Wage and Tax Statement received from their employer. The Medicare
  program uses the EIN to identify businesses. The establishment of a standard for a unique employer
  identifier was published in the May 31, 2002 Federal register, with a compliance date of July 30, 2004.

**A new Mandatory Insurer Reporting Law (Section 111 of Public Law 110-173) requires group health
plan insurers, third party administrators, and plan administrators or fiduciaries of self-insured/self-
administered group health plans to report, as directed by the Secretary of the Department of Health and
Human Services, information that the Secretary requires for purposes of coordination of benefits. The
law also imposes this same requirement on liability insurers (including self-insurers), no-fault insurers
and workers' compensation laws or plans. Two key elements that will be required to be reported are
SSNs (or HICNs) and EINs. In order for Medicare to properly coordinate Medicare payments with
other insurance and/or workers' compensation benefits, Medicare relies on the collection of both the
SSN or HICN and the EIN, as applicable.**

As a subscriber (or spouse or family member of a subscriber) to a group health plan arrangement, your SSN
and/or HICN will likely be requested in order to meet the requirements of P.L. 110-173 if this information is
not already on file with your insurer. Similarly, individuals who receive ongoing reimbursement for medical
care through no-fault insurance or workers' compensation or who receive a settlement, judgment or award
from liability insurance (including self-insurance), no-fault insurance, or workers' compensation will be asked
to furnish information concerning their SSN and/or HICN and whether or not they (or the injured party, if the
settlement, judgment or award is based upon an injury to someone else) are Medicare beneficiaries.
Employers, insurers, third party administrators, etc. will be asked for EINs.

To confirm that this ALERT is an official Government document and for further information on the mandatory
reporting requirements under this law, please visit the CMS website at www.cms.hhs.gov/MandatoryInsRep.

MMSEA111AlertSSNandHICNandEINcollection062308final

APPENDIX 9

CMS Alert re Social Security Numbers – August 18, 2009

The Centers for Medicare & Medicaid Services (CMS) is the federal agency that oversees the Medicare program. Many Medicare beneficiaries have other insurance in addition to their Medicare benefits. Sometimes, Medicare is supposed to pay after the other insurance. However, if certain other insurance delays payment, Medicare may make a "conditional payment" so as not to inconvenience the beneficiary, and recover after the other insurance pays.

Section 111 of the Medicare, Medicaid and SCHIP Extension Act of 2007 (MMSEA), a new federal law that became effective January 1, 2009, requires that liability insurers (including self-insurers), no-fault insurers, and workers' compensation plans report specific information about Medicare beneficiaries who have other insurance coverage. This reporting is to assist CMS and other insurance plans to properly coordinate payment of benefits among plans so that your claims are paid promptly and correctly.

We are asking you to the answer the questions below so that we may comply with this law.

Please review this picture of the Medicare card to determine if you have, or have ever had, a similar Medicare card.

Section I

Are you presently, or have you ever been, enrolled in Medicare Part A or Part B?	☐Yes	☐No

If yes, please complete the following. If no, proceed to Section II.

Full Name: *(Please print the name exactly as it appears on your SSN or Medicare card if available.)*

Medicare Claim Number:		Date of Birth (Mo/Day/Year)		-		-		
Social Security Number: *(If Medicare Claim Number is Unavailable)*	- -		Sex	☐Female	☐Male

Section II

I understand that the information requested is to assist the requesting insurance arrangement to accurately coordinate benefits with Medicare and to meet its mandatory reporting obligations under Medicare law.

_____   _____
Claimant Name (Please Print)   Claim Number

_____
Name of Person Completing This Form If Claimant is Unable (Please Print)

_____   _____
Signature of Person Completing This Form   Date

If you have completed Sections I and II above, stop here. If you are refusing to provide the information requested in Sections I and II, proceed to Section III.

Section III

_____   _____
Claimant Name (Please Print)   **Claim Number**

For the reason(s) listed below, I have not provided the information requested. I understand that if I am a Medicare beneficiary and I do not provide the requested information, I may be violating obligations as a beneficiary to assist Medicare in coordinating benefits to pay my claims correctly and promptly.

Reason(s) for Refusal to Provide Requested Information:

_____

_____

_____

_____

_____   _____
Signature of Person Completing This Form   **Date**

APPENDIX 10

CMS Revised HICN SSN Form – August 18, 2009

Page 1 of 2

The Centers for Medicare & Medicaid Services (CMS) is the federal agency that oversees the Medicare program. Many Medicare beneficiaries have other private group health plan (GHP) insurance in addition to their Medicare benefits. There are federal rules that determine whether Medicare or the other GHP insurance pays first.

Section 111 of the Medicare, Medicaid and SCHIP Extension Act of 2007 (MMSEA), a new federal law that became effective January 1, 2009, requires that group health insurers, claims processing third-party administrators, and certain employer self-funded/self-administered plans report specific information about Medicare beneficiaries who have other group coverage. This reporting is to assist CMS and other health insurance plans to properly coordinate payment of benefits among plans so that your claims are paid promptly and correctly.

We are asking you to the answer the questions below so that we may comply with this law.

Please review this picture of the Medicare card to determine if you, a spouse, or other family members covered by your group health plan have, or has ever had, a similar Medicare card.

Section I:

Are you presently, or have you ever been, enrolled in Medicare Part A or Part B?	☐Yes	☐No

If yes, please complete the following. If no, proceed to Section II.

Full Name: *(Please print the name exactly as it appears on your SSN or Medicare card if available.)*

Medicare Claim Number:	Date of Birth (Mo/Day/Year)

Social Security Number: *(If Medicare Claim Number is Unavailable)*	Sex ☐Female ☐Male

Section II:

Do you have a spouse that is presently, or has ever been, enrolled in Medicare Part A or Part B?	☐Yes	☐No

If yes, please complete the following. If no, proceed to Section III.

Full Name: *(Please print the name exactly as it appears on their SSN or Medicare card if available.)*

Medicare Claim Number:	Date of Birth (Mo/Day/Year)

Social Security Number: *(If Medicare Claim Number is Unavailable)*	Sex ☐Female ☐Male

Section III:

Do you have another covered family member that is presently, or has ever been, enrolled in Medicare Part A or Part B?	☐Yes	☐No

If yes, please complete the following. If no, proceed to Section IV. If additional space is needed for completion of this section, please attach another sheet.

Full Name: *(Please print the name exactly as it appears on their SSN or Medicare card if available.)*

Relationship *(Dependent child, domestic partner, etc.)*:

Medicare Claim Number:	Date of Birth (Mo/Day/Year)

Subscriber ID: XXXXXXXXXX

| Social Security Number: (If Medicare Claim Number is Unavailable) | | | | - | | - | | | | Sex | ☐Female | ☐Male |

Full Name: *(Please print the name exactly as it appears on their SSN or Medicare card if available.)*

| | | | | | | | | | | | | | | | | | | | | | | | | |

Relationship *(Dependent child, domestic partner, etc.)*:

| Medicare Claim Number: | | | - | | | | - | | Date of Birth (Mo/Day/Year) | | | - | | - | | | |

| Social Security Number: (If Medicare Claim Number is Unavailable) | | | | - | | - | | | | Sex | ☐Female | ☐Male |

Full Name: *(Please print the name exactly as it appears on their SSN or Medicare card if available.)*

| | | | | | | | | | | | | | | | | | | | | | | | | |

Relationship *(Dependent child, domestic partner, etc.)*:

| Medicare Claim Number: | | | - | | | | - | | Date of Birth (Mo/Day/Year) | | | - | | - | | | |

| Social Security Number: (If Medicare Claim Number is Unavailable) | | | | - | | - | | | | Sex | ☐Female | ☐Male |

Section IV:
I understand that the information requested is to assist my insurer, third-party administrator or group health plan to accurately coordinate benefits with Medicare and to meet its mandatory reporting obligations under Medicare law.

_____   _____
Subscriber Name (Please Print)   Subscriber's Plan ID

_____
Name of Person Completing This Form (Please Print)

_____   _____
Signature of Person Completing This Form   Date

If you have completed Sections I – IV above, stop here. If you are refusing to provide the information requested in Sections I – IV, proceed to Section V.

Section V:

_____   _____
Subscriber Name (Please Print)   Subscriber's Plan ID

For the reason(s) listed below, I have not provided the information requested. I understand that if I am a Medicare beneficiary and I do not provide the requested information, I may be violating obligations as a beneficiary to assist Medicare in coordinating benefits to pay my claims correctly and promptly.

Reason(s) for Refusal to Provide Requested Information:
_____

_____

_____   _____
Name of Person Completing This Form (Please Print)   Signature of Person Completing This Form / Date

Subscriber ID: XXXXXXXXXX

APPENDIX 11

Request to Healthcare Providers to Rebill Medicare

[INSERT DATE]

[Insert Name of Health Care Provider]
[Insert Address of Health Care Provider]

RE: Beneficiary Name: [INSERT Last Name, First Name, Middle Initial]
    HIC#: [NOT Social Security #]
    Date of Birth: [Insert Date of Birth]
    Policy/Claim Number: [Insert Claim #]
      Date of Illness/Injury: [Insert Accident Date]

Dear Coordination of Benefits Contractor:

I have presented a liability claim against the following liability plan:

[Insert Name of Company]
[Insert Address]
[Insert Claim Number]

The liability plan is still investigating the accident and cannot promptly pay. It is requested that you rebill Medicare at this time. Upon any settlement, award, judgment or other payment by the liability plan related to this accident, the appropriate Medicare contactor will be notified and the parties will agree on reimbursement to the Medicare Trust Fund at that time.

Thank you for your prompt attention to this matter.

Regards,

[Insert Signatory Name]
[Insert Signatory Title]

[Insert Medicare Beneficiary Name]

cc: [Liability Plan]
     [Medicare – COBC]

APPENDIX 12

Medicare Questionnaire (OMB Form #938-0214)

DEPARTMENT OF HEALTH AND HUMAN SERVICES
CENTERS FOR MEDICARE & MEDICAID SERVICES

QUESTIONS CALL: 1-800-999-1118

MEDICARE QUESTIONNAIRE FOR BENEFICIARIES 65 OR OVER

NAME: **JOHN Q. PUBLIC**

DATE OF BIRTH: **7/23/1935**

MEDICARE NUMBER: **987654321X**

INSTRUCTIONS: This form will be read by a computer. Please print as shown below. Stay within the boxes. Use CAPITAL letters. Mark boxes with an X. **USE BLACK OR BLUE INK.**

EXAMPLE | A | B | C | | | 1 | 2 | 3 | |

SECTION A - INFORMATION ABOUT YOU

1) On **7/21/2000**, will YOU be working? YES [X]   NO [ ]   (If NO, go to SECTION B)

2) Do YOU have any group health plan coverage through your current employer?
   YES [X]   NO [ ]   (If NO, go to SECTION B)

3) How many employees, including yourself, work for your employer?
   [ ] Don't know   [X] 20 or more   [ ] Less than 20 (If less than 20, STOP, go to SECTION B)
   Please provide information about the employer and the employer group health plan in the spaces below:

EMPLOYER NAME: **MEGACONGLOMERATE INC.**

ADDRESS: **123 MAIN STREET**

ADDRESS: **ASTRA BUILDING**

CITY: **ANYTOWN**   STATE: **NY**   ZIP: **00000**

NAME OF GROUP HEALTH PLAN: **ABC INSURANCE CO**

ADDRESS: **456 FIRST AVE**

ADDRESS:

CITY: **GOTHAM CITY**   STATE: **NY**   ZIP: **99999**

GROUP IDENTIFICATION NUMBER:

POLICY NUMBER:

4) Does your employer group health plan cover prescription drugs? YES [X]   NO [ ]   (If NO, go to SECTION B)
   Please use your insurance card to provide the following information if available:

Rx GROUP: **ZPQR52213**   Rx PCN:

MEMBER ID: **597612073**   Rx BIN: **995544**

SECTION B - INFORMATION ABOUT YOUR HUSBAND/WIFE

1) On **3/23/2005**, will you be receiving any group health plan coverage through the current employment of your husband/wife? YES [ ]   NO [X]   N/A [ ]   (If NO or N/A, STOP, go to SECTION C)

Husband/Wife's First Name:

Husband/Wife's Social Security Number: | | | — | | | — | | | |

Husband/Wife's Middle Initial   Husband/Wife's Last Name:

SECTION B - INFORMATION ABOUT YOUR HUSBAND/WIFE, CONTINUED

2) How many employees work for your husband/wife's employer? (Please include your husband/wife).

Don't know ☐　　20 or more ☐　　less than 20 ☐　　(if less than 20, **STOP**, go to **SECTION C**)

Please provide information about the employer and the employer group health plan in the spaces below:

EMPLOYER NAME

ADDRESS

ADDRESS

CITY　　　　　　　　　　　　　　　　　　STATE　ZIP

NAME OF GROUP HEALTH PLAN

ADDRESS

ADDRESS

CITY　　　　　　　　　　　　　　　　　　STATE　ZIP

GROUP IDENTIFICATION NUMBER

POLICY NUMBER

3) Does your husband/wife's employer's group health plan cover prescription drugs?　YES ☐　NO ☐
(If **NO, STOP**, go to **SECTION C**)

Please use your husband/wife's insurance card to provide the following information if available:

Rx GROUP　　　　　　　　　　　　　　　　Rx PCN

MEMBER ID　　　　　　　　　　　　　　　　Rx BIN

SECTION C - MORE INFORMATION ABOUT YOU

1) Are **YOU** receiving **Black Lung** Benefits?　　　　YES ☐　　NO ☒
2) Are **YOU** receiving **Worker's Compensation** Benefits?　YES ☐　　NO ☒
3) Are **YOU** receiving treatment for an injury or illness which another party could be held responsible or could be covered under no-fault, automobile, or liability insurance?　YES ☐　　NO ☒

STOP　If you answered **YES** to any of these questions, go to **SECTION D**.
If you answered **NO** to all of these questions, sign and return only this page.

Your Signature　John Public

AREA CODE　PHONE NUMBER
2 1 2 - 2 1 2 - 2 1 2 1

DEPARTMENT OF HEALTH AND HUMAN SERVICES
CENTERS FOR MEDICARE & MEDICAID SERVICES

QUESTIONS CALL: 1-800-999-1118

MEDICARE QUESTIONNAIRE FOR BENEFICIARIES 65 OR OVER, CONTINUED

NAME	DATE OF BIRTH	MEDICARE NUMBER
JOHN Q PUBLIC	07/23/1935	987654321X

SECTION D - MORE INFORMATION ABOUT YOU, CONTINUED

1) If **YOU** are getting **Black Lung** (Coal Miner's) Medical Benefits, print the date the benefits began.

   M M   D D   Y Y Y Y

2) If **YOU** are now getting any medical services related to an illness or injury which occured on the job, for which **YOU** have or will file a **Workers' Compensation** claim, print the date of the illness or injury.

   M M   D D   Y Y Y Y

Please provide information about the employer, insurance carrier, and attorney in the spaces below :

EMPLOYER NAME

ADDRESS

ADDRESS

CITY | STATE | ZIP

NAME OF INSURANCE CARRIER

ADDRESS

ADDRESS

CITY | STATE | ZIP

POLICY or CLAIM NUMBER

NAME OF ATTORNEY (If Applicable)

ADDRESS

ADDRESS

CITY | STATE | ZIP

BRIEF DESCRIPTION OF ILLNESS OR INJURY

Sample

(TURN PAGE OVER)

SECTION D - MORE INFORMATION ABOUT YOU, CONTINUED

3) If **YOU** are now getting any treatment for an illness or injury for which another party could be held liable, please print the date of illness or injury: ☐☐ — ☐☐ — ☐☐☐☐
M M   D D   Y Y Y Y

NAME OF INSURANCE CARRIER

ADDRESS

ADDRESS

CITY   STATE   ZIP

POLICY or CLAIM NUMBER

NAME OF ATTORNEY (If Applicable)

ADDRESS

ADDRESS

CITY   STATE   ZIP

BRIEF DESCRIPTION OF ILLNESS OR INJURY

4) If **YOU** are now getting any treatment for an illness or injury which could be covered under **no-fault** or **automobile insurance**, print the date the of illness or injury: ☐☐ — ☐☐ — ☐☐☐☐
M M   D D   Y Y Y Y

NAME OF INSURANCE CARRIER

ADDRESS

ADDRESS

CITY   STATE   ZIP

POLICY or CLAIM NUMBER

NAME OF ATTORNEY (If Applicable)

ADDRESS

ADDRESS

CITY   STATE   ZIP

BRIEF DESCRIPTION OF ILLNESS OR INJURY

Your Signature   AREA CODE   PHONE NUMBER

Sample

OMB NO. 0938-0214

APPENDIX 13

Letter to Medicare Notifying of Abandonment or Denial of Claim

[INSERT DATE]

Medicare – Coordination of Benefits
P.O. Box 33847
Detroit, MI 48232

Medicare Secondary Payer Recovery Contractor – NGHP
P.O. Box 138832
Oklahoma City, OK 73113

RE: Beneficiary Name: [INSERT Last Name, First Name, Middle Initial]
   HIC#: [NOT Social Security #]
   Date of Birth: [Insert Date of Birth]
   Policy/Claim Number: [Insert Claim #]
      Date of Illness/Injury: [Insert Accident Date]

Dear Coordination of Benefits Contractor and Medicare Secondary Payer Recovery Contractor:

The [Insert Liability Carrier] previously notified COBC on [INSERT DATE] about its potential status as a primary plan and has now determined after its investigation that it is not responsible for the Medicare beneficiary, [INSERT CLAIMANT NAME] injuries. Consequently, The [Insert Liability Carrier] will make no payment, nor obligate itself to make any payment to the Medicare beneficiary and has closed its file. Medicare is therefore primary with regard to this accident.

Thank you for your prompt attention to this matter.

Regards,

[Insert Liability Claims Examiner Name]
Claims Adjuster

cc: [Insert Medicare Beneficiary Name]

APPENDIX 14

COBC Acknowledgement Letter

COBC Acknowledgement Letter

CENTERS for MEDICARE & MEDICAID SERVICES

MEDICARE - Coordination of Benefits
1-800-999-1118 or (TTY/TDD): 1-800-318-8782

****FIRST CLASS MAIL- R:2446 T: P: F:49799   November 08, 2010

FRANCO SIGNOR LAW FIRM 2746 DELWARE AVE
KENMORE NY 14217

DEAR JEFF SIGNOR:

RE: Beneficiary Name: ▮▮▮▮▮▮▮▮▮▮
HIC#: ▮▮▮▮▮▮▮▮

Medicare has been advised that you have been retained to represent the above beneficiary for matters arising out of the above referenced illness/injury. In order to accurately update the beneficiary's records, we need you to confirm the information below. *A prompt response is necessary.*

**Employer Name:
**Address:
**Address:
**City: **State: **Zip:
Name of Group Health Plan/Insurance Carrier: GALLAGHER BASSET
Address: PO BOX 6330
Address:
City: OAKBROOK TERRAC State: IL Zip: 60181
Policy Number: 003632295204GB01   **Policy Holder:
**Insurance Type: [___] Hospital Only   [___] Medical Only   [___] Medical and Hospital
Date Coverage Began: 03/20/2009   Date of Illness or Injury: 03/20/2009

**Prescription Drug Group ID: **Prescription Drug PCN:
**Prescription Drug Member ID: **Prescription Drug BIN:

* Please note that the fields marked with asterisks "*" above indicate that no information is currently on file and should be provided by you on the attached questionnaire.

Medicare acknowledges that you may file a claim and/or a civil action against a third party on your client's behalf, seeking damages for injuries he/she received and medical expenses he/she incurred as a result of the above illness/injury.

To ensure a timely response, please call our toll free customer service line at: 1-800-999-1118 or 1-800-318-8782 for the hearing impaired or use the enclosed questionnaire and courtesy reply envelope to supply us with any information requiring a change to your records. Failure to respond could result in the incorrect payment of medical claims. If the above information accurately reflects the information regarding other insurance coverage, there is no need to reply to this inquiry.

Continued   Page I-1

COBC Acknowledgement Letter

We would like to take this opportunity to advise you of the applicability of the Medicare Secondary Payer Laws. Per 42 U.S.C. 1395y (b) (2) and 1862 (b)(2)(A)(ii) of the Act, Medicare is precluded from paying for a beneficiary's medical expenses when payment "has been made or can reasonably be expected to be made . . . under a Workers' Compensation plan, an automobile or liability insurance policy or plan (including a self-insured plan) or under no-fault insurance." However, Medicare may pay for a beneficiary's covered medical expenses conditioned on reimbursement to Medicare from proceeds received pursuant to a third party liability settlement, award, judgment or recovery. ▓▓▓▓▓▓▓▓▓▓

In these instances, Medicare's reimbursement is reduced by a pro rata share of procurement costs. It is in your and your client's best interest to keep Medicare's payment and the obligation to satisfy Medicare's claim in mind when negotiating and accepting a final dollar amount in settlement of the claim with the third party. Medicare's claim must be paid up front out of settlement proceeds before any distribution occurs. Moreover, Medicare must be paid within 60 days of receipt of proceeds from the third party. Interest may be assessed, if Medicare is not repaid in a timely manner. Repayment of Medicare's conditional payments must be made to the local Medicare contractor or the lead contractor handling this case.

Upon receipt of your response to his letter, we will aly update your client's Medicare file, and promptly issue an attorney package to you which includes the name, address and telephone number of the lead Medicare contractor that will handle the specifics of this case to recovery, and a release form to be forwarded to the lead contractor.

If you have any questions regarding this letter or any questions regarding Medicare as a secondary payer for services, please call (800) 999-1118.

CC: ▓▓▓▓▓▓▓

NOTICE TO PATIENT ABOUT THE COLLECTION AND USE OF MEDICARE INFORMATION (PRIVACY ACT STATEMENT)

The Social Security Act mandates the collection of this information. The purpose of collecting this information is to properly pay medical insurance benefits to you or on your behalf.

Information collected may be given to health insurance providers and suppliers of services (and their authorized billing agents) directly or through fiscal intermediaries or carriers, for administration of title XVIII; and to an individual or organization for a research evaluation, or epidemiological project related to the prevention of disease or disability, or the restoration or maintenance of health.

The identification number we are using is your Medicare Health Insurance Number. While furnishing the information on this form is voluntary, the Medicare program may not be able to make accurate claims payment when the requested information is not available in its records.

Public Law 100-503, the Computer Matching and Privacy Protection Act of 1988 permits the government to verify information by way of computer matches. Anyone who knowingly and willfully makes or causes to be made a false statement or representation of a material fact for use in determining a right to payment under the Social Security Act commits a crime punishable under Federal law by fine, imprisonment, or both.

According to the Paperwork Reduction Act of 1995, no persons are required to respond to a collection of information unless it displays a valid OMB control number. The valid OMB control number for this information collection is 0938-0214. The time required to complete this information collection is estimated to average 5 minutes per responder, including the time to review instructions, search existing data resources, gather the data needed, and complete and review the information collection. If you have any suggestions for improving this form, please write to: CMS, Attn: PRA Reports Clearance Officer, 7500 Security Boulevard, Baltimore, Maryland 21244-1850.

COBC Acknowledgement Letter

MEDICARE SECONDARY PAYER DEVELOPMENT

NAME

MEDICARE HEALTH INSURANCE CLAIM NUMBER

INSTRUCTIONS: This form will be read by a computer. Please print as shown below. Stay within the boxes. Use CAPITAL letters. Mark boxes with an X. **USE BLACK OR BLUE INK.**

EXAMPLE | A | B | C | | | 1 | 2 | 3 | |

SECTION A - INFORMATION ABOUT YOU

1) Do YOU have any group health plan coverage based upon your current employment?

YES ☐   NO ☐   (If NO, go to SECTION B)

2) How many employees, including yourself, work for the employer from whom you have health insurance?

Don't Know ☐   1-19 ☐   20-99 ☐   100 or More ☐   (If less than 20, go to SECTION B)

Please provide information about the employer and the employer group health plan in the spaces below

EMPLOYER NAME

ADDRESS

ADDRESS

CITY   STATE   ZIP

NAME OF GROUP HEALTH PLAN

ADDRESS

ADDRESS

CITY   STATE   ZIP

DATE INSURANCE COVERAGE BEGAN   POLICY NUMBER

☐ ☐ – ☐ ☐ – ☐ ☐ ☐ ☐
M M   D D   Y Y Y Y

TYPE OF INSURANCE HOSPITAL/MEDICAL ☐   HOSPITAL ONLY ☐   MEDICAL ONLY (DOCTOR/SUPPLIER) ☐

3) Does your group health plan cover prescription drugs? YES ☐   NO ☐   (If NO, go to SECTION B)

Please use your insurance card to provide the following information if available

Rx GROUP   Rx PCN

MEMBER ID   Rx BIN

SECTION B - INFORMATION ABOUT YOUR SPOUSE/OTHER FAMILY MEMBER

1) Do YOU have any group health plan coverage based upon your spouse's/other family member's current employment?   YES ☐   NO ☐   (If NO, go to SECTION C)

2) How many employees, including your spouse/other family member, work for the employer from whom they have health insurance?   Don't Know ☐   1-19 ☐   20-99 ☐   100 or more ☐
(If less than 20, go to SECTION C)

Page I-3

COBC Acknowledgement Letter

SECTION B - INFORMATION ABOUT YOUR SPOUSE/OTHER FAMILY MEMBER, CONTINUED

Policy Holder/Subscriber's First Name

Policy Holder/Subscriber's Social Security Number

Policy Holder/Subscriber's Last Name

Please provide information about the employer and the employer group health plan in the spaces below

EMPLOYER NAME

ADDRESS

ADDRESS

CITY   STATE   ZIP

NAME OF GROUP HEALTH PLAN

ADDRESS

ADDRESS

CITY   STATE   ZIP

DATE INSURANCE COVERAGE BEGAN   POLICY NUMBER

M M — D D — Y Y Y Y

TYPE OF INSURANCE: HOSPITAL/MEDICAL ☐   HOSPITAL ONLY ☐   MEDICAL ONLY (DOCTOR/SUPPLIER) ☐

3) Does your family member/spouse's group health plan cover prescription drugs?

     YES ☐   NO ☐   (IF NO, STOP go to SECTION C)

Please use your insurance card to provide the following information, if available

Rx GROUP   Rx PCN

MEMBER ID   Rx BIN

SECTION C - MORE INFORMATION ABOUT YOU

1) Are YOU receiving **Black Lung** Benefits?   YES ☐   NO ☐

2) Are YOU receiving **Workers' Compensation** benefits?   YES ☐   NO ☐

3) Are YOU receiving treatment for an injury or illness which another party could be held liable or could be covered under no-fault or auto insurance?   YES ☐   NO ☐

STOP   If YOU answered YES to any questions in this section, go to SECTION D

If YOU answered NO to all of these questions, sign below and return this form only.

Your Signature   AREA CODE   PHONE NUMBER

Page I-4

(CONTINUED ON NEXT PAGE)

OMB # 0938-0214

COBC Acknowledgement Letter

MEDICARE SECONDARY PAYER DEVELOPMENT, CONTINUED

NAME: MEDICARE HEALTH INSURANCE CLAIM NUMBER

SECTION D - MORE INFORMATION ABOUT YOU

1) If YOU are getting **Black Lung** (Coal Miner's) Medical Benefits, print the date the benefits began.

M M — D D — Y Y Y Y

2) If YOU are now receiving any medical services related to an illness or injury which occurred on the job, for which YOU have or will file a **Workers' Compensation** claim, print the date of illness or injury.

M M — D D — Y Y Y Y

Please provide information about the employer and the employer, insurance carrier, and attorney in the spaces below.

EMPLOYER NAME

ADDRESS

ADDRESS

CITY   STATE   ZIP

NAME OF INSURANCE CARRIER

ADDRESS

ADDRESS

CITY   STATE   ZIP

POLICY or CLAIM NUMBER

NAME OF ATTORNEY (If Applicable)

ADDRESS

ADDRESS

CITY   STATE   ZIP

BRIEF DESCRIPTION OF ILLNESS OR INJURY

Page I-5

(TURN PAGE OVER)

COBC Acknowledgement Letter

SECTION D - MORE INFORMATION ABOUT YOU, CONTINUED

3) If YOU are now getting any treatment for an illness or injury for which another party could be held liable, please print the date of illness or injury

M M — D D — Y Y Y Y

NAME OF INSURANCE CARRIER

ADDRESS

ADDRESS

CITY   STATE   ZIP

POLICY or CLAIM NUMBER

NAME OF ATTORNEY (If Applicable)

ADDRESS

ADDRESS

CITY   STATE   ZIP

BRIEF DESCRIPTION OF ILLNESS OR INJURY

4) If YOU are now getting any treatment for an illness or injury which could be covered under no-fault or automobile insurance, print the date the of illness or injury

M M — D D — Y Y Y Y

NAME OF INSURANCE CARRIER

ADDRESS

ADDRESS

CITY   STATE   ZIP

POLICY or CLAIM NUMBER

NAME OF ATTORNEY (If Applicable)

ADDRESS

ADDRESS

CITY   STATE   ZIP

BRIEF DESCRIPTION OF ILLNESS OR INJURY

Your Signature   AREA CODE   PHONE NUMBER

APPENDIX 15

MSPRC Rights and Responsibilities Letter

MSPRC

 Learn about your letter at *www.msprc.info*

[BENEFNAME M BENELNAME]   [DATE]
[MADD1 MADD2]
[MCITY MSTATE MZIP]

SUBJECT: Medicare Secondary Payer Rights and Responsibilities
           Beneficiary's Name [BENEFNAME M BENELNAME]
           HIC#: [CLAIMNUM]
           Date of Incident: [TCI DATE]
           Case #: [Remas Case#]

Dear [BENEFNAME M BENELNAME]:

Please note that if we know that you have an attorney or other individual representing you in this matter, we are sending him/her a copy of this letter. If you have an attorney or other representative for this matter and his/her name is not at the end of this letter indicating that he/she is receiving a copy, please contact us immediately. If you have any questions regarding this letter and are represented by an attorney or other individual in this matter, you may wish to talk to your representative before contacting us.

We understand that you have made a claim against other insurance or workers' compensation. This letter is to let you know:

- What your responsibilities are as a Medicare beneficiary in connection with your claim;
- What information we need if you have a representative;
- What information we are requesting regarding your claim;
- What information we need if there is a settlement, judgment, award or other payment for your claim (or if your claim is dismissed or otherwise abandoned).

NOTE: This letter also tells you about other information we will send to you regarding claims Medicare paid on your behalf on or after the date of your incident/injury, and provides information for mailing or faxing information to us.

Your Responsibilities as a Medicare Beneficiary

- When no-fault insurance, liability insurance or workers' compensation is available to you, it must pay before Medicare pays. Some examples of no-fault and liability insurance include automobile or homeowners' medical payments coverage or personal injury protection, automobile liability or no-fault insurance, liability insurance which pays you because another individual or entity is negligent, malpractice insurance, etc.

- Medicare makes "conditional" payments while your insurance or workers' compensation claim is pending to ensure that you receive the medical services you need in a timely manner.
- Once you receive a settlement, judgment, award, or other payment from the liability insurance, no-fault insurance or workers' compensation, the conditional payments Medicare made on your behalf must be repaid to the Medicare program. Medicare should be repaid before funds are disbursed for other purposes. (The applicable law can be found at 42 U.S.C. 1395y(b)(2)(A) & (B).)

Information We Need If You Have a Representative

If someone is acting as your representative (that is, an attorney or other individual who is acting on your behalf), you should have the following information sent to us so we can communicate directly with your representative as well as with you.

- If your representative is an attorney, he/she should send us a copy of the agreement you signed when you retained the attorney. The agreement should also be signed or countersigned and dated by the attorney; be on the attorney's letterhead (or have a cover letter from the attorney); and have your name and Medicare Health Insurance Claim Number (the number on your Medicare card) at the top of the document. This will act as proof that this attorney is representing you, may act on your behalf, and receive your Medicare claims information directly from us.
- If someone other than an attorney is your representative, you must send a letter that is signed and dated, telling us that he/she is your representative and the date of the incident or injury for which he/she is acting as your representative. Please include your name and Medicare Health Insurance Claim Number at the top of the letter so that we can easily associate your agreement with your file. Your representative must also sign and date the letter to show that he/she has agreed to represent you. (Model language for proof of representation is available on our website at www.msprc.info.)

As we stated at the beginning of this letter, if we have information that you have a representative, we are copying him/her on this letter. Your representative can take care of submitting this information to us. (However, if your representative's name is not shown at the end of this letter, please contact us immediately and give a copy of this letter to your representative.)

Information Requested Regarding Your Insurance or Workers' Compensation Claim

We are requesting that your representative send us the name, address, and telephone number of the insurer or workers' compensation carrier involved and, if available, the policy number, claim number, and claim adjuster's name. (If you do not have a representative, we ask that you send us this information.)

If we have a name and address for the insurer or workers' compensation, we are copying them on this letter. However, we may not have more specific information, such as the claims adjuster you are working with, so we are requesting that you send us the complete information.

Information We Need If There Is a Settlement, Judgment, Award, or Other Payment (or If Your Claim Is Dismissed or Otherwise Abandoned)

Once you have a settlement, judgment, award, or other payment for your claim, if you have a representative, he/she should send us the following information. (If you do not have a representative, you will need to send us this information.)

- A copy of the settlement, judgment, award or other document regarding payment indicating the appropriate date and the total amount of the settlement, judgment, award or other payment.
- An itemized statement of attorney fees and other procurement costs that you are paying.

If your claim has been dismissed or otherwise abandoned without a settlement, judgment, award, or other payment, please send us any documentation of these actions so that we may close our record of this incident.

Information Regarding Claims Medicare Paid On Your Behalf on or After Your Date of Incident

Beneficiary representatives often ask us what "conditional" payments Medicare made on or after your date of incident. "Conditional" payments are those Medicare payments that are related to your pending insurance or workers' compensation claim.

Within sixty-five days from the date of this letter, you will receive a Conditional Payment Letter (CPL) which will show you the conditional payments Medicare has made on your behalf at that time (an interim conditional payment amount). If you have an attorney or other representative, and we have appropriate proof of representation, we will also send a copy of this information to your representative. If we do not have the appropriate proof of representation, only you will receive the CPL; and you should supply a copy to your representative. (Please see the section above for information on appropriate proof of representation documentation.)

If your claim is for no-fault insurance or workers' compensation benefits, a copy of the CPL will be sent to the insurer or workers' compensation carrier if we have that information.

Please do not submit a request for a CPL because we will send one to you automatically as soon as the information is available. A separate request will not make the information available faster.

Once we send the CPL, we will also post this conditional payment information under the "MyMSP" tab of the www.mymedicare.gov website. The information at www.mymedicare.gov will be updated weekly with any newly processed claims. If you wish, you can also keep track of the medical expenses that were paid by Medicare, and if you have an attorney or other representative, provide him/her with this information. This may assist him/her with finalizing your settlement.

Mailing or Faxing Information to the MSPRC

Please use a copy of the enclosed "Correspondence Cover Sheet" whenever you or your representative submit any correspondence pertaining to the incident identified in the subject field of this letter. This cover sheet includes our address information and is pre-filled with information that will facilitate processing your correspondence. If you do not include a copy of this cover sheet, please include your name and your Medicare Health Insurance Claim Number (the number on your Medicare card) on all correspondence. This will allow us to associate the correspondence with the appropriate records.

Attached is a Privacy Act Statement that explains your privacy rights. You may be interested in the enclosed brochure about the MSPRC.

Sincerely,
MSP Recovery Contractor

Enclosures:
Privacy Statement
Medicare Secondary Payer Recovery Contractor Brochure
Correspondence Cover Sheet

[Copies to: Attorney/Other Representative, No-Fault Insurance (if information is available), Workers' Compensation Entity (if information is available)]

NOTICE TO BENEFICIARY ABOUT THE COLLECTION AND
USE OF MEDICARE INFORMATION
(PRIVACY ACT STATEMENT)

The Social Security Act mandates the collection of this information. The purpose of collecting this information is to properly pay medical insurance benefits to you or on your behalf.

Information collected may be given to health insurance providers and suppliers of services (and their authorized billing agents) directly or through fiscal intermediaries or carriers, for administration of Title XVIII; and to an individual or organization for a research evaluation, or epidemiological project related to the prevention of disease or disability, or the restoration or maintenance of health.

The identification number we are using is your Medicare Health Insurance Number. While furnishing the information on this form is voluntary, the Medicare program may not be able to make accurate claims payment when the requested information is not available in its records.

Public Law 100-503, the computer Matching and privacy Protection Act of 1988, permits the government to verify information by way of computer matches. Anyone who knowingly and willfully makes, or causes to be made, a false statement or representation of a material fact for use in determining a right to payment under the Social Security Act commits a crime punishable under Federal law by fine, imprisonment, or both.

According to the paperwork Reduction Act of 1995, no persons are required to respond to a collection of information unless it displays a valid OMB control number. The valid OMB control number for this information is 0938-0214. The time required to complete this information collection is estimated to average 5 minutes per responder, including the time to review instructions, search existing data resources, gather the data needed, and complete and review the information collection. If you have any suggestions for improving this form, please write to: CMS, Attn: PRA Reports Clearance Officer, 7500 Security Boulevard, Baltimore, Maryland 21244-1850.

APPENDIX 16

MSPRC Consent to Release Form

Medicare Consent

CONSENT TO RELEASE

The language below should be used when you, a Medicare beneficiary, want to authorize someone other than your attorney or other representative to receive information, including identifiable health information, from the Centers for Medicare & Medicaid Services (CMS) related to your liability insurance (including self-insurance), no-fault insurance or workers' compensation claim.

I _____, (print your name exactly as shown on your Medicare card) hereby authorize the CMS, its agents and/or contractors to release, upon request, information related to my injury/illness and/or settlement for the specified date of injury/illness to the individual and/or entity listed below:

CHECK ONLY ONE OF THE FOLLOWING TO INDICATE WHO MAY RECEIVE INFORMATION AND THEN PRINT THE REQUESTED INFORMATION:
(If you intend to have your information released to more than one individual or entity, you must complete a separate release for each one.)

☐ Insurance Company   ☐ Workers' Compensation Carrier   ☐ Other: _____
                                                                    (Explain)

Name of entity: _____

Contact for above entity: _____
Address: _____
                               _____

Telephone: _____

CHECK ONE OF THE FOLLOWING TO INDICATE HOW LONG CMS MAY RELEASE YOUR INFORMATION (The period you check will run from when you sign and date below.):

☐ One Year   ☐ Two Years   ☐ Other: _____
                                          (Provide a specific period of time)

I understand that I may revoke this "consent to release information" at any time, in writing.

MEDICARE BENEFICIARY INFORMATION AND SIGNATURE:

Beneficiary Signature: _____   Date: _____

Note: If the beneficiary is incapacitated, the submitter of this document will need to include documentation establishing the authority of the individual signing on the beneficiary's behalf. Please visit www.msprc.info for further instructions.

Medicare Health Insurance Claim Number: (the number on your Medicare Card): _____

Date of Injury/Illness: _____

Page C-1

A16-1

APPENDIX 17

MSPRC Cover Sheet

MSPRC Coversheet

MSPRC

CENTERS for MEDICARE & MEDICAID SERVICES

Learn about your letter at *www.msprc.info*

Correspondence Cover Sheet

Beneficiary's Name: _____

HIC#: _____

Date of Incident: _____

Case ID#: _____

This cover sheet is for your use when mailing or faxing in correspondence to the MSPRC. Please retain a COPY of this cover sheet for any future correspondence. The information above will ensure accuracy when handling your case documentation.

Please indicate the type of correspondence you are submitting to the MSPRC to facilitate routing. Check all that apply:

- [ ] Check
- [ ] Settlement Information
- [ ] Retainer agreement or other authorization documentation
- [ ] Other:

Note: A Conditional Payment Letter is sent automatically, as soon as the information is available. Separate requests for initial Conditional Payment Amounts will not make Conditional Payment information available sooner.

In order to accurately associate claims to your case, please include a description of the injury. (ie: Knee, Physical Therapy, Slip and Fall, Lumbar Injury...)

ICD-9 Diagnosis Code	ICD-9 Diagnosis Description

Submit correspondence to the appropriate MSPRC address listed below:

Liability Insurance or No Fault Insurance:

MSPRC – NGHP
PO Box 138832
Oklahoma City, OK 73113

Workers' Compensation:

Workers' Compensation MSP Recovery
MSPRC WC
PO Box, 33831
Detroit, MI 48232-5831

Page F-1

A17-1

APPENDIX 18

MSPRC Model Proof of Representation

[Enter date]

MSPRC – NGHP
P.O. Box 138832
Oklahoma City, OK 73113

Re: <u>**PROOF OF REPRESENTATION**</u>

Dear Medicare Secondary Payer Recovery Contractor:

Type of Medicare Beneficiary Representative (Check one below and the print the requested information):
☐ Individual other than an Attorney: Name:
☐ Attorney* Relationship to the Medicare Beneficiary: Personal Injury Attorney
☐ Guardian* Firm or Company Name:
☐ Conservator* Address:
☐ Power of Attorney*

Telephone: _____

Note – If you have an attorney, your attorney may be able to use his/her retainer agreement instead of this language. (If the beneficiary is incapacitated, his/her guardian, conservator, power of attorney etc. will need to submit documentation other than this model language.) Please visit www.msprc.info for further instructions

Medicare Beneficiary Information and Signature/Date:

Beneficiary's Name (please print exactly as shown on your Medicare card): _____

Beneficiary's Health Insurance Claim Number (number on your Medicare card):_____

Date of Illness/Injury for which the beneficiary has filed a liability insurance, no-fault insurance or workers' compensation claim:

_____

Beneficiary Signature:

_____

Date Signed: _____

Representative Signature/Date:

Representative's Signature:

_____

Date signed: _____

APPENDIX 19

MSPRC Conditional Payment Letter – *Example*

Learn about your letter at *www.msprc.info*

PLEASE REFRAIN FROM MAKING PAYMENT AT THIS TIME

RE: Name of Beneficiary:
HIC#:
Date of Injury/Illness/Incident:

Dear

Please note that, if we know that you have an attorney or other individual representing you in this matter, we are sending him/her a copy of this letter. If you have an attorney or other representative for this matter and his/her name is not shown as a "cc" at the end of this letter (indicating that he/she is receiving a copy), please contact us immediately. If you have any questions regarding this letter and are represented by an attorney or other person in this matter, you may wish to talk to your representative before contacting us.

This letter follows a previous letter notifying you/your attorney of Medicare's priority right of recovery as defined under the Medicare Secondary Payer provisions. Because you were involved in an automobile, slip and fall, medical malpractice, or some other type of liability claim, the medical expenses are subject to reimbursement to Medicare from proceeds received pursuant to a third party liability settlement, award, judgment, or recovery.

However, we request that you/your attorney refrain from sending any monies to Medicare prior to submission of settlement information and receipt of a demand/recovery calculation letter from our office. This will eliminate underpayments, overpayments, and/or associated delays.

Currently, Medicare has paid   in conditional payments related to your claim. Attached you/your attorney will find a listing of claims that comprise this total. Please take a look at this listing and let us know if you/your attorney disagree with the inclusion of any claim in whole or in part and explain the reasons why you/your attorney disagree(s).

Please be advised that we are still investigating this case file to obtain any other outstanding Medicare conditional payments. Therefore, the enclosed listing of current conditional payments (including a response of a zero amount) is not a final listing and will need to be updated once we receive final settlement information from you. It would be in your best interest to keep Medicare's payments and the statutory obligation to satisfy Medicare in mind when the final dollar amount is negotiated and accepted in resolution of the claim with the third party.

If the case has settled, please furnish our office with a copy of:

1) The settlement agreement from the third party payer showing the total amount of the settlement, signed and dated, AND

2) Your closing statement reflecting the actual amount of the attorney's fees and costs (excluding medical bills).

Thank you for your assistance and cooperation in this matter. If you have any questions regarding this matter, please contact us at   (TTY/TDD: 1-866-677-7294 for the hearing and speech impaired).

Sincerely,

Medicare Secondary Payer Recovery Contractor

Enclosures: Payment Summary Form
cc:

SGLLCPNGHP

Payment Summary Form

REPORT NUMBER:
CONTRACTOR:

BENEFICIARY NAME:
BENEFICIARY HICN:

DATE:

CASE ID:
CASE TYPE:
DATE OF INCIDENT:

TOS	ICN	LINE	PROCESSING CONTRACTOR	PROVIDER NAME	DIAGNOSIS CODE	FROM DATE	TO DATE	TOTAL CHARGES	REIMBURSED AMOUNT	CONDITIONAL PAYMENT

SUM OF TOTAL CHARGES:
TOTAL CONDITIONAL PAYMENT:

APPENDIX 20

MSPRC Payment Summary Detail Form

Payment Summary Form

REPORT NUMBER: 5
CONTRACTOR: MEDICARE SECONDARY PAYER RECOVERY CONTRACTOR

BENEFICIARY NAME:
BENEFICIARY HICN:

DATE: 09/28/2009

CASE ID:
CASE TYPE: LIABILITY
DATE OF INCIDENT: 02/19/2008

TOS	ICN	LINE	PROCESSING CONTRACTOR	PROVIDER NAME	DIAGNOSIS CODE	FROM DATE	TO DATE	TOTAL CHARGES	REIMBURSED AMOUNT	CONDITIONAL PAYMENT
71	86010810100464O	1	805	NICOLETTO, WILLIAM B	7391,7210,72 33,7392	04/07/2008	04/07/2008	$50.00	$28.34	$28.34
71	86010810200360	1	805	NICOLETTO, WILLIAM B	7391,7210,72 33,7392	04/08/2008	04/08/2008	$50.00	$22.70	$22.70
71	86010811200385O	1	805	NICOLETTO, WILLIAM B	7391,7210,72 33,7392	04/14/2008	04/14/2008	$50.00	$28.34	$28.34
71	86070814204656O	1	805	NICOLETTO, WILLIAM B	7391,7210,72 33,7392	04/15/2008	04/15/2008	$50.00	$28.34	$28.34
71	86010811400824O	1	805	NICOLETTO, WILLIAM B	7391,7210,72 33,7392	04/18/2008	04/18/2008	$50.00	$28.34	$28.34
71	86010811900541O	1	805	NICOLETTO, WILLIAM B	7391,7210,72 33,7392	04/23/2008	04/23/2008	$50.00	$28.34	$28.34
71	86090820372429O	1	805	GLEIMER, BARRY S	7234,7262,84 70,8471	05/15/2008	05/15/2008	$225.00	$20.00	$20.00
71	86090820372433O	1	805	GLEIMER, BARRY S	7234,7262,84 70,8471	05/29/2008	05/29/2008	$60.00	$20.00	$20.00
71	86090820372438O	1	805	GLEIMER, BARRY S	8471,7262,84 70	06/12/2008	06/12/2008	$100.00	$20.00	$20.00
71	86020826943771O	1	12402	GLEIMER, BARRY S	7234,7262,84 70	06/19/2008	06/19/2008	$60.00	$20.00	$20.00
71	86020823446158O	1	805	ASHBY, JOHN	7234,3540,35 42	08/05/2008	08/05/2008	$600.00	$20.00	$20.00
71	86020831788028O	1	12402	ROTHMAN, SIMON	7230,7211,72 211	11/05/2008	11/05/2008	$466.55	$373.24	$373.24
71	86020904355977O	1	12402	KALLINY, MOHSEN A	7234,72211,8 470	12/12/2008	12/12/2008	$175.00	$105.45	$105.45
71	86020906138587O	1	12402	S JERSEY MUSCUL OSKELETAL INS	7234,7220	01/09/2009	01/09/2009	$2,464.00	$249.92	$249.92

Payment Summary Form

REPORT NUMBER: 1
CONTRACTOR: MEDICARE SECONDARY PAYER RECOVERY CONTRACTOR

BENEFICIARY NAME:
BENEFICIARY HICN:

DATE: 09/28/2009

CASE ID:
CASE TYPE: LIABILITY
DATE OF INCIDENT: 02/19/2008

TOS	ICN	LINE	PROCESSING CONTRACTOR	PROVIDER NAME	DIAGNOSIS CODE	FROM DATE	TO DATE	TOTAL CHARGES	REIMBURSED AMOUNT	CONDITIONAL PAYMENT
71	860209061385870	2	12402	S JERSEY MUSCUL OSKELETAL INS	7234,7220	01/09/2009	01/09/2009	$368.00	$0.00	$0.00
71	860209050511250	1	12402	KALLINY, MOHSEN A	7220,7234	01/09/2009	01/09/2009	$600.00	$81.10	$81.10
71	860909078135300	1	12402	GHAUL, MARK R	7234	01/09/2009	01/09/2009	$875.00	$55.62	$55.62
71	860909078135300	2	12402	RUSSO, CARMEN	7234	01/09/2009	01/09/2009	$437.50	$55.62	$55.62
71	860809069001620	1	12402	NICOLETTO, WILLIAM B	7391,7210,72 33,7392	02/25/2009	02/25/2009	$50.00	$28.96	$28.96
71	860809069001610	1	12402	NICOLETTO, WILLIAM B	7391,7210,72 33,7392	02/27/2009	02/27/2009	$50.00	$28.96	$28.96
82	090897019011000	1	16003	AT HOME MEDICAL EQUIPMENT LLC	7220,7234	03/03/2009	03/03/2009	$55.00	$31.13	$31.13
71	860809068224210	1	12402	NICOLETTO, WILLIAM B	7391,7210,72 33,7392	03/03/2009	03/03/2009	$50.00	$28.96	$28.96
82	09105702748000	1	16003	AT HOME MEDICAL EQUIPMENT LLC	7220,7234	03/03/2009	03/03/2009	$502.63	$402.10	$402.10
71	860809070157350	1	12402	NICOLETTO, WILLIAM B	7391,7210,72 33,7392	03/04/2009	03/04/2009	$50.00	$28.96	$28.96
71	860909082733700	1	12402	KALLINY, MOHSEN A	7248,7202,72 24,7244	03/05/2009	03/05/2009	$100.00	$52.99	$52.99
71	860209069355940	1	12402	BONJER, BRUCE	72210,72252	03/06/2009	03/06/2009	$472.09	$377.67	$377.67
71	860109072011670	1	12402	NICOLETTO, WILLIAM B	7391,7210,72 33,7392	03/06/2009	03/06/2009	$50.00	$28.96	$28.96
71	860109075208360	1	12402	NICOLETTO, WILLIAM B	7391,7210,72 33,7392	03/09/2009	03/09/2009	$50.00	$28.96	$28.96
71	860809077174070	1	12402	NICOLETTO, WILLIAM B	7391,7210,72 33,7392	03/11/2009	03/11/2009	$50.00	$28.96	$28.96
71	860809078189670	1	12402	NICOLETTO, WILLIAM B	7391,7210,72 33,7392	03/13/2009	03/13/2009	$50.00	$28.96	$28.96

Payment Summary Form

REPORT NUMBER:

CONTRACTOR: MEDICARE SECONDARY PAYER RECOVERY CONTRACTOR

DATE: 09/28/2009

BENEFICIARY NAME:

BENEFICIARY HICN:

CASE ID:

CASE TYPE: LIABILITY

DATE OF INCIDENT: 02/19/2008

TOS	ICN	LINE	PROCESSING CONTRACTOR	PROVIDER NAME	DIAGNOSIS CODE	FROM DATE	TO DATE	TOTAL CHARGES	REIMBURSED AMOUNT	CONDITIONAL PAYMENT
71	86080909603090960	1		IAM B	33,7392					
71	86080909603091040	1	12402	NICOLETTO, WILL IAM B	7391,7210,72 33,7392	03/16/2009	03/16/2009	$50.00	$28.96	$28.96
71	86080909616350560	1	12402	NICOLETTO, WILL IAM B	7391,7210,72 33,7392	03/20/2009	03/20/2009	$50.00	$28.96	$28.96
71	86020909234389890	1	12402	NICOLETTO, WILL IAM B	7391,7210,72 33,7392	03/23/2009	03/23/2009	$50.00	$28.96	$28.96
71	86020909234389890	1	12402	GLEIMER, BARRY S	7244,7260,72 62	03/26/2009	03/26/2009	$25.00	$0.00	$0.00
71	86020909234389890	2	12402	GLEIMER, BARRY S	7244,7260,72 62	03/26/2009	03/26/2009	$40.00	$12.38	$12.38
71	86020909234389890	3	12402	GLEIMER, BARRY S	7260,7244,72 62	03/26/2009	03/26/2009	$60.00	$24.25	$24.25
71	86020909234389890	4	12402	GLEIMER, BARRY S	7260,7244,72 62	03/26/2009	03/26/2009	$30.00	$0.00	$0.00
71	86020910516153530	1	12402	ARMSTRONG, JAME S M	7234	03/27/2009	03/27/2009	$875.00	$111.23	$111.23
71	86090911064740480	1	12402	KALLINY, MOHSEN A	7220,7234	03/27/2009	03/27/2009	$600.00	$81.10	$81.10
71	86020911887614140	1	12402	S JERSEY MUSCUL OSKELETAL INS	7220,7234	03/27/2009	03/27/2009	$2,587.00	$249.92	$249.92
71	86020911887614140	2	12402	S JERSEY MUSCUL OSKELETAL INS	7220,7234	03/27/2009	03/27/2009	$579.00	$0.00	$0.00
71	86090909680303390	1	12402	GLEIMER, BARRY S	7244,81209	03/30/2009	03/30/2009	$25.00	$0.00	$0.00
71	86090909680303390	2	12402	GLEIMER, BARRY S	7244,81209	03/30/2009	03/30/2009	$40.00	$12.38	$12.38
71	86090909680303390	3	12402	GLEIMER, BARRY	81209,7244	03/30/2009	03/30/2009	$60.00	$24.25	$24.25

Payment Summary Form

DATE: 09/28/2009

REPORT NUMBER:

CONTRACTOR: MEDICARE SECONDARY PAYER RECOVERY CONTRACTOR

BENEFICIARY NAME:
BENEFICIARY HICN:

CASE ID:
CASE TYPE: LIABILITY
DATE OF INCIDENT: 02/19/2008

TOS	ICN	LINE	PROCESSING CONTRACTOR	PROVIDER NAME	DIAGNOSIS CODE	FROM DATE	TO DATE	TOTAL CHARGES	REIMBURSED AMOUNT	CONDITIONAL PAYMENT
71	860909096803400	1	12402	GLEIMER, BARRY S	7244,81209	04/01/2009	04/01/2009	$120.00	$48.50	$48.50
71	860909096803400	2	12402	GLEIMER, BARRY S	81209	04/01/2009	04/01/2009	$30.00	$22.34	$22.34
71	860109096217160	1	12402	NICOLETTO, WILLIAM B	7391,7210.72 33,7392	04/01/2009	04/01/2009	$50.00	$28.96	$28.96
71	860209113770970	1	12402	GLEIMER, BARRY S	7244	04/03/2009	04/03/2009	$25.00	$0.00	$0.00
71	860209113770970	2	12402	GLEIMER, BARRY S	7244	04/03/2009	04/03/2009	$40.00	$12.38	$12.38
71	860209113770970	3	12402	GLEIMER, BARRY S	7244	04/03/2009	04/03/2009	$120.00	$48.50	$48.50
82	091057027470000	1	16003	AT HOME MEDICAL EQUIPMENT LLC	7220,7234	04/03/2009	04/03/2009	$389.09	$311.27	$311.27
82	091057027470000	2	16003	AT HOME MEDICAL EQUIPMENT LLC	7220,7234	04/03/2009	04/03/2009	$46.10	$36.88	$36.88
71	860209113770990	1	12402	GLEIMER, BARRY S	7244	04/08/2009	04/08/2009	$25.00	$0.00	$0.00
71	860209113770990	2	12402	GLEIMER, BARRY S	7244	04/08/2009	04/08/2009	$40.00	$12.38	$12.38
71	860209113770990	3	12402	GLEIMER, BARRY S	7244	04/08/2009	04/08/2009	$120.00	$48.50	$48.50
71	860809110051990	1	12402	NICOLETTO, WILLIAM B	7391,7210.72 33,7392	04/14/2009	04/14/2009	$50.00	$28.96	$28.96
71	860209120702470	1	12402	KALLINY, MOHSEN A	7248,7210.72 34,7244	04/28/2009	04/28/2009	$100.00	$52.99	$52.99
82	091277014820000	1	16003	AT HOME MEDICAL	7220,7234	05/06/2009	05/06/2009	$136.00	$48.40	$48.40

Payment Summary Form

REPORT NUMBER:
CONTRACTOR: MEDICARE SECONDARY PAYER RECOVERY CONTRACTOR

DATE: 09/28/2009

BENEFICIARY NAME:
BENEFICIARY HICN:

CASE ID:
CASE TYPE: LIABILITY
DATE OF INCIDENT: 02/19/2008

TOS	ICN	LINE	PROCESSING CONTRACTOR	PROVIDER NAME	DIAGNOSIS CODE	FROM DATE	TO DATE	TOTAL CHARGES	REIMBURSED AMOUNT	CONDITIONAL PAYMENT
71	86020914159966O	1	12402	CITTA-PIETROLUN GO, T EQUIPMENT LLC	7244	05/15/2009	05/15/2009	$250.00	$101.50	$101.50
71	86020914159966O	2	12402	CITTA-PIETROLUN GO, T	7244	05/15/2009	05/15/2009	$125.00	$46.08	$46.08
71	86020914159966O	3	12402	CITTA-PIETROLUN GO, T	7244	05/15/2009	05/15/2009	$800.00	$215.04	$215.04
71	86020914159966O	4	12402	CITTA-PIETROLUN GO, T	7244	05/15/2009	05/15/2009	$800.00	$326.02	$326.02
71	86020914159966O	5	12402	CITTA-PIETROLUN GO, T	7244	05/15/2009	05/15/2009	$300.00	$82.62	$82.62
71	86020915578002B0	1	12402	KALLINY, MOHSEN A	7268	06/02/2009	06/02/2009	$100.00	$0.00	$0.00
71	86020915578002B0	4	12402	KALLINY, MOHSEN A	7268	06/02/2009	06/02/2009	$25.00	$0.00	$0.00
71	86020915578002B0	5	12402	KALLINY, MOHSEN A	7268	06/02/2009	06/02/2009	$150.00	$0.00	$0.00
71	86020915578149O	1	12402	GLEIMER, BARRY S	72210,3542,7 1841,7234	06/02/2009	06/02/2009	$125.00	$52.99	$52.99
71	86020920469653O	1	12402	KALLINY, MOHSEN A	7242	06/02/2009	06/02/2009	$150.00	$46.26	$46.26
82	09180707372000	1	16O03	AT HOME MEDICAL EQUIPMENT LLC	7220,7234	06/18/2009	06/18/2009	$136.00	$48.40	$48.40
71	86020919603378O	1	12402	BRENNAN, MARK D	7244	07/10/2009	07/10/2009	$750.00	$50.32	$50.32
71	86020919603378O	2	12402	RUSSO, CARMEN N	7244	07/10/2009	07/10/2009	$375.00	$50.32	$50.32
71	86020920469654O	1	12402	KALLINY, MOHSEN A	7248,72252,7 234,7244	07/22/2009	07/22/2009	$100.00	$32.37	$32.37

APPENDIX 21

MSPRC Payment Summary Form – *Example of Lined Out*

Payment Summary Form

REPORT NUMBER: EMCAN-55
CONTRACTOR: MEDICARE SECONDARY PAYER RECOVERY CONTRACTOR

BENEFICIARY NAME:
BENEFICIARY HICN

CASE ID:
CASE TYPE: LIABILITY
DATE OF INCIDENT: 08/08/2005

Handwritten annotations (top):
- 786.50 = Chest Pain
- 922.10 = Contusion - Chest Wall
- 845.10 "Sprain/Strain - Ankle/foot
- 722.93 = Spinal Stenosis - Lumbar
- 715.97 = Osteoarthrosis   DATE: 02/24/2010
- 719.47 = Joint Pain

TOS	ICN	LINE	PROCESSING CONTRACTOR	PROVIDER NAME	DIAGNOSIS/ICD	FROM DATE	TO DATE	TOTAL CHARGES	REIMBURSED AMOUNT	CONDITIONAL PAYMENT
40	20522702266902	0	390	VIRTUA WEST JERSEY HOSPITALS B ERLIN	9221,84510	08/09/2005	08/09/2005	$1,644.60	$162.09	$162.09
40	20523001983602	0	390	COOPER UNIVERSITY HOSPITAL	78650	08/12/2005	08/12/2005	$713.00	$26.35	$26.35
71	86020523074606O	1	805	SHACK, EVAN T	78650	08/09/2005	08/09/2005	$62.00	$11.82	$11.82
71	86020523990229S0	1	805	SHACK, EVAN T	71947	08/09/2005	08/09/2005	$40.00	$7.66	$7.66
71	86020524220317O	1	805	RYAN, JOHN J	84510,88909	08/09/2005	08/09/2005	$267.00	$51.27	$51.27
71	86090522909040I0	1	805	ANGELO, MARK	9221 78650	08/12/2005	08/12/2005	$75.00	$45.26	$45.26
71	86090522908401I0	2	805	ANGELO, MARK	78650	08/12/2005	08/12/2005	$83.00	$23.46	$23.46
71	86090525027904O	3	805	HOCHBERG, ROBER T D	78650	08/12/2005	08/12/2005	$56.00	$9.57	$9.57
71	86090523100270O	1	805	ANGELO, MARK	78650	08/15/2005	08/15/2005	$75.00	$45.26	$45.26
71	86020523590775O	1	805	ANGELO, MARK	78650	08/19/2005	08/19/2005	$75.00	$45.26	$45.26
71	86090524149098O	1	805	KERNER, SHELDON P	72293 71947	08/25/2005	08/25/2005	$55.00	$13.45	$13.45
71	86090523160298O	2	805	KERNER, SHELDON P	72293 71947	08/26/2006	08/26/2006	$35.00	$7.70	$7.70
71	86090523149096O	0	805	KERNER, SHELDON P	71947 72293	08/26/2006	08/26/2006	$84.00	$24.40	$24.40
71	87110709558626O	1	865	HANSEN, C	72293 78650,2720.4 1401	04/03/2007	04/03/2007	$1,200.00	$386.62	$386.62
71	87110709558626O	2	865	HANSEN, C	78650,2720.4 1401	04/03/2007	04/03/2007	$250.00	$70.46	$70.46
71	87110709558626O	3	865	HANSEN, C	78650,2720.4 1401	04/03/2007	04/03/2007	$250.00	$63.91	$63.91
71	87110709558626O	4	865	HANSEN, C	78650,2720.4	04/03/2007	04/03/2007	$450.00	$91.82	$91.82

* Unrelated charges — Spinal Stenosis, Osteoarthritis, Joint Pain, Ankle/foot Pain.

A21-1

Payment Summary Form

REPORT NUMBER: RMCAN-SS
CONTRACTOR: MEDICARE SECONDARY PAYER RECOVERY CONTRACTOR

DATE: 02/24/2010

BENEFICIARY NAME:
BENEFICIARY HICN:

CASE ID:
CASE TYPE: LIABILITY
DATE OF INCIDENT: 08/08/2005

TOS	ICN	LINE	PROCESSING CONTRACTOR	PROVIDER NAME	DIAGNOSIS/ICD	FROM DATE	TO DATE	TOTAL CHARGES	REIMBURSED AMOUNT	CONDITIONAL PAYMENT
71	87110709585862560	5	865	HANSEN, C	1401 78650,2720.4	04/03/2007	04/03/2007	$340.00	$108.80	$108.80
71	87110709585862560	6	865	HANSEN, C	78650,2720.4 1401	04/03/2007	04/03/2007	$447.50	$110.65	$110.65
71	860908287695410	1	805	LEUZZI, ROSEMARIE A	462,78650	10/07/2008	10/07/2008	$190.00	$77.57	$77.57
71	860908287695410	2	805	LEUZZI, ROSEMARIE A	462,78650	10/07/2008	10/07/2008	$33.00	$0.00	$0.00
71	860908287695410	3	805	LEUZZI, ROSEMARIE A	78650	10/07/2008	10/07/2008	$83.00	$20.10	$20.10

SUM OF TOTAL CHARGES: $6,441.10
TOTAL CONDITIONAL PAYMENT: $1,379.82

APPENDIX 22

Example Letter to MSPRC Dealing with Relatedness

DATE

Medicare Secondary Payer Recovery Contractor
VIA FAX: (734) 957-0998
Auto/Liability
P.O. Box 33828
Detroit, Michigan 48232-5828

RE: Beneficiary: XXXX
     Medicare Number: XXXX
     Date of Incident: 01/26/2007

Dear Medicare Secondary Payer Recovery Contractor:

ABC Inc. is the liability insurance plan responsible for this accident. We settled the case with the Medicare beneficiary, XXXX on or about XXXX for $15,000. A copy of the settlement agreement is enclosed for your files along with the executed consent from the Medicare beneficiary.

We received from the MSPRC the Payment Summary form for the Medicare beneficiary and after review have noted some discrepancies. We attach the Payment Summary Form and would like your consideration in removing certain of the charges that are unrelated to the accident. We have identified the unrelated charges by marking it with a "?". A copy is enclosed.

The Medicare beneficiary injured her ankle when she was struck by a hand truck carrying retail product. There were no other injuries. These are the unrelated ICD-9 codes:

ICD-9	Reason
75612	Congenital back - (Spondylolisthesis)
7242	Low back degenerative condition
72402	Lumbar pain - degenerative condition
72210	Degenerative low back condition
3532	Cervical pain - degenerative condition
4130	Angina (heart problem)
71509	Osteoarthritis (degenerative condition)
72885	Back muscle spasm
71699	Arthritis
5990	Urinary tract infection
78909	Abdomen and pelvis pain
7881	Dysuria (bladder issues)
5739	Disorder of the liver
78900	Abdomen and pelvis pain
59651	Hypertonicity of bladder
78843	Nocturia (bladder issues)
2449	Thyroid
25000	Diabetes
2720	Metabolic issues
4019	Hypertension

Please review and advise the undersigned of the final reimbursement amount. Please keep in mind that pursuant to Section 50.5 of the MSP Manual, **"There should be no recovery of benefits paid for services rendered after the date of a liability insurance settlement."** Consequently, we would expect the final reimbursement payment statement to not contain any medical related charges post October 1, 2008.

We look forward to your response.

Regards,

XXXXXX

Encl.
cc: XXXXX

APPENDIX 23

MSPRC Final Demand Letter

Final Demand Letter

 **MSPRC**

 Learn about your letter at *www.msprc.info*

Letter Date

Name
Address 1
Address 2
City, state, zip code

RE: Beneficiary Name:
Medicare Number:
Case Identification Number:
Insurer Claim Number:
Insurer Policy Number:
Date of Incident:
Demand Amount:

Dear   :

Please note that if we know that you have an attorney or other individual representing you in this matter, we are sending him/her a copy of this letter. If you have an attorney or other representative for this matter and his/her name is not shown as a "cc" at the end of this letter (indicating that he/she is receiving a copy), please contact us immediately. If you have any questions regarding this letter and are represented by an attorney or other individual in this matter, you may wish to talk to your representative and make sure that he/she has received a copy of this letter before contacting us.

We are writing to you because we learned that you have made a liability claim relating to an accident, illness, injury, or incident occurring on or about [MSP Effective Date] and obtained a recovery. We have determined that you are required to repay the Medicare program [Medicare Demand Amount] for the cost of medical care it paid relating to your liability recovery. (The term "recovery" includes a settlement, judgment, award, or any other type of recovery.)

Please read this entire letter, as it contains important information, including:

- An explanation of why you need to repay Medicare and the way we determined the amount you are required to repay (Parts I and II);
- Instructions for repaying Medicare if you agree that there has been an overpayment and accept the amount we have determined you owe. (Part III);
- Instructions for requesting waiver of recovery (for the full or a part of the amount of this demand) or appeal (if you disagree that an overpayment exists or with the amount of the overpayment we have determined you owe). (Part IV). Please note that Medicare will

Final Demand Letter

🔔 Learn about your letter at *www.msprc.info*

not initiate any recovery action while your request for waiver of recovery or appeal is
pending;
- Interest charges that apply if you do not repay Medicare within sixty (60) days from the
date of this letter and certain actions Medicare may decide to take if you fail to repay the
amount you owe (Part V);
- Whom you should contact if you have questions about this letter (Part VI).

I. Why am I required to repay Medicare?

You are required to repay Medicare because Medicare paid for medical care you received related
to your liability recovery. The Medicare Secondary Payer (MSP) law allows Medicare to pay for
medical care received by a Medicare beneficiary who has or may have a liability claim.
However, the law also requires Medicare to recover those payments if payment of a liability
settlement, judgment, recovery, or award has been or could be made. Congress passed the MSP
law because it wanted to make sure that the Medicare Trust Funds would have enough money to
pay for medical care that beneficiaries may need in the future. Congress decided that, if a
liability recovery was available to pay for a Medicare beneficiary's medical care, then that
money should be used to pay for the care and any amounts already paid by Medicare should be
refunded to the Medicare Trust Funds.

If you would like to read the MSP law, you can find it in Title 42 of the United States Code,
Section 1395y(b)(2). You can also find the regulations that explain how the Medicare program
recovers amounts it is owed under the MSP law in Title 42 of the Code of Federal Regulations,
beginning at Section 411.20. You can also learn more about how the MSP law works by
contacting your local Social Security office or by visiting www.medicare.gov

II. How did Medicare decide how much money I owe?

The Medicare program paid [Medicare Overpayment Amount] for medical care related to your
liability recovery. We have enclosed a list of the payments Medicare made related to your
recovery with this letter. The Medicare program generally reduces the amount a Medicare
beneficiary is required to repay to take into account the costs (such as attorney's fees) paid by the
beneficiary to obtain his or her liability recovery. You can find the formula we use to decide how
much the amount of this reduction should be at 42 C.F.R., sub-section 411.37. We have applied
the formula and determined that the amount you owe Medicare is [Medicare Demand Amount].

This letter relates only to money paid from your current recovery. If, in the future, you receive
additional money from this liability recovery, or any other liability recovery, you must let us
know.

III. If I accept this determination, how do I repay Medicare what I owe?

Final Demand Letter

MSPRC

Learn about your letter at *www.msprc.info*

As stated, Medicare has calculated an overpayment of Insert [Medicare Demand Amount], with repayment requested within sixty (60) days of the date of this letter, [Letter Date]. Please send a check or money order for [Medicare Demand Amount] made payable to Medicare, to us at the address listed at the end of this letter. Please make sure to include your name and Medicare number on the check or money order and include a copy of this letter with your payment.

The amount requested in this letter may not include payments received prior to the issuance of this demand letter dated [Letter Date]. Upon issuing a check, please deduct previous payments made to the MSPRC for the above referenced debt.

Please continue reading for information regarding your rights with respect to this overpayment and what happens if you do not repay Medicare timely (including the accrual and assessment of interest).

IV. What rights do I have if I disagree with the amount this letter says I owe or think that I should not have to repay Medicare for some other reason?

Right to Request a Waiver -You have the right to request that the Medicare program waive recovery of the amount you owe in full or in part. Your right to request a waiver is separate from your right to appeal our determination, and you may request both a waiver and an appeal at the same time. The Medicare program may waive recovery of the amount you owe if you can show that you meet both of the following conditions:

1. This overpayment (for purposes of requesting waiver of recovery, the amount you owe is considered an overpayment) was not your fault, because the information you gave us with your claims for Medicare benefits was correct and complete as far as you knew; and when the Medicare payment was made, you thought that it was the right payment;

    AND

2. Paying back this money would cause financial hardship or would be unfair for some other reason.

If you believe that both of these conditions apply to you, you should send us a letter that explains why you think you should receive a waiver of recovery of the amount you owe. If you request a waiver, we will send you a form asking for more specific information about your income, assets, expenses, and the reasons why you believe you should receive a waiver. Medicare will not initiate any recovery action while your request for waiver is pending. If we are unable to grant your request for a waiver, we will send you a letter that explains the reason(s) for our decision and the steps you will need to follow to appeal that decision if it is less than fully favorable to you.

Final Demand Letter

Learn about your letter at *www.msprc.info*

Right to Appeal- You also have the right to appeal our determination if you disagree that you owe Medicare as explained in Part I of this letter, or if you disagree with the amount that you owe Medicare ([Medicare Demand Amount]) as explained in Part II of this letter. To file an appeal, you should send us a letter explaining why you think the amount you owe Medicare is incorrect and /or any reason(s) why you disagree with our determination. Medicare will not initiate any recovery action while your appeal request is pending. Once we receive your request, we will decide whether our determination that you must repay Medicare [Medicare Demand Amount] is correct and send you a letter that explains the reasons for our decision. Our letter will also explain the steps you will need to follow to appeal that decision if it is less than fully favorable to you.

You have 120 days from receipt of this letter [Letter Date] to file an appeal. We must assume that you received this letter within five (5) days of the date of the letter [Letter Date] unless you furnish us with proof of the contrary.

If you do not already have an attorney or other representative and you want help with your request for waiver or appeal, you can have a friend, lawyer, or someone else help you. Some lawyers do not charge unless you win your case. There are groups, such as lawyer referral service that can help you find a lawyer. There are also groups, such as legal aid services, that will provide free legal services if you qualify.

V. What happens if I do not repay Medicare the amount I owe?

If you do not repay Medicare in full by [Due Date], you will be required to pay interest on any remaining balance, from the date of this letter, at a rate of [Interest Rate] per year as determined by federal regulation. If the debt is not fully resolved within 60 days of the date of this letter, interest is due and payable for each full 30 day period the debt remains unresolved. By law, all payments are applied to interest first, principal second. You can find the regulation that explains interest charges at 42 C.F.R., sub-section 411.24(m).

If you choose to appeal this determination or request a full or partial waiver of recovery, you may wish to repay Medicare the full amount or the amount you believe you owe within sixty (60) days of the date of this letter to avoid the assessment of interest. Interest accrues on any unpaid balance, which may include any amount you are determined to owe once a decision is reached on your request for waiver of recovery or appeal. If you receive a waiver of recovery or if you are successful in appealing our decision, Medicare will refund any excess amounts you have paid. Medicare will not initiate any recovery action while your request for waiver or appeal is pending.

If you can't repay Medicare in one payment, you may ask us to consider whether to allow you to pay in regular installments. If you make installment payments, you should be aware that your payments will be applied to any interest due first and then to the outstanding principal amount.

Final Demand Letter

🐾 Learn about your letter at *www.msprc.info*

The provisions of the Debt Collection Improvement Act of 1996 apply to Medicare debt. Recovery actions may include collection by Treasury offset against any monies otherwise payable to the debtor by any agency of the United States (for example, tax refunds or federal benefits), among other collection methods. If Medicare intends to take collection action (including referral to Treasury), you will be provided with appropriate notice. This notice will include information concerning appropriate steps to avoid such actions.

VI. Who should I contact if I have questions about this letter?

If you have any questions concerning this matter, please call the Medicare Secondary Payer Recovery Contractor (MSPRC) at 1-866-677-7220 (TTY/TDD: 1-866-677-7294 for the hearing and speech impaired) or you may contact us in writing at the address below. If you contact us in writing, please be sure to include the beneficiary's name, Medicare Health Insurance Claim Number (this is the number found on the beneficiary's red, white and blue Medicare card), and the date of the incident. Providing us with this information will help us respond more quickly to any questions you may have.

Medicare Secondary Payer Recovery Contractor
Liability
PO Box 138832
Oklahoma City, OK 73113

Sincerely,

MSPRC

CC:

Enclosure: Payment Summary Form

APPENDIX 24

Conditional Payment Notice (CPN)

 Learn about your letter at *www.msprc.info*

insert date

insert name
insert address 1
insert address 2
insert city, state, zip code

Conditional Payment Notice (CPN)

Beneficiary Name: insert name
Medicare Number: insert HICN
Case Identification Number:
Date of Incident: insert DOI
Response Due Date: Insert Response Due Date

THIS IS NOT A BILL. DO NOT SEND PAYMENT AT THIS TIME.

Dear insert name:

If we know you have an attorney or other individual representing you in this matter, we are sending him/her a copy of this letter. If you have an attorney or other representative for this matter and his/her name is not shown as a "cc" at the end of this letter (indicating that he/she is receiving a copy), please contact us immediately. If you have any questions regarding this letter and are represented by an attorney or other individual in this matter, you may wish to talk to your representative before contacting us.

The Centers for Medicare & Medicaid Services (CMS) has been notified that you have received a settlement, judgment, award or other payment related to your case with the above referenced date of incident. (Usually this notification is from the insurer, workers' compensation entity, if applicable, or a beneficiary's attorney or representative.)

If the settlement, judgment, award or other payment has not been distributed to you or your attorney/representative to date, please alert the MSPRC immediately.

To date, the Medicare Secondary Payer Recovery Contractor (MSPRC) has determined that Medicare has paid *at least* Insert Conditional Payment Amount in conditional payments related to your case, based upon the available information. The total conditional payments may increase if Medicare paid for additional items and/or services related to your case. This notice is being issued to you to ensure that we have all the correct information to determine the amount Medicare may recover.

Conditional Payment Notice

🦇 Learn about your letter at *www.msprc.info*

Please note: If the underlying claim involves ingestion, exposure, implantation, or other non-trauma based injury, this conditional payment amount will need to be revised. Please provide the MSPRC with a description of the injury in addition to all other items requested so that we may associate the appropriate claims with the case.

We have posted this conditional payment information under the "MyMSP" tab of the www.mymedicare.gov website. The information at www.mymedicare.gov will be updated weekly with any changes or newly processed claims.

What does Medicare need from you?

1. **Please review the enclosed conditional payment summary form and if the items and/or services listed are correct, please skip to step 3.**

2. **If the items and/or services listed are NOT related to your case, please submit disputes by** Insert Response Due Date.
   - Please note that Medicare has determined that the items and/or services listed on the enclosed conditional payment summary form are related to your case. If you believe that some of the items and/or services listed on the conditional payment summary form are **NOT** related to your case, please submit documentation explaining why you believe certain items and/or services are **NOT** related.

   - The documentation you submit must be able to show that the items and/or services you are disputing were not *claimed* or *released* in connection with the claim you made for liability insurance, no-fault insurance, or workers' compensation. This will typically include at least a copy of the claim submitted to your insurer (or workers' compensation) and settlement documentation.

If you have questions about whether items and/or services listed on your conditional payment summary form were claimed or released, consider speaking with your attorney or representative. If you do not have an attorney or representative, please contact the MSPRC for clarification.

The option to submit disputes before the MSPRC issues the recovery demand letter does NOT affect your appeal rights, which will be explained in the demand letter once it is issued.

3. **Please submit ALL procurement cost information if you have not already done so.**
   - Required procurement cost information includes:
     - The settlement date,
     - The settlement amount,
     - Attorney fees and other costs you have paid (costs for medical records, expert testimony, etc).

Important! If settlement information is not received by Insert Response Due Date, you will receive a demand letter requesting repayment of all conditional payments related to your case without a proportionate reduction for fees or costs, if applicable.
For further directions, please see http://www.msprc.info/forms/Final_Settlement_Detail.pdf.

Conditional Payment Notice

MSPRC

Learn about your letter at *www.msprc.info*

4. Please submit information on additional settlements relating to the date of incident listed above.

- Please notify the MSPRC If you have received more than one settlement, judgment award, or other payment for the incident that occurred on insert DOI.

- Please also notify the MSPRC about *pending* settlements, or *pending* claims for the incident that occurred on insert DOI.

Please provide all requested documentation by Insert Response Due Date to the address below. Be sure to include all of the following in your response.

1. All proof of representation documentation, if not already submitted.
2. A description of the injury.
3. Proof of any items and/or services that are NOT related to your case, if applicable.
4. All settlement documentation if you are providing proof of any items and/or services not related to your case.
5. Procurement costs and fees paid by the beneficiary.
6. Documentation for any additional or pending settlements, judgments, awards, or other payments related to the incident that occurred on insert DOI.

Please mail the requested information to the address below or fax the information to 1-405-869-3309. If you have any questions concerning this matter, please call the Medicare Secondary Payer Recovery Contractor (MSPRC) at 1-866-677-7220 (TTY/TDD: 1-866-677-7294 for the hearing and speech impaired). When sending any correspondence please provide the Beneficiary Name, Medicare Health Insurance Claim Number (the number on the Medicare card) and Case Identification Number (if known). This will allow us to associate the correspondence to the appropriate records.

MSPRC NGHP
PO Box 138832,
Oklahoma City, OK 73113

Sincerely,

MSPRC

insert cc:

Enclosure: Payment Summary Form

APPENDIX 25

Zero Pay Letter

 Learn about your letter at *www.msprc.info*

Beneficiary:
Medicare Number:
Date of Incident:
Case Identification Number:

Dear :

You recently contacted us by   seeking information related to the above-referenced case because the case has a settlement, judgment, or award.

A review of Medicare's records indicates Medicare did not pay any claims related to the settlement, judgment or award for the above-referenced incident. We did receive the date of settlement, judgment, or award and have closed our file.

Although the file is closed, please understand that Medicare has no responsibility to pay for any claims related to the settlement, judgment, or award for the above-referenced incident that were incurred from the date of the incident until the day after the case was finalized. Medicare has no responsibility for these claims as they should be paid out of any settlement, judgment, or award proceeds.

If you have any questions concerning this matter, please call the Medicare Secondary Payer Recovery Contractor (MSPRC) at   (TTY/TDD: 1-866-677-7294 for the hearing and speech impaired) or you may contact us in writing at the address below. If you contact us in writing, please be sure to include the beneficiary's name and Medicare number.

Sincerely,

cc:

SGLB34NGHP

RCB341

APPENDIX 26

CMS Affidavit

CMS Affidavit

The Centers for Medicare & Medicaid Services (CMS) is the federal agency that oversees the Medicare program. Many Medicare beneficiaries have other insurance in addition to their Medicare benefits. Sometimes, Medicare is supposed to pay after the other insurance. However, if certain other insurance delays payment, Medicare may make a "conditional payment" so as not to inconvenience the beneficiary, and recover after the other insurance pays.

Section 111 of the Medicare, Medicaid and SCHIP Extension Act of 2007 (MMSEA), a new federal law that became effective January 1, 2009, requires that liability insurers (including self-insurers), no-fault insurers, and workers' compensation plans report specific information about Medicare beneficiaries who have other insurance coverage. This reporting is to assist CMS and other insurance plans to properly coordinate payment of benefits among plans so that your claims are paid promptly and correctly.

We are asking you to the answer the questions below so that we may comply with this law.

Please review this picture of the Medicare card to determine if you have, or have ever had, a similar Medicare card.

Section I

Are you presently, or have you ever been, enrolled in Medicare Part A or Part B?	☐Yes	☐No
If yes, please complete the following. If no, proceed to Section II.		
Full Name: *(Please print the name exactly as it appears on your SSN or Medicare card if available.)*		

Medicare Claim Number:		**Date of Birth** (Mo/Day/Year)	- -
Social Security Number: *(If Medicare Claim Number is Unavailable)*	- -	**Sex**	☐Female ☐Male

Section II

I understand that the information requested is to assist the requesting insurance arrangement to accurately coordinate benefits with Medicare and to meet its mandatory reporting obligations under Medicare law.

_____   _____
Claimant Name (Please Print)   **Claim Number**

_____
Name of Person Completing This Form If Claimant is Unable (Please Print)

_____   _____
Signature of Person Completing This Form   **Date**

If you have completed Sections I and II above, stop here. If you are refusing to provide the information requested in Sections I and II, proceed to Section III.

CMS Affidavit

Section III

_____   _____
Claimant Name (Please Print)   **Claim Number**

For the reason(s) listed below, I have not provided the information requested. I understand that if I am a Medicare beneficiary and I do not provide the requested information, I may be violating obligations as a beneficiary to assist Medicare in coordinating benefits to pay my claims correctly and promptly.

Reason(s) for Refusal to Provide Requested Information:

_____

_____

_____

_____

_____   _____
Signature of Person Completing This Form   **Date**

APPENDIX 27

CMS Memorandum regarding Providing Social Security Numbers, August 24, 2009

CENTERS for MEDICARE & MEDICAID SERVICES

CMS Office of Financial Management/Financial Services Group

August 24, 2009

**The Medicare Secondary Payer Mandatory Reporting Provisions in
Section 111 of the Medicare, Medicaid and SCHIP Extension Act of 2007 (the MMSEA)
(See 42 U.S.C. 1395y(b)(7)&(b)(8))**

ALERT: Compliance Guidance Regarding Obtaining Individual HICNs and/or SSNs for Non-Group Health Plan (NGHP) Reporting Under 42 U.S.C. 1395y(b)(8)

Persons with Medicare need to be aware that workers' compensation plans, no-fault insurance and liability insurance (including self-insurance) (Non-Group Health Plan (NGHP) Insurance Arrangements) are now required to report data necessary to identify Medicare beneficiaries for whom the NGHP is responsible for paying primary to Medicare. Reporting entities have access to a query function which can assist them in: 1) verifying a Medicare Health Insurance Claim Number (or HICN) for a given Medicare beneficiary; **or** 2) determining whether or not an individual is a Medicare beneficiary if the individual furnishes his/her Social Security Number (SSN).

Some NGHP reporting entities have advised the Centers for Medicare & Medicaid Services (CMS) that they are having difficulties in obtaining either the HICN or SSN from some claimants. The CMS is providing the attached model language (with a picture of a Medicare card), to assist reporting entities in obtaining this information and being compliant with Section 111.

Claimants should routinely cooperate in furnishing either their HICN (or SSN if they do not have a HICN available) as requested. If an individual refuses to furnish either a HICN or SSN, and the NGHP reporting entity chooses to use the attached model language, CMS will consider the reporting entity compliant for purposes of its next Section 111 file submission if:

- A signed copy of the model language in the format provided is obtained (even if the individual is later discovered to be a Medicare beneficiary).

- With respect to that same individual, the reporting entity has the model language (with the picture of the Medicare ID card) re-signed and dated at least once every 12 months in cases where ongoing responsibility for medicals (ORM) applies.

- The reporting entity should retain this documentation.

NOTE:

This process does not provide a "safe harbor" to any reporting entity attempting to use it to avoid reporting MSP data about an individual known to the reporting entity to be a Medicare beneficiary. Also note that reporting entities are not required to use the specific model language provided by CMS.

APPENDIX 28

NGHP Alert for Liability Insurance: Who Must Report

Office of Financial Management/Financial Services Group

February 24, 2010

ALERT for Liability Insurance (Including Self-Insurance), No-Fault Insurance, and Workers' Compensation: WHO MUST REPORT

This document provides information regarding who/what entity is a MMSEA Section 111 Responsible Reporting Entity (RRE) for Liability Insurance (Including Self-Insurance), No-Fault Insurance, and Workers' Compensation.

The July 31, 2009 draft "Who Must report" language generated many comments from the industry. While the definitions set forth in the draft language would have reduced the number of RREs in situations involving a deductible, they still allowed for the possibility of both the insured and insurer reporting with respect to ORM or a TPOC amount if it involved a deductible. Additionally, CMS received many comments indicating continuing confusion regarding who would be the RRE in situations involving a deductible, particularly when factoring in the draft language regarding TPAs. Lastly, the comments indicated confusion regarding the term "payment" – many assuming the term automatically equated to "funding" rather than physical payment. CMS believes that the instructions below eliminate reporting by both the insured and insurer due to deductible issues and address the other issues which received comments.

This following language replaces Section 7.1 of the NGHP User Guide regarding "Who Must Report". Additionally, see the changes to Appendix G at the end of this document.

Who Must Report

General:

- 42 U.S.C. 1395y(b)(8) provides that the "applicable plan" is the RRE and defines "applicable plan" as follows:

  > "APPLICABLE PLAN- In this paragraph, the term `applicable plan' means the following laws, plans, or other arrangements, including the fiduciary or administrator for such law, plan, or arrangement:
  > (i) Liability insurance (including self-insurance).
  > (ii) No fault insurance.
  > (iii) Workers' compensation laws or plans."

1

- You must use the information in this Section as well as the applicable statutory language in conjunction with Appendix G (Definitions and Reporting Responsibilities) in order to determine if you are a RRE for purposes of these new provisions. The statutory language is available in Appendix F.

  See Appendix G for changes made to the second paragraph under "Liability Self-Insurance" and the paragraph for "Workers' Compensation Law or Plan".

- CMS is aware that the industry generally does not use the term "plan" or some other CMS definitions such as the definitions for "no-fault insurance" or "self-insurance". However, CMS is constrained by the language of the applicable statute and CMS' regulations. **It is critical that you understand and utilize CMS' definitions for purposes of Section 111 when reviewing and implementing Section 111 instructions.**

- Corporate structure and RREs:

  1. An entity <u>may not</u> register as an RRE for a sibling in its corporate structure.

  2. An entity <u>may</u> register as an RRE for itself or for any direct subsidiary in its corporate structure.

  3. A parent entity <u>may</u> register as an RRE for any subsidiary in its corporate structure regardless of whether or not the parent would otherwise qualify as an RRE.

  4. For purposes of this rule regarding corporate structure and RREs, a captive is considered a subsidiary of its parent entity and a sibling of any other subsidiary of its parent.

  5. A subsidiary <u>may not</u> register as an RRE for its parent.

  6. The general concept is that an entity may only register for another entity if that second entity is below it in the direct line of the corporate structure. For example an entity may register for a direct subsidiary or the subsidiary of that subsidiary.

  7. Example:

     o Facts –
       - Parent Company/Holding Company "A" has 4 subsidiaries (S1, S2, S3, S4).
       - "A" does not meet the definition of an RRE.
       - S1, S2, S3, and S4 meet the definition of an RRE for self-insurance or otherwise.
       - S1 has a captive insurance company (S1 Captive).
       - S1 Captive meets the definition of an RRE.

     o "A" may register as RRE for any combination of S1, S2, S3, S4. (See #3 above.)

2

- o "A" registers as the RRE for S1, it may report for any of S1's subsidiaries such as S1 Captive. (See #2 & #3.)

- o "A" may, but is not required to, designate S1, S2, S3, S4 or S1 Captive as its agent for reporting purposes for the subsidiaries for which it registers as an RRE. (See Section 7.2 on Use of Agents.)

- o S1, S2, S3, S4 and S1 Captive may each register separately as RREs and designate "A" or any of its sibling subsidiaries or S1 Captive as its agent for reporting purposes. (See #2 above & Section 7.2 on Use of Agents.)

- o S1, S2, S3, and S4 may not register as the RRE for each other. (See #1 above.)

- o S2, S3, and S4 may not register as the RRE for S1 Captive. (See #4 above.)

- o S1 Captive may not register as the RRE for S1 (its parent) or for any of the other subsidiaries. (See # 5 & #6.)

- **"Deductible" vs. "Self-Insured Retention" (SIR):**

  - o "Deductible" refers to the risk the insured retains with respect the coverage provided by the insurer.

  - o "Self-Insured Retention" refers to the risk the insured retains that is not included in the coverage provided by the insurer.

- **"Payment":**

  When referring to **"payment"** of an ORM or TPOC **in this "Who Must Report" section,** the reference is to actual physical payment rather than to who/which entity ultimately funds the payment.

- Third Party Administrators (TPAs):

  - o Third party administrators (TPAs) as defined by CMS for purposes for 42 U.S.C. 1395y(b)(7) & (8) are never RREs for purposes of 42 U.S.C. 1395y(b)**(8)** [liability (including self-insurance), no-fault, and workers' compensation reporting] **based solely upon their status as this type of TPA.** (Note that for purposes of 42 U.S.C. 1395y (b)**(7)** reporting for group health plan arrangements, this type of TPA is automatically an RRE.)

  - o However, while entities which meet this definition of a TPA generally only act as agents for purposes of the liability insurance (including self-insurance), no-fault insurance, or workers' compensation reporting they may, under specified circumstances, also be an RRE. See, for example, the discussion of State established "assigned claims funds."

○ Although it may contract with a TPA or other entity as its agent for actual file submissions for reporting purposes, the RRE is limited to the "applicable plan". An RRE may not by contract or otherwise limit its reporting responsibility. The applicable plan must either report directly or contract with the TPA or some other entity to submit data as its agent. Where an RRE uses another entity for claims processing or other purposes, it may wish to consider contracting with that entity to act as its agent for reporting purposes.

○ Example: Liability insurer hires a TPA to process claims. The TPA is a separate legal entity, makes payment decisions based upon the facts of each case, issues payment. The RRE is the liability insurer. The liability insurer may not shift its RRE responsibility to the TPA.

Acquisition/ Divestiture or Sale (Not Under Bankruptcy Liquidation):

An entity which is an RRE is acquired by another entity. The acquiring entity is the RRE as of the effective date of acquisition. The acquiring entity is the RRE with respect to **acquired** claims, including ORM.

Bankruptcy:

Where an RRE has filed for bankruptcy, it remains the RRE to the extent that settlements, judgments, awards or other payments are paid to or on behalf of the injured party after approval by a bankruptcy court. However, bankruptcy does not eliminate reporting obligations for bankrupt companies or their insurer, regardless of whether a bankrupt company or insurer is the RRE, for payments made pursuant to court order or after lifting the stay.

Deductible Issues vs. Re-insurance, Stop Loss Insurance, Excess Insurance, Umbrella Insurance, etc.:

- **Generally, the insurer is the RRE for Section 111 reporting.**

- See the change to the second paragraph under "Liability Self-Insurance" in Appendix G ("Definitions and Reporting Responsibilities") at the end of this document.

- Where an entity engages in a business, trade, or profession, deductible amounts are self-insurance for MSP purposes. **However,** where the self-insurance in question is a deductible, and the insurer is responsible for Section 111 reporting with respect to the policy, it is responsible for reporting both the deductible and any amount in excess of the deductible. The deductible is not reported as "self-insurance"; it is reported under the applicable policy number. The total of both the deductible and any amount in excess of the deductible is reported. (Please note that government entities are considered to be entities engaged in a business.)

- If an insured entity engages in a business, trade, or profession and acts without recourse to its insurance, it is responsible for Section 111 reporting with respect to those actions. For

4

NGHP ALERT FOR LIABILITY INSURANCE: WHO MUST REPORT

example: A claim is made against Company X which has insurance through Insurer Y. Company X settles the claim without informing its insurer. Company X is responsible for Section 111 reporting for the claim regardless of whether or not the settlement amount is within the deductible or in excess of the deductible.

- For re-insurance, stop loss insurance, excess insurance, umbrella insurance, guaranty funds, patient compensation funds, etc. which have responsibility beyond a certain limit, the key in determining whether or not reporting for 42 U.S.C. 1395y(b)(8) is required for these situations is whether or not the payment is to the injured claimant/representative of the injured claimant vs. payment to the self-insured entity to reimburse the self-insured entity. Where payment is being made to reimburse the self-insured entity, the self-insured entity is the RRE for purposes a settlement, judgment, award or other payment to or on behalf of the injured party and no reporting is required by the insurer reimbursing the self-insured entity.

- See also, the subsection addressing Workers' Compensation

Foreign Insurers (Including Self-Insurance): CMS will issue a separate ALERT addressing foreign insurers.

Fronting Policies:

The intent with "fronting" policies is that the insurer will not ultimately retain any risk under the insurance policy. The expectation of both the insured and the insurer is that the insured will retain the ultimate risk under the insurance policy for all claims. Where the insured pays the claim, the insured is the RRE. Where the insurer pays the claim, the insurer is the RRE.

Liquidation (settlement, judgement, award or other payment obligation against the entity in liquidation):

- To the extent that settlement, judgment, award, or other payment to or on behalf of the injured party is **funded** from the assets of the entity in liquidation, the entity in liquidation is the RRE.

- To the extent that a portion of a settlement, judgment, award or other payment obligation to or on behalf of the injured party is **funded** by another entity from that other entity's assets (for example, payment by a state guarantee fund), the entity that makes payment is the RRE.

- To the extent that a payment does not fully satisfy the entity in liquidation's debt to the injured party, the amount reported is the amount paid. Any subsequently approved interim or final payments would be handled in the same manner. That is, they would be reported as additional TPOC amounts.

Multiple Defendants:

- Where there are multiple defendants involved in a settlement, an agreement to have one of the defendant's insurer(s) issue any payment in obligation of a settlement, judgment, award or other does not shift RRE responsibility to the entity issuing the payment. All RREs involved in the settlement remain responsible for their own reporting.

- For a settlement, judgment, award or other payment with joint and several liability, each insurer must report the total settlement, judgment, award, or other payment – not just its assigned or proportionate share.

Multi-National Organizations, Foreign Nations, American Indian, Alaskan Native Tribes:

Liability insurance (including self-insurance), no-fault insurance and workers compensation plans associated with multi-national organizations, foreign nations, American Indian and Alaskan Native tribes are subject to the MSP provisions and must be reported accordingly.

Self-Insurance Pools:

- RRE for liability insurance or workers' compensation self-insurance pools -- Entities self-insured in whole or in part with respect to liability insurance or workers' compensation may elect, where permitted by law, to join with other similarly situated entities in a self-insurance pool such as a joint powers authority (JPA).

- "Review or approval authority" means that the self-insured entity has the ability to affect the payment or other terms of the settlement, judgment, award or other payment (including ORM).

- If all three of the characteristics below are met, the RRE is the self-insurance pool:

  1. The self-insurance pool is a separate legal entity.

  2. The self-insurance pool has full responsibility to resolve and pay claims using pool funds.

  3. The self-insurance pool resolves and pays claims without review or approval authority by the participating self-insured entity. When a self-insured entity in the self-insurance pool (including, for example, a JPA) has the review or approval authority for the payment of claims and/or negotiated resolutions, the self-insurance pool is not the RRE, the individual self-insured members are the RREs.

- Exception: Where the statute authorizing the establishment of a self-insurance pool stipulates that said self-insurance pool shall be licensed and regulated in the same manner as liability insurance (or workers' compensation, where applicable), then the self-insurance pool is the RRE. Absent meeting this exception, unless all three of the characteristics specified under the preceeding bullet apply to the self-insurance pool, the participating self-insured entity is the RRE.

- Where the individual members are the RREs, each of the members would have the option of using the self-insured pool (or another entity) as its agent for purposes of Section 111 reporting.

- Example: A self-insurance pool meets the three characteristics specified above for some members of the pools but not for others. The self-insurance pool provides administrative services only (ASO) for certain members. The RRE is the self-insurance pool only for those

6

members for which it meets the three characteristics specified above. Each member who receives ASO from the self-insurance pool is a separate RRE for its settlements, judgment, awards, or other payments. The self-insurance pool is not the RRE for such members.

State established "assigned claims fund": RRE for a State established "assigned claims fund" which provides benefits for individuals injured in an automobile accident that do not qualify for personal injury protection/medical payments protection from an automobile insurance carrier:

- "Review or approval authority" means that the State agency has the ability to affect the payment or other terms of the settlement, judgment, award or other payment (including ORM).

- Where there is a State agency which resolves and pays the claims using State funds or funds obtained from others for this purpose, the established agency is the RRE.

- Where there is a State agency which designates an authorized insurance carrier to resolve and pay the claims using State-provided funds without State agency review and/or approval, the designated carrier is the RRE. (Note: This would be an example of the rare situation where a TPA entity would also be an RRE for NGHP.)

- Where there is a State agency which designates an authorized insurance carrier to resolve and pay the claims using State-provided funds but the State agency retains review or approval authority, the State agency is the RRE.

- Example: A State agency pays no-fault claims using a State fund which is not under the agency's control. Additionally, the State agency designates an insurance carrier to resolve liability insurance claims, but the State agency retains payment responsibility. The State agency is the RRE for both the liability insurance and the no-fault insurance. It may report both types of insurance under a single RRE ID # or obtain a separate RRE ID # for each type of insurance.

Subrogation by an Insurer:

- Fact pattern:
  - Insurer A pays claim of its insured under the terms of its contract. The insurer is the RRE and reports the payment.
  - Insurer A may file a subrogation claim (on behalf of its insured/the injured party) against another insurer B.
  - Assume insurer B indemnifies insurer A for the payment it previously made. The indemnification payment is not reportable by either insurer.

Workers' Compensation:

- See the change to the "Workers' Compensation Law or Plan" paragraph of Appendix G ("Definitions and Reporting Responsibilities") at the end of this document.

- Appendix G provides, in part: *"For purposes of the reporting requirements at 42 U.S.C. 1395y(b)(8), a workers' compensation law or plan means a law or program administered by*

7

a State (defined to include commonwealths, territories and possessions of the United States) or the United States to provide compensation to workers for work-related injuries and/or illnesses. The term includes a similar compensation plan established by an employer that is funded by such employer directly or indirectly through an insurer to provide compensation to a worker of such employer for a work-related injury or illness."

- Where "workers' compensation law or plan" means *"a law or program administered by a State (defined to include commonwealths, territories and possessions of the United States) or the United States to provide compensation to workers for work-related injuries and/or illnesses,"* the following rules apply:

  o Where the applicable law or plan authorizes an employer to purchase insurance from an insurance carrier and the employer does so, follow the rules in the subsection for "Deductible Issues vs. Re-insurance, Stop Loss Insurance, Excess Insurance, Umbrella Insurance, etc."

  o Where the applicable law or plan authorizes an employer to self-insure and the employer does so independently of other employers, follow the rules in the subsection for "Deductible Issues vs. Re-insurance, Stop Loss Insurance, Excess Insurance, Umbrella Insurance, etc." (Here the reference is to "self-insurance" other than a "deductible.")

  o Where the applicable law or plan authorizes employers to join with other employers in self-insurance pools (e.g., joint powers authorities) and the employer does so, follow the rules in the subsection for "Self-Insurance Pools".

  o Where the applicable law or plan establishes a State/Federal agency with sole responsibility to resolve and pay claims, the established agency is the RRE.

  o In situations where the applicable law or plan authorizes employers to self-insure or to purchase insurance from an insurance carrier and also establishes a State/Federal agency to assume responsibility for situations where the employer fails to obtain insurance or to properly self-insure –

    - "Review or approval authority" means that the agency has the ability to affect the payment or other terms of the settlement, judgment, award or other payment (including ORM).

    - Where such State/Federal agency itself resolves and pays the claims using State/Federal funds or funds obtained from others for this purpose, the established agency is the RRE.

    - Where such State/Federal agency designates an authorized insurance carrier to resolve and pay the claim using State/Federal-provided funds without State/Federal agency review and/or approval, the designated carrier is the RRE.

    - Where such State/Federal agency designates an authorized insurance carrier to resolve and pay the claim using State/Federal-provided funds but State/Federal

8

agency retains review or approval authority, the State/Federal agency is the RRE.

- Where "workers' compensation law or plan" refers to "*a similar compensation plan established by an employer that is funded by such employer directly or indirectly through an insurer to provide compensation to a worker of such employer for a work-related injury or illness*" follow the rules for insurer or self-insured, as applicable, including the rules for self-insurance pools. (Here the reference is to "self-insurance" other than a "deductible.")

Note: For Appendix G – 1) The second paragraph under "Liability Self-Insurance" is revised in this ALERT. See the last sentence of this paragraph. 2) The paragraph for "Workers' Compensation Law or Plan" is also being revised in this ALERT. See the last two sentences of the paragraph.

Appendix G – MMSEA Section 111 Definitions and Reporting Responsibilities
Attachment A – Definitions and Reporting Responsibilities

(Attachment A to the Supporting Statement for the MMSEA Section 111 Paperwork Reduction Act (PRA) Federal Register (FR) Notice published February 13, 2009.)

SUPPORTING DOCUMENT FOR PRA PACKAGE FOR MEDICARE SECONDARY PAYER REPORTING RESPONSIBILITIES FOR SECTION 111 OF THE MEDICARE, MEDICAID, AND SCHIP EXTENSION ACT OF 2007

Note: The second paragraph under Liability Self-Insurance was revised subsequent to the initial publication of this Attachment on August 1, 2008.

DEFINITIONS AND REPORTING RESPONSIBILITIES

GROUP HEALTH PLAN (GHP) ARRANGEMENTS (42 U.S.C. 1395y(b)(7)) --

INSURER
For purposes of the reporting requirements at 42 U.S.C.1395y(b)(7), an insurer is an entity that, in return for the receipt of a premium, assumes the obligation to pay claims described in the insurance contract and assumes the financial risk associated with such payments. In instances where an insurer does not process GHP claims but has a third party administrator (TPA) that does, the TPA has the responsibility for the reporting requirements at 42 U.S.C. 1395y(b)(7).

THIRD PARTY ADMINISTRATOR (TPA)
For purposes of the reporting requirements at 42 U.S.C.1395y(b)(7), a TPA is an entity that pays and/or adjudicates claims and may perform other administrative services on behalf of GHPs (as defined at 42 U.S.C. 1395y(b)(1)(A)(v)), the plan sponsor(s) or the plan insurer. A TPA may perform these services for, amongst other entities, self-insured employers, unions, associations, and insurers/underwriters of such GHPs. If a GHP is self-funded and self-administered for certain purposes but also has a TPA as defined in this paragraph, the TPA has the responsibility for the reporting requirements at 42 U.S.C. 1395y(b)(7).

USE OF AGENTS FOR PURPOSES OF THE REPORTING REQUIREMENTS AT 42 U.S.C. 1395y(b)(7):

10

For purposes of the reporting requirements at 42 U.S.C. 1395y(b)(7), agents may submit reports on behalf of :

- Insurers for GHPs
- TPAs for GHPs
- Employers with self-insured and self-administered GHPs

Accountability for submitting the reports in the manner and form stipulated by the Secretary and the accuracy of the submitted information continues to rest with each of the above-named entities.

The CMS will provide information on the format and method of identifying agents for reporting purposes.

LIABILITY INSURANCE (INCLUDING SELF-INSURANCE), NO-FAULT INSURANCE, AND WORKERS' COMPENSATION (42 U.S.C. 1395y(b)(8)) --

INSURER
For purposes of the reporting requirements for 42 U.S.C. 1395y(b)(8), a liability insurer (except for self-insurance) or a no-fault insurer is an entity that, in return for the receipt of a premium, assumes the obligation to pay claims described in the insurance contract and assumes the financial risk associated with such payments. The insurer may or may not assume responsibility for claims processing; however, the insurer has the responsibility for the reporting requirements at 42 U.S.C. 1395y(b)(8) regardless of whether it uses another entity for claim processing.

CLAIMANT:
For purposes of the reporting requirements at 42 U.S.C. 1395y(b)(8), "claimant" includes: 1) an individual filing a claim directly against the applicable plan, 2) an individual filing a claim against an individual or entity insured or covered by the applicable plan, or 3) an individual whose illness, injury, incident, or accident is/was at issue in "1)" or "2)".

APPLICABLE PLAN:
For purposes of the reporting requirements at 42 U.S.C. 1395y(b)(8), the "applicable plan" as defined in subsection (8)((F) has the responsibility for the reporting requirements at 42 U.S.C. 1395y(b)(8). For workers' compensation information this would be the Federal agency, the State agency, or self-insured employer or the employer's insurer.

NO-FAULT INSURANCE:
Trade associations for liability insurance, no-fault insurance and workers' compensation have indicated that the industry's definition of no-fault insurance is narrower than CMS' definition. For purposes of the reporting requirements at 42 U.S.C. 1395y(b)(8), the definition of no-fault insurance found at 42 C.F.R. 411.50 is controlling.

LIABILITY SELF-INSURANCE:
42 U.S.C. 1395y(b)(2)(A) provides that an entity that engages in a business, trade or profession shall be deemed to have a self-insured plan if it carries its own risk (whether by a failure to obtain insurance, or otherwise) in whole or in part. Self-insurance or deemed self-insurance can be demonstrated by a settlement, judgment, award, or other payment to satisfy an alleged claim (including any deductible or co-pay on a liability insurance, no-fault insurance, or workers' compensation law or plan) for a business, trade or profession. See also 42 C.F.R. 411.50.

Special Considerations where liability self-insurance which is a deductible or co-payment for liability insurance, no-fault insurance, or workers' compensation is paid to the insurer or workers' compensation entity for distribution (rather than directly to the claimant): As indicated in the definition of "liability self-insurance," such deductibles and co-payments constitute liability self-insurance, and require reporting by the self-insured entities. However, in order to avoid two entities reporting where the deductibles and/or co-payments are physically being paid by the insurance company or workers' compensation rather than the self-insured entity, CMS has determined that the liability insurance company, no-fault insurance company, or workers' compensation, as appropriate, must include the self-insurance deductible or co-pay in the amount it reports. [*The following sentence is hereby deleted:* Note that this rule only applies where the self-insurance deductible or co-pay is paid to the insurer for distribution rather than directly to the claimant.]

WORKERS' COMPENSATION LAW OR PLAN

For purposes of the reporting requirements at 42 U.S.C. 1395y(b)(8), a workers' compensation law or plan means a law or program administered by a State (defined to include commonwealths, territories and possessions of the United States) or the United States to provide compensation to workers for work-related injuries and/or illnesses. The term includes a similar compensation plan established by an employer that is funded by such employer directly or indirectly through an insurer to provide compensation to a worker of such employer for a work-related injury or illness. [*The following sentence is hereby deleted*: Where such a plan is directly funded by the employer, the employer has the responsibility for the reporting requirements at 42 U.S.C. 1395y(b)(8). Where such a plan is indirectly funded by the employer, the insurer has the responsibility for the reporting requirements at 42 U.S.C. 1395y(b)(8).]

USE OF AGENTS FOR PURPOSES OF THE REPORTING REQUIREMENTS AT 42 U.S.C. 1395y(b)(8):

Agents may submit reports on behalf of:

- Insurers for no-fault or liability insurance
- Self-insured entities for liability insurance
- Workers' compensation laws or plans

Accountability for submitting the reports in the manner and form stipulated by the Secretary and the accuracy of the submitted information continues to rest with each of the above-named entities.

TPAs of any type (including TPAs as defined for purposes of the reporting requirements at 42 U.S.C. 1395y(b)(7) for GHP arrangements) have no reporting responsibilities for purposes of the reporting requirements at 42 U.S.C. 1395y(b)(8) for liability insurance (including self-insurance), no-fault insurance, or workers' compensation. Where an entity reports on behalf of another entity required to report under 42 U.S.C. 1395y(b)(8), it is doing so as an agent of the second entity.

CMS will provide information on the format and method of identifying agents for reporting purposes.

APPENDIX 29

Medicare Revised Implementation Timeline for Certain Liability Insurance TPOC, dated September 30, 2011

CENTERS for MEDICARE & MEDICAID SERVICES

Office of Financial Management/Financial Services Group

September 30, 2011

Medicare Secondary Payer Mandatory Reporting Provisions in
Section 111 of the Medicare, Medicaid, and SCHIP Extension Act of 2007 (MMSEA)
(See 42 U.S.C. 1395y(b)(7)&(b)(8))

ALERT

Revised Implementation Timeline for Certain Liability Insurance (Including Self-Insurance) Total Payment Obligation to the Claimant (TPOC) Settlements, Judgments, Awards or Other Payments

The Centers for Medicare & Medicaid Services (CMS) has delayed Section 111 reporting for certain liability insurance (including self-insurance) TPOC settlements, judgments, awards, or other payments. The implementation date for reporting will be based on the TPOC amount. Below is a schedule of the new dates.

TPOC Amount	TPOC Date On or After	Section 111 Reporting Required in the Quarter Beginning
TPOCs over $100,000	October 1, 2011	January 1, 2012
TPOCs over $50,000	April 1, 2012	July 1, 2012
TPOCs over $25,000	July 1, 2012	October 1, 2012
All TPOCs over min. threshold	October 1, 2012	January 1, 2013

The CMS has not changed any other MMSEA Section 111 implementation dates. See the applicable MMSEA Section 111 User Guide. In addition, other relevant information, including explanations of TPOC, ORM, and a Responsible Reporting Entity, can be found in the User Guide. (Note: This delay is optional).

The content of this ALERT supersedes the content of the existing User Guide (Version 3.2) and will be incorporated into the next version of the User Guide. After full implementation of the Section 111 reporting requirements, CMS will use the normal notice of proposed rulemaking process for establishing any penalties.

APPENDIX 30

MMSEA Abbreviated Claim Input Data Fields

MMSEA Section 111
Liability Insurance (Including Self-Insurance) No-Fault Insurance, Workers' Compensation
Claim Input File Detail Record - 2220 bytes

Field #	Name	Description
1	Record Identifier	
2	DCN	Each record shall have a unique DCN within the file submitted. The DCN only needs to be unique within the current file being submitted. DCN will be supplied back by COBC on corresponding response file records for tracking purposes.
3	Action Type	Action to be performed. Valid values: 0 = Add 1 = Delete 2 = Update/Change 3 = Update for additional, separate TPOC Report Note: For changes/corrections to the initial TPOC report use "2." Some settlements, judgments, or awards provide for additional awards/payment if certain criteria are met. This would be an example of a situation where "3" would be used.
4	Injured Party HICN	Medicare Health Insurance Claim Number
5	Injured Party SSN	Social Security Number
6	Injured Party Last Name	Surname of Injured Party
7	Injured Party First Name	Given or first name of Injured Party.
8	Injured Party Middle Init	First letter of Injured Party middle name.
9	Injured Party Gender	Code to reflect the sex of the injured party. Valid values: 1 = Male 2 = Female 0 = Unknown
10	Injured Party DOB	Date of Birth of Injured Party
11	Reserved for Future Use	
12	CMS Date of Incident (DOI)	Date of Incident (DOI) as defined by CMS: For an automobile wreck or other accident, the date of incident is the date of the accident. For claims involving exposure (including, for example, occupational disease and any associated cumulative injury) the DOI is the date of first exposure. For claims involving ingestion (for example, a recalled drug), it is the date of first ingestion. For claims involving implants, it is the date of the implant (or date of the first implant if there are multiple implants). Note: CMS' definition of DOI generally differs from the definition routinely used by the insurance/workers' compensation industry (Field 13) only for claims involving exposure, ingestion, or implants.

13	**Industry Date of Incident (DOI)**	Date of Incident (DOI) used by the insurance/workers' compensation industry: For an automobile wreck or other accident, the date of incident is the date of the accident. For claims involving exposure, ingestion, or implantation, the date of incident is the date of last exposure, ingestion, or implantation. Note: The definition of DOI routinely used by the insurance/workers' compensation industry DOI generally differs from the definition which CMS must use (Field 12) only for claims involving exposure, ingestion, or implants. For future expansion to ICD-10 Codes.
14	**Reserved for Future Use**	
15	**Alleged Cause of Injury, Incident, or Illness**	ICD-9-CM (International Classification of Diseases, Ninth Revision, Clinical Modification) External Cause of Injury Code "E Code" describing the alleged cause of injury/illness (E800-E999).
16	**Reserved for Future Use**	
17	**State of Venue**	US postal abbreviation corresponding to the US State whose state law controls resolution of the claim. If the state of venue is in dispute at the time an RRE reports acceptance on ongoing responsibility for medicals, the RRE should use its best judgment regarding the state of venue and submit updated information, if applicable, when the ongoing responsibility is terminated or further reporting is required because of a settlement, judgment, award or payment other than payment made under the ongoing responsibility for medicals.
18	**Reserved for Future Use**	
19	**ICD-9 Diagnosis Code 1**	ICD-9-CM (International Classification of Diseases, Ninth Revision, Clinical Modification) Diagnosis Code describing the alleged injury/illness.
20	**Reserved for Future Use**	
21	**ICD-9 Diagnosis Code 2**	See explanation for Field 19. May include additional ICD-9 Diagnosis Code or ICD-9 External Cause of Injury Codes "E Code" (E800-E999) if applicable. Provide if available/applicable.
22	**Reserved for Future Use**	
23	**ICD-9 Diagnosis Code 3**	See explanation for Field 19 and 21 Provide if available/applicable.
24	**Reserved for Future Use**	
25	**ICD-9 Diagnosis Code 4**	See explanation for Field 19 and 21 Provide if available/applicable.
26	**Reserved for Future Use**	

27	ICD-9 Diagnosis Code 5	See explanation for Field 19 and 21 Provide if available/applicable.
28	Reserved for Future Use	
29	ICD-9 Diagnosis Code 6	See explanation for Field 19 and 21 Provide if available/applicable.
30	Reserved for Future Use	
31	ICD-9 Diagnosis Code 7	See explanation for Field 19 and 21 Provide if available/applicable.
32	Reserved for Future Use	
33	ICD-9 Diagnosis Code 8	See explanation for Field 19 and 21 Provide if available/applicable.
34	Reserved for Future Use	
35	ICD-9 Diagnosis Code 9	See explanation for Field 19 and 21 Provide if available/applicable.
36	Reserved for Future Use	
37	ICD-9 Diagnosis Code 10	See explanation for Field 19 and 21 Provide if available/applicable.
38	Reserved for Future Use	
39	ICD-9 Diagnosis Code 11	See explanation for Field 19 and 21 Provide if available/applicable.
40	Reserved for Future Use	
41	ICD-9 Diagnosis Code 12	See explanation for Field 19 and 21 Provide if available/applicable.
42	Reserved for Future Use	
43	ICD-9 Diagnosis Code 13	See explanation for Field 19 and 21 Provide if available/applicable.
44	Reserved for Future Use	
45	ICD-9 Diagnosis Code 14	See explanation for Field 19 and 21 Provide if available/applicable.
46	Reserved for Future Use	
47	ICD-9 Diagnosis Code 15	See explanation for Field 19 and 21 Provide if available/applicable.
48	Reserved for Future Use	
49	ICD-9 Diagnosis Code 16	See explanation for Field 19 and 21 Provide if available/applicable.
50	Reserved for Future Use	
51	ICD-9 Diagnosis Code 17	See explanation for Field 19 and 21 Provide if available/applicable.
52	Reserved for Future Use	
53	ICD-9 Diagnosis Code 18	See explanation for Field 19 and 21 Provide if available/applicable.
54	Reserved for Future Use	
55	ICD-9 Diagnosis Code 19	See explanation for Field 19 and 21 Provide if available/applicable.
56	Reserved for Future Use	
57	Description of Illness/Injury	Free-form text description of illness or injury. Include description of major body part injured (e.g. head, arm, leg, etc.) and cause of illness/injury.

58	Product Liability Indicator	Indicates whether injury, illness or incident was allegedly caused by/contributed to by a particular product. Some product liability situations involve a product which allegedly results in situations involving falls or other accidents. Others may involve exposure to, implantation of, or ingestion of a particular product. Valid values: 1 = No 2 = Yes, but not a mass tort situation. 3 = Yes, and is a mass tort situation.
59	Product Generic Name	Generic name of product alleged to be cause of injury, illness or incident.
60	Product Brand Name	Brand name of product alleged to be cause of injury, illness or incident.
61	Product Manufacturer	Maker of product named in Fields 59 and/or 60 above.
62	Product Alleged Harm	Free-form description of harm allegedly caused by product named in Fields 59 and/or 60 above.
63	Reserved for Future Use	
Self-Insurance Information - Information required to: 1) indicate if the reportable event involves "self-insurance" as defined by CMS; and 2) if yes, specific information regarding the self-insured individual or entity.		
64	Self Insured Indicator	Indication of whether the reportable event involves self- insurance as defined by CMS. Valid values: Y = Yes N = No Self-insurance is defined in "Attachment A - Definitions and Reporting Responsibilities" to the Supporting Statement for the FR PRA Notice (CMS-10265) for this mandatory reporting and is available in Appendix H of this User Guide. You must use this definition of self-insurance for purposes of this reporting.
65	Self-Insured Type	Identifies whether the self- insured is an organization or individual. Valid values: I = Individual O = Other than Individual (e.g. business, corporation, organization, company, etc.)
66	Policyholder Last Name	Surname of policyholder.
67	Policyholder First Name	Given/First name of policyholder.
68	DBA Name	"Doing Business As" Name of self-insured organization/business.
69	Legal Name	Legal Name of self-insured organization/business.
70	Reserved for Future Use	
Plan Information		

71	Plan Insurance Type	Type of insurance coverage or line of business provided by the plan policy or self-insurance. Valid values: D = No-Fault E = Workers' Compensation L = Liability Note: When selecting "no-fault" as the type of insurance, you must use the CMS definition of no-fault insurance found at 42 CFR 411.50. This definition is different from the industry definition which is generally limited to certain automobile insurance. "No fault insurance means insurance that pays for medical expenses for injuries sustained on the property or premises of the insured, or in the use, occupancy, or operation of an automobile, regardless of who may have been responsible for causing the accident. This insurance includes but is not limited to automobile, homeowners, and commercial 445 'medical payments coverage', 'personal injury protection', or 'medical expense coverage.' See 42 CFR 411.50"
72	TIN	Federal Tax Identification Number of the "applicable plan," whether liability insurance (including self-insurance), no- fault insurance or a workers' compensation law or plan. Must have a corresponding entry with associated Office Code/Site ID on the TIN Reference File.
73	Office Code/Site ID	RRE-defined code to uniquely identify variations in insurer addresses/claim offices/Plan Contact Addresses. Defined by RRE. Used to uniquely specify different addresses associated with one TIN. If only one address will be used per reported TIN, leave blank. Must have a corresponding entry with associated TIN on the TIN Reference File. A record must be submitted on the TIN Reference File for each unique TIN/Office Code combination.
74	Policy Number	The unique identifier for the policy under which the underlying claim was filed. RRE defined. If liability self- insurance or workers' compensation self-insurance, fill with 0's if you do not have or maintain a specific number reference.
75	Claim Number	The unique claim identifier by which the primary plan identifies the claim. If liability self- insurance or workers' compensation self-insurance, fill with 0's if you do not have or maintain a claim number reference.
76	Plan Contact Department Name	Name of department for the Plan Contact to which claim-related communication and correspondence should be sent.

77	Plan Contact Last Name	Surname of individual that should be contacted at the Plan for claim-related communication and correspondence.
78	Plan Contact First Name	Given or first name of individual that should be contacted at the Plan for claim-related communication and correspondence.
79	Plan Contact Phone	Telephone number of individual that should be contacted at the Plan for claim-related communication. Format with 3-digit area code followed by 7-digit phone number with no dashes or other punctuation (e.g. 1112223333).
80	Plan Contact Phone Extension	Telephone extension number of individual that should be contacted at the Plan for claim- related communication.
81	No-Fault Insurance Limit	Dollar amount of limit on no-fault insurance. Specify dollars and cents with implied decimal. No formatting (no $ or , or .) For example, a limit of $10,500.00 should be coded as 00001050000. Fill with all 9's if there is no dollar limit. Fill with all 0's if Plan Insurance Type (Field 71) is E (Workers' Compensation) or L (Liability Insurance (including Self- Insurance)).
82	Exhaust Date for Dollar Limt for No-Fault	Date on which limit was reached or benefits exhausted for No- Fault Insurance Limit (Field 81). Insurance
83	Reserved for Future Use	
Injured Party's Attorney or Other Representative Information		
Attorney/Representative information required only if injured party has a representative.		
84	Injured Party Representative Indicator	Code indicating the type of Attorney/Other Representative information provided. Valid values: A = Attorney G = Guardian/Conservator P = Power of Attorney O = Other Space = None
85	Representative Last Name	Surname of representative.
86	Representative First Name	Given or first name of representative.
87	Representative Firm Name	Representative's firm name.
88	Representative TIN	Representative's Federal Tax Identification Number (TIN). If representative is part of a firm, supply the firm's Employer Identification Number (EIN), otherwise supply the representative's Social Security Number (SSN).
89	Representative Mailing Address Line 1	First line of the mailing address for the representative named above.
90	Representative Mailing Address Line 2	Second line of the mailing address of the representative named above.
91	Representative City	Mailing address city for the representative named above.
92	Representative State	US Postal abbreviation state code for the representative named above.

93	**Representative Mail Zip Code**	5-digit Zip Code for the representative named above.
94	**Representative Mail Zip+4**	4-digit Zip+4 code for the representative named above.
95	**Representative Phone**	Telephone number of the representative named above. Format with 3-digit area code followed by 7-digit phone number with no dashes or other punctuation (e.g. 1112223333).
96	**Representative Phone Extension**	Telephone extension number of representative named above.
97	**Reserved for Future Use**	
Settlement, Judgment, Award or Other Payment Information		
98	**ORM Indicator**	Indication of whether there is on- going responsibility for medicals (ORM). Fill with Y if there is ongoing responsibility for medicals. Valid values: Y - Yes N - No The Y value remains in this field even when an ORM Termination Date (Field 99) is submitted in this same record or a subsequent record.
99	**ORM Termination Date**	Date ongoing responsibility for medicals ended, where applicable. Only applies to records previously submitted (or submitted in this record where ongoing responsibility for medicals and termination of such responsibility are reported in this same submission) with ORM Indicator = Y. ORM Termination Date is not applicable if claimant retains the ability to submit/apply for payment for additional medicals related to the claim. See Sections 11.6 and 11.7 of the User Guide for information concerning extensions/exceptions regarding reporting ORM When an ORM termination date is submitted, the ORM indicator in Field 98 must remain as Y.
100	**TPOC Date**	Initial date of Total Payment Obligation to the Claimant (TPOC) without regard to ongoing responsibility for medicals (ORM). Date payment obligation was established. This is the date the obligation is signed if there is a written agreement unless court approval is required. If court approval is required it is the later of the date the obligation is signed or the date of court approval. If there is no written agreement it is the date the payment (or first payment if there will be multiple payments) is issued.

101	TPOC Amount	Total Payment Obligation to the Claimant (TPOC) amount: Dollar amount of the total payment obligation to the claimant. If there is a structured settlement, the amount is the total payout amount. If a settlement provides for the purchase of an annuity, it is the total payout from the annuity. For annuities base the total amount upon the time period used in calculating the purchase price of the annuity or the minimum payout amount (if there is a minimum payout), whichever calculation results in the larger amount. When this record includes information reflecting ongoing responsibility for medicals (either current or terminated), fill with zeroes unless there is a TPOC date/amount for a settlement, judgment, award, or other payment in addition to/apart from the information which must be reported with respect to responsibility for ongoing medicals. 445 Note: Remember to use theproper Action Code (Field 3) to distinguish an initial TPOC report from the report of additional, separate TPOC. amounts, where applicable.
102	Funding Delayed Beyond TPOC Start Date	If funding for the Total Payment Obligation to Claimant is delayed, provide actual or estimated date of funding.
103	Reserved for Future Use	

Claimant Information 1

This section is only required if the Claimant is not the Injured Party/Medicare Beneficiary. The claimant may be the beneficiary's estate, or other claimant in the case of wrongful death or survivor action. Additional claimants must be listed on the Auxiliary Record. **Fill the entire section (Fields 104-117) with spaces if not supplying Claimant 1 information.**
(This section is not used when the injured party/Medicare beneficiary is alive and an individual is pursuing a claim on behalf of the beneficiary.   See the section for Injured Party's Attorney or Other Representative Information.)

104	Claimant 1 Relationship	Relationship of the claimant to the injured party/Medicare beneficiary. Valid values: E = Estate F = Family O = Other Space = Not applicable (rest of the section will be ignored)
105	Claimant 1 TIN	Federal Tax Identification Number (TIN), Employer Identification Number (EIN) or Social Security Number (SSN) of Claimant 1. Must not match injured party named above or other claimant(s) listed on the Auxiliary Record.
106	Claimant 1 Last Name	Surname of Claimant 1.
107	Claimant 1 First Name	Given/First name of Claimant 1.

108	Claimant 1 Middle Initial	First letter of Claimant 1's middle name.
109	Claimant 1 Mailing Address Line 2	First line of the mailing address for the claimant named above.
110	Claimant 1 Mailing Address Line 2	Second line of the mailing address of the claimant named above.
111	Claimant 1 City	Mailing address city for the claimant named above.
112	Claimant 1 State	US Postal abbreviation state code for the claimant named above.
113	Claimant 1 Zip	5-digit Zip Code for the claimant named above.
114	Claimant 1 Zip+4	4-digit Zip+4 code for the claimant named above.
115	Claimant 1 Phone	Telephone number of the claimant named above. Format with 3-digit area code followed by 7-digit phone number with no dashes or other punctuation (e.g. 1112223333).
116	Claimant 1 Phone extension	Telephone extension number of the claimant named above.
117	Reserved for Future Use	

Claimant 1 Attorney/Other Representative Information
This section is only required if Claimant 1 has a representative. **Fill the entire section (Fields 118-130) with spaces if not supplying Claimant 1 representative information.**

118	Claimant 1 (C1) Representative Indicator	Code indicating the type of Attorney/Other Representative information provided for Claimant 1. Valid values: A = Attorney G = Guardian/Conservator P = Power of Attorney O = Other Space = Not applicable (rest of the section will be ignored)
119	C1 Representative Last Name	Surname of C1 representative.
120	C1 Representative First Name	Given/First name of C1 representative.
121	C1 Representative Firm Name	Representative's firm name.
122	C1 Representative TIN	C1 representative's Federal Tax Identification Number (TIN). If representative is part of a firm, supply the firm's Employer Identification Number (EIN), otherwise supply the representative's Social Security Number (SSN).
123	C1 Representative Mail Address 1	First line of the mailing address for the C1 representative named above.
124	C1 Representative Mailing Address 2	Second line of the mailing address of the C1 representative named above.
125	C1 Representative Mailing City	Mailing address city for the C1 representative named above.
126	C1 Representative State	US Postal abbreviation state code for the C1 representative named above.
127	C1 Representative Zip	5-digit Zip Code for the C1 representative named above.
128	C1 Representative Zip+4	4-digit Zip+4 code for the C1 representative named above.

129	C1 Representative Phone	Telephone number of the C1 representative named above. Format with 3-digit area code followed by 7-digit phone number with no dashes or other punctuation (e.g. 1112223333).
130	C1 Representative Phone Extension	Telephone extension number of the C1 representative named above.
131	Reserved for Future Use	

APPENDIX 31

CMS Memorandum – Medicare Secondary Payer – Worker's Compensation – Information, dated 5/11/2011

DEPARTMENT OF HEALTH & HUMAN SERVICES
Centers for Medicare & Medicaid Services
7500 Security Boulevard, Mail Stop C3-14-00
Baltimore, Maryland 21244-1850

CMS/
CENTERS for MEDICARE & MEDICAID SERVICES

MEMORANDUM

DATE: May 11, 2011

FROM: Acting Director
Financial Services Group
Office of Financial Management

SUBJECT: Medicare Secondary Payer--Workers' Compensation--INFORMATION

TO: Consortium Administrator for Financial Management and Fee-for-Service
Operations

The purpose of this memorandum is to reiterate guidance provided in the Centers for Medicare & Medicaid Services' (CMS') July 23, 2001, July 11, 2005, and April 25, 2006 procedure memoranda regarding CMS' Workers' Compensation Medicare Set-aside Agreement (WCMSA) proposal review thresholds, which can be found on CMS' Web site at: http://www.cms.gov/WorkersCompAgencyServices.

Submission of a WCMSA proposal to CMS for review and approval is a recommended process. There are no statutory or regulatory provisions requiring that a WCMSA proposal be submitted to CMS for review. However, if an entity chooses to use the WCMSA review process, CMS requests that it comply with the established policies and procedures referenced on its Web site. Claimants, employers, carriers, and their representatives should be encouraged regularly to monitor this dedicated workers' compensation Web site for changes in policies and procedures.

With respect to these policies and procedures, it is critically important to note the following information:

1. Medicare reviews certain workers' compensation (WC) settlements in order to protect Medicare's interests under the Medicare Secondary Payer Statute [codified at 42 U.S.C. Section 1395y] and its implementing regulations. [Ref: 7/23/01 Memo Q1(c))]. **Note:** A WCMSA should not be submitted to CMS when the resolution of the workers' compensation claim results in the medical portion of the claim is being left open.

2. A WCMSA meets CMS' criteria for review when the following thresholds are met:

   - The claimant is currently a **Medicare beneficiary** and the total settlement amount is **greater than $25,000; OR**
   - The claimant has a "reasonable expectation" of Medicare enrollment **within 30 months of the settlement date and** the anticipated total settlement amount for future medical expenses and disability/lost wages over the life or duration of the settlement agreement is expected to be **greater than $250,000.**

Page 2 – Consortium Administrator

3. The CMS no longer reviews new WCMSA proposals if the above thresholds are not met. However, CMS wishes to stress that these threshold requirements reflect a CMS operational workload standard. These requirements do not constitute a substantive dollar or "safe harbor" threshold. It remains true that Medicare beneficiaries still must consider Medicare's interests in all WC cases and ensure that Medicare is the secondary payer to WC in such cases.

4. Both the beneficiary and non-beneficiary review thresholds are subject to change. [Ref: 7/11/05 Memo Q2; 4/25/06 Memo]. CMS reserves the right to modify or eliminate these thresholds, doing so relative to a proper consideration of Medicare's interests.

Your staff may direct questions or concerns on the above referenced policies and procedures to Frank Johnson of my staff at (410) 786-2892.

Charlotte Benson

Charlotte Benson

APPENDIX 32

CMS Policy Memo, 4/21/2003

DEPARTMENT OF HEALTH & HUMAN SERVICES
Centers for Medicare & Medicaid Services
7500 Security Boulevard, Mail Stop C2-21-15
Baltimore, Maryland 21244-1850

Center for Medicare Management

TO: All Regional Administrators

FROM: Director
           Center for Medicare Management

SUBJECT: Medicare Secondary Payer -- Workers' Compensation (WC) Frequently
           Asked Questions

Questions raised are paraphrased below. This memorandum will be posted on the Centers for Medicare & Medicaid Services' (CMS) website.

1) **What statutory law, regulations, or Federal case law supports/allows CMS to review proposed settlements of injured workers who are not Medicare beneficiaries?**

Answer: Section 1862(b)(2) of the Social Security Act (the Act) (42 USC 1395y(b)(2)) requires that Medicare payment may not be made for any item or service to the extent that payment has been made under a workers' compensation (WC) law or plan. Medicare does not pay for an individual's WC related medical services when that individual received a WC settlement, judgment, or award that includes funds for future medical expenses, until all such funds are properly expended.

Because Medicare does not pay for an individual's WC related medical services when the individual receives a WC settlement that includes funds for future medical expenses, it is in that individual's interests to consider Medicare at the time of settlement. Once CMS agrees to a Medicare set-aside amount, the individual can be certain that Medicare's interests have been appropriately considered.

2) **When dealing with a WC case, what is "a reasonable expectation" of Medicare enrollment within 30 months?**

4/22/2003

Page 2 – All Regional Administrators

Answer: Situations where an individual has a "reasonable expectation" of Medicare enrollment for any reason include but are not limited to:

    a) The individual has applied for Social Security Disability Benefits;

    b) The individual has been denied Social Security Disability Benefits but anticipates appealing that decision;

    c) The individual is in the process of appealing and/or re-filing for Social Security Disability Benefits;

    d) The individual is 62 years and 6 months old (i.e., may be eligible for Medicare based upon his/her age within 30 months); or

    e) The individual has an End Stage Renal Disease (ESRD) condition but does not yet qualify for Medicare based upon ESRD.

3) How does Medicare determine its interests in WC cases when the parties to the settlement do not explicitly state how much of the settlement is for past medical expenses and how much is for future medical expenses?

Answer: A settlement that does not specifically account for past versus future medical expenses will be considered to be entirely for future medical expenses once Medicare has recovered any conditional payments it made. This means that Medicare will not pay for medical expenses that are otherwise reimbursable under Medicare and are related to the WC case, until the entire settlement is exhausted.

Example: A beneficiary is paid $50,000 by a WC carrier, and the parties to the settlement do not specify what the $50,000 is intended to pay for. If there is no CMS approved Medicare set-aside arrangement, Medicare will consider any amount remaining after recovery of its conditional payments as compensation for future medical expenses.

Additionally, please note that any allocations made for lost wages, pre-settlement medical expenses, future medical expenses, or any other settlement designations that do not consider Medicare's interests, will not be approved by Medicare.

4) What's the difference between commutation and compromise cases? And can a single WC case possess both?

Answer: When a settlement includes compensation for future medical expenses, it is referred to as a " WC commutation case." When a settlement includes compensation for medical expenses incurred prior to the settlement date, it is referred to as a "WC compromise case." A WC settlement can have both a compromise aspect as well as a commutation aspect.

4/22/2003

Additionally, a settlement possesses a commutation aspect if it does not provide for future medical expenses when the facts of the case indicate the need for continued medical care related to the WC illness or injury.

Page 3 – All Regional Administrators

Example: The parties to a settlement may attempt to maximize the amount of disability/lost wages paid under WC by releasing the WC carrier from liability for medical expenses. If the facts show that this particular condition is work-related and requires continued treatment, Medicare will not pay for medical services related to the WC injury/illness until the entire settlement has been used to pay for those services.

5) When a state WC judge approves a WC settlement, will Medicare accept the terms of that settlement?

Answer: Medicare will generally honor judicial decisions issued after a hearing on the merits of a WC case by a court of competent jurisdiction. If a court or other adjudicator of the merits specifically designates funds to a portion of a settlement that is not related to medical services (e.g., lost wages), then Medicare will accept that designation.

However, a distinction must be made where a court or other adjudicator is only approving a settlement that incorporates the parties' settlement agreements. Medicare cannot accept the terms of the settlement as to an allocation of funds of any type if the settlement does not adequately address Medicare's interests. If Medicare's interests are not reasonably considered, Medicare will refuse to pay for services related to the WC injury (and otherwise reimbursable by Medicare) until such expenses have exhausted the amount of the entire WC settlement. Medicare will also assert a recovery claim, if appropriate.

6) What is the expected time frame for the regional offices (ROs) to review and make their decisions regarding proposed WC settlements?

Answer: ROs seek to review and make a decision regarding proposed WC settlements within 45 to 60 days, from the time that all necessary/required documentation has been submitted.

7) May administrative fees/expenses for administration of the Medicare set-aside arrangement and/or attorney costs specifically associated with establishing the Medicare set-aside arrangement be charged to the set-aside arrangement?

Answer: Yes, such fees and costs may be charged to the arrangement if all the following are true:
   a) They are related to the Medicare set-aside itself;
   b) They are reasonable in amount; and

4/22/2003

c) They are included in the proposed Medicare set-aside arrangement submitted to CMS and incorporated into the Medicare set-aside approved by CMS.

It is important to note that all administrative fees and other costs and expenses associated with the disability/lost wages portion of the settlement and/or the portion of the settlement that provides for medical services that are not covered by Medicare cannot be charged to the Medicare set-aside arrangement.

Page 4 – All Regional Administrators

Note: This question and answer does not address attorney fees and costs in connection with procurement of the WC settlement from the WC carrier

8) May a beneficiary self-administer his or her own Medicare set-aside arrangement?

Answer: Yes, if this is permitted under state law. It should be noted though, that a self-administered arrangement is subject to the same rules/requirements as any other set-aside arrangement.

9) In WC cases that use structured Medicare set-aside arrangements (i.e., settlement monies are apportioned over fixed or defined periods of time), will Medicare agree to cover the beneficiary when it has not been verified whether the funds as apportioned in the arrangement have been exhausted?

Answer: No, Medicare does not make any payments until the contractor responsible for monitoring the individual's case can verify that the funds apportioned to the period, including any carry-forward amount, have been completely exhausted as set forth in the Medicare set-aside arrangement.

Additionally, please note that any structured set-aside arrangement agreed to by the parties will not be approved by Medicare if the settlement has not adequately considered Medicare's interests.

10) In a structured Medicare set-aside arrangement where payments are made at regular intervals to cover expenses incurred during those periods, how should an administrator account for unspent funds during a given period?

Answer: If funds are not exhausted during a given period then the excess funds must be carried forward to the next period. The threshold after which Medicare would begin to pay claims related to the injury would then be increased in any subsequent period by the amount of the carry-forward.

Example: A structured set-aside is designed to pay $20,000 per year over the next 10 years for an individual's Medicare covered services. Medicare would begin paying covered expenses in any given year after this $20,000 is exhausted. However, in 2003 the injured

4/22/2003

individual needs only $15,000 to cover all related expenses. The administrator would need to carry-forward the excess $5,000 into 2004. Therefore, in 2004 a total of $25,000 of Medicare covered expenses would need to be spent for services otherwise reimbursable by Medicare before Medicare would begin to cover WC related expenses, but only for the balance of 2004. This carry-forward process continues until the accumulated carry-forward plus the payment for a given year is exhausted.

Page 5 – All Regional Administrators

11) If a beneficiary or injured individual's physical condition substantially improves, may the administrator of the Medicare set-aside arrangement release or reduce the amounts of the set-aside?

Answer: The administrator of the CMS approved Medicare set-aside arrangement cannot release or reduce the set-aside amounts without approval from CMS. If the treating physician concludes that the beneficiary's medical condition has substantially improved, then the beneficiary (or his/her representative) may submit a written request to the appropriate CMS RO asking for a reduction of the Medicare set-aside arrangement. This request must include supporting documentation from the treating physician(s). Once the RO receives all pertinent documentation, the RO will then evaluate the request and make a decision. The RO decision is final and not subject to administrative appeal.

12) What are an attorney's ethical and legal obligations when his or her client effectively ignores Medicare's interests in a WC case?

Answer: Attorneys should consult their national, state, and local bar associations for information regarding their ethical and legal obligations. Additionally, attorneys should review applicable statutes and regulations, including, but not limited to, 42 CFR 411.24(e) and 411.26.

13) From where can CMS recover funds if Medicare's interests are ignored in a WC case?

Answer: The CMS has a direct priority right of recovery against any entity, including a beneficiary, provider, supplier, physician, attorney, state agency, or private insurer that has received any portion of a third party payment directly or indirectly. The CMS also has a subrogation right with respect to any such third party payment. See, for example, 42 CFR 411.24(b), (e), and (g) and 42 CFR 411.26.

14) If Medicare rejects a proposed Medicare set-aside arrangement, how can the parties to a WC settlement appeal this rejection?

4/22/2003

Answer: The CMS has no formal appeals process for rejection of a Medicare set-aside arrangement. However, when CMS does not believe that a proposed set-aside adequately protects Medicare's interests, the parties may provide the RO with additional information/documentation in order to justify their proposal. If the additional information does not convince the RO to approve the set-aside arrangement, and the parties proceed to settle the case despite the ROs objections, then Medicare will not recognize the settlement. Medicare will exclude its payments for the medical expenses related to the injury or illness until such time as WC settlement funds expended for services otherwise reimbursable by Medicare exhaust the entire settlement. At this point, when Medicare denies a particular beneficiary's claim, the beneficiary may appeal that particular claim denial through Medicare's regular administrative appeals process. Information on applicable appeal rights is provided at the time of each claim denial.

Page 6 – All Regional Administrators

15) When the parties to a WC settlement present CMS with documentation that is intended to support and justify their proposed Medicare set-aside amounts, will Medicare accept a "life care plan" or similar evaluation prepared by a non-treating physician?

Answer: Yes, Medicare will consider accepting a life care plan or similar evaluation from a non-treating physician, if the physician does all of the following:
   a) Examines the WC claimant;
   b) Reviews the claimant's medical records;
   c) Contacts any of the claimant's treating physicians (if applicable);
   d) Is available to answer CMS' questions;
   e) Prepares a report that summarizes the above; and
   f) Offers a written medical opinion as to all of the reasonably anticipated future medical needs of the claimant related to the claimant's work injury.

Please note that such a life care plan or evaluation is not automatically conclusive. The CMS may not credit the report if there is information that calls the evaluation or plan into question for some reason, such as contrary evidence, internal conflicts, or if the plan is not credible on its face.

16) If a current Medicare beneficiary has outstanding WC related claims that were not paid prior to the settlement and are not covered in that settlement, will Medicare or the Medicare set-aside arrangement pay those claims?

Answer: No, Medicare cannot pay because it is secondary to the WC settlement and the Medicare set-aside arrangement cannot pay because it is created solely for future medical expenses related to the WC case. Medical expenses incurred prior to the

settlement need to be accounted for in the compromise portion of the settlement. These services should be known to the parties. The provider/supplier will typically have billed

4/22/2003

Medicare and/or the WC carrier for these services and the beneficiary's representative will have made inquiries about outstanding related claims.

In addition, to the extent Medicare has made any conditional payments, Medicare will recover those payments pursuant to 42 CFR 411.47.

17) When an annuity is included in a settlement for an injured individual (who is not yet a Medicare beneficiary), how does Medicare determine whether the value of the annuity meets the $250,000 monetary threshold?

Answer: Medicare determines the value of an annuity based on how much the annuity is expected to pay over the life of the settlement, not on the Present Day Value (PDV) or cost of funding that annuity.

Page 7 – All Regional Administrators

Example: A settlement is to pay $15,000 per year for the next 20 years to an individual who has a "reasonable expectation" of Medicare enrollment within 30 months. This settlement is to be funded with an annuity that will cost $175,000. The RO will review this settlement because the total settlement to be paid is greater than $250,000 ($15,000 per year x 20 years = $300,000). It is immaterial for Medicare's purposes that the PDV or cost ($175,000) to fund this settlement is less than $250,000.

18) Is there a means by which an injured individual can permanently waive his or her right to certain specific services related to a WC case, and thereby reduce the amount of a Medicare set-aside arrangement?

Answer: No, the ROs cannot approve settlements that promise not to bill Medicare for certain services in lieu of including those services in a Medicare set-aside arrangement. This is true even if the claimant/beneficiary offers to execute an affidavit or other legal document promising that Medicare will not be billed for certain services if those services are not included in the Medicare set-aside arrangement.

19) Does CMS require that a Medicare set-aside arrangement be established in situations that involve both a WC claim and a third party liability claim?

Answer: Third party liability insurance proceeds are also primary to Medicare. To the extent that a liability settlement is made that relieves a WC carrier from any future medical expenses, a CMS approved Medicare set-aside arrangement is appropriate. This set-aside would need sufficient funds to cover future medical expenses incurred once the total third party liability settlement is exhausted. The only exception to establishing a Medicare set-aside arrangement would be if it can be documented that the beneficiary does not require any further WC claim related medical services. A Medicare set-aside arrangement is also unnecessary if the medical portion of the WC claim remains open, and WC continues to be responsible for related services once the liability settlement is exhausted.

20) **If the settling parties of a WC case contend that a WC settlement is not intended to compensate an injured individual for future medical expenses, does CMS still require that a Medicare set-aside arrangement be established?**

Answer: It is <u>unnecessary</u> for the individual to establish a set-aside arrangement for Medicare if all of the following are true:

   a) The facts of the case demonstrate that the injured individual is only being compensated for past medical expenses (i.e., for services furnished prior to the settlement);

   b) There is no evidence that the individual is attempting to maximize the other aspects of the settlement (e.g., the lost wages and disability portions of the settlement) to Medicare's detriment; and

   c) The individual's treating physicians conclude (in writing) that to a reasonable degree of medical certainty the individual will no longer require any Medicare-covered treatments related to the WC injury.

Page 8 – All Regional Administrators

However, if Medicare made any conditional payments for work-related services furnished prior to settlement, then Medicare would require recovery of those payments. In addition, Medicare will not pay for any services furnished prior to the date of the settlement for which it has not already paid.

21) **If a beneficiary or injured individual dies before the Medicare set-aside arrangement is completely exhausted, what happens to the remaining money?**

Answer: Once the RO and the contractor responsible for monitoring the beneficiary's case ensure that all of the beneficiary's claims have been paid, then any amount left over in the beneficiary's Medicare set-aside arrangement may be disbursed pursuant to state law, once Medicare's interests have been protected. This may involve holding the Medicare set-aside arrangement open for some period after the date of death, as providers, physicians, and other suppliers are permitted to submit their initial bill to Medicare for a period ranging from 15-27 months after the date of service.

22) **What happens if one of the parties settling a WC case refuses to involve CMS, even though Medicare has an interest in the case?**

Answer: In these situations, the "cooperative" settling party should notify the appropriate CMS RO. Where the RO believes it is appropriate, the RO will then send the "uncooperative" party a letter (via certified mail) conveying that Medicare's interests must be considered in the WC settlement.

The ROs should inform the "uncooperative" settling party that: "Pursuant to 42 CFR 411.24(g), CMS has a right of action to recover its payments from any entity, including a beneficiary, provider, supplier, physician, attorney, state agency, or private insurer that has received a third party payment. Moreover, pursuant to 42 CFR 411.26, CMS is subrogated to any individual, provider, supplier, physician, private insurer, state agency, attorney, or any other entity entitled to payment by a third party payer. Therefore, pursuant to 42 CFR 411.24(b), CMS may initiate recovery against the parties listed under 42 CFR 411.26 as soon as it learns that payment has been made or could be made under workers' compensation."

Additionally, if Medicare's interests are not adequately considered in any settlement, then Medicare may refuse to pay for services related to the WC injury until such time as expenses for such services have exhausted the amount of the entire WC settlement.

23) Who should the parties settling a WC case contact in the RO?

Answer: The first report of attorney representation of a Medicare beneficiary for a WC claim should be made to the CMS Coordination of Benefits (COB) Contractor. Attorneys can call the COB Contractor from 8am-8pm, Monday - Friday, Eastern Time; the toll-free number is 1-800-999-1118.

Page 9 – All Regional Administrators

Settling parties should also contact the CMS RO responsible for a particular state (contact information is provided in an attachment to these questions and answers) for approval of a Medicare set-aside arrangement. The inquiry should be directed to the attention of the Regional Office Medicare Secondary Payer Coordinator, who will forward the inquiry to the appropriate RO if a transfer is necessary. (WC set-aside responsibilities are generally, but not always, assigned based upon RO responsibility for contractor oversight over the lead fiscal intermediary for WC recoveries for a particular state. This may or may not be the same RO as the one with general responsibilities for a particular state.)

All RO questions on the issues addressed in these "questions and answers" should be directed to Fred Grabau at (410) 786-0206.

Thomas L. Grissom

Attachment

4/22/2003

Page 10 – All Regional Administrators

cc: All ARA's for Financial Management
        ARA for DHPP RO VII
        All RO MSP Coordinators

Page 11 – All Regional Administrators

bcc: Paul Olenick
 Martha Kuespert
 Fred Grabau
 Eve Fisher
 Tina Merritt
 Barbara Wright
 Betty Noble
 Hugh Hill
 Joan Fowler
 Harry Gamble
 Donna Kettish

4/22/2003

MEDICARE SECONDARY PAYER REGIONAL OFFICE COORDINATORS
(WORKERS' COMPENSATION CONTACTS)

NAME	REGIONAL OFFICE	PHONE
James Bryant	I--Boston	617-565-1331
Thomas Hatchfield		617-565-1254
Sedric Goutier		617-565-1228
Jerry Kerr	II--New York	212-264-3760
	III--Philadelphia	
Catherine McCoy		215-861-4250
Maria Kuehn		215-861-4306
Juanita Dixon	IV--Atlanta	404-562-7313
Geraldine Taylor		404-562-7311
	V--Chicago	
Janice Edwards		312-886-3256
Barry Thomas	VI--Dallas	214-767-6455
Doug Rundle	VII--Kansas City	816-426-5783
Cindy Christensen	VIII--Denver	303-844-7095
Rosie Sagum	IX--San Francisco	415-744-3655
Tom Bosserman		415-744-4907
Jean Tsutakawa	X--Seattle	206-615-2382
Jonella Windell		206-615-2385

Note: If the caller is simply contacting Medicare for the first time in order to report workers' compensation coverage (as opposed to seeking out RO approval of a proposed Medicare set-aside arrangement), then the caller should contact the Coordination of Benefits Contractor at 1-800-999-1118.

STATES IN EACH REGION

I.	BOSTON	Connecticut Maine Massachusetts New Hampshire Rhode Island Vermont	VI.	DALLAS	Arkansas Louisiana New Mexico Oklahoma Texas
II.	NEW YORK	New Jersey New York Puerto Rico Virgin Islands	VII	KANSAS CITY	Iowa Kansas Missouri Nebraska
III.	PHILA.	Delaware Dist. Of Columbia Maryland Pennsylvania Virginia West Virginia	VIII	DENVER	Colorado Montana North Dakota South Dakota Wyoming
IV.	ATLANTA	Alabama North Carolina South Carolina Florida Georgia Kentucky Mississippi Tennessee	XI.	SAN FRAN	American Samoa Arizona California Guam Hawaii Nevada
V.	CHICAGO	Illinois Indiana Michigan Minnesota Ohio Wisconsin	X.	SEATTLE	Alaska Idaho Oregon Washington Utah

APPENDIX 33

CMS Memorandum to All Regional Administrators, *Workers' Compensation Commutation of Future Benefits*, July 23, 2001 [Patel Memo]

JUL 23 2001

To: All Associate Regional Administrators
        Attention: Division of Medicare

From: Deputy Director
        Purchasing Policy Group
        Center for Medicare Management

SUBJECT: Workers' Compensation: Commutation of Future Benefits

Medicare's regulations (42 CFR 411.46) and manuals (MIM 3407.7&3407.8 and MCM 2370.7 & 2370.8) make a distinction between lump sum settlements that are commutations of future benefits and those that are due to a compromise between the Workers' Compensation (WC) carrier and the injured individual. This Regional Office letter clarifies the Centers for Medicare & Medicaid Services (CMS) policy regarding a number of questions raised recently by several Regional Offices (RO) concerning how the RO should evaluate and approve WC lump sum settlements to help ensure that Medicare's interests are properly considered.

Regional Office staff may choose to consult with the Regional Office's Office of the General Counsel (OGC) on WC cases because these cases may entail many legal questions. OGC should become involved in WC cases if there are legal issues which need to be evaluated or if there is a request to compromise Medicare's recovery claim or if the Federal Claims Collection Act (FCCA) delegations require such consultation. Because most WC carriers typically dispute liability in WC compromise cases, it is very common that Medicare later finds that it has already made conditional payments. (A conditional payment means a Medicare payment for which another payer is responsible.) If Medicare's conditional payments are more than $100,000 and the beneficiary also wishes Medicare to compromise its recovery under FCCA (31U.S.C.3711), the case must be referred to Central Office and then forwarded to the Department of Justice. It is important to note in all WC compromise cases that all pre-settlement and post-settlement requests to compromise **any** Medicare recovery claim amounts must be submitted to the RO for appropriate action. Regional Offices must comply with general CMS rules regarding collection of debts (please reference the Administrator's March 27, 2000 memo re: New instructions detailing your responsibilities for monies owed to the government).

Medicare is secondary payer to WC, therefore, it is in Medicare's best interests to learn the existence of WC situations as soon as possible in order to avoid making mistaken payments. The use of administrative mechanisms[1] sometimes referred to by attorneys as Medicare Set-

---

[1] Although 42 CFR 411.46 requires that all WC settlements must adequately consider Medicare's interests, 42 CFR 411.46 does not mandate what particular type of administrative mechanism should be used to set-aside monies for Medicare including a self-administered arrangement (State law permitting). Of course, if an arrangement is self-administered, then the injured individual/beneficiary **must** adhere to

Page 2 – All Associate Regional Administrators

aside Trusts (hereafter referred to as "set-aside arrangements") in WC commutation cases enables Medicare to identify WC situations that would otherwise go unnoticed, which in turn prevents Medicare from making mistaken payments.

Set-aside arrangements are used in WC commutation cases, where an injured individual is disabled by the event for which WC is making payment, but the individual will not become entitled to Medicare until some time after the WC settlement is made. Medicare learns of the existence of a primary payer (WC) as soon as possible when Medicare reviews a proposed set-aside arrangement at or about the time of WC settlement. In such cases, Medicare greatly increases the likelihood that no Medicare payment is made until the set-aside arrangement's funds are depleted. These set-aside arrangements provide both Medicare and its beneficiaries security with regard to the amount that is to be used to pay for an individual's disability related expenses. It is important to note that set-aside arrangements are **only** used in WC cases that possess a commutation aspect; they are not used in WC cases that are strictly or solely compromise cases.

Lump sum compromise settlements represent an agreement between the WC carrier and the injured individual to accept less than the injured individual would have received if he or she had received full reimbursement for lost wages and life long medical treatment for the injury or illness. In a typical lump sum compromise case between a WC carrier and an injured individual, the WC carrier strongly disputes liability and usually will not have voluntarily paid for all the medical bills relating to the accident. Generally, settlement offers in these cases are relatively low and allocations for income replacement and medical costs may not be disaggregated. Such agreements, rather than being based on a purely mathematical computation, are based on other factors. These may include whether there was a preexisting condition, whether the accident was really work related, or whether the individual was acting as an employee, or performing work-related duties at the time the accident occurred.

One of the distinctions that Medicare's regulations and manuals make between compromise and commutation cases is the absence of controversy over whether a WC carrier is liable to make payments. A significant number of WC lump-sum cases are commutations of future WC benefits where typically there is no controversy between the injured individual and the WC carrier over whether the WC carrier is actually liable to make payments. An absence of controversy over whether a WC carrier is liable to make payments is not the only distinction that Medicare's manuals and regulations make between compromise and commutation cases. Thus, lump-sum settlements should not automatically be considered as compromise cases simply because a WC carrier does not admit to being liable in the settlement agreement. Conversely, lump-sum settlements should not automatically be considered as commutation

the same rules/requirements as any other administrator of a set-aside arrangement.

Page 3 - All Associate Regional Administrators

cases simply because a WC carrier does admit to being liable in a settlement agreement. Therefore, an admission of liability by the WC carrier is not the sole determining factor of whether or not a case is considered a compromise or commutation.

WC commutation cases are settlement awards intended to compensate individuals for **future** medical expenses required because of a work-related injury or disease. In contrast, WC compromise cases are settlement awards for an individual's current or past medical expenses that were incurred because of a work-related injury or disease. Therefore, settlement awards or agreements that intend to compensate an individual for any medical expenses after the date of settlement (i.e., future medical expenses) are commutation cases.

It is important to note that a single WC lump-sum settlement agreement can possess both WC compromise and commutation aspects. That is, some single lump-sum settlement agreements can designate part of a settlement for an injured individual's future medical expenses and simultaneously designate another part of the settlement for all of the injured individual's medical expenses up to the date of settlement. This means that a commutation case may possess a compromise aspect to it when a settlement agreement also stipulates to pay for all medical expenses up to the date of settlement. Conversely, a compromise case may possess a commutation aspect to it when a settlement agreement also stipulates to pay for future medical expenses. Therefore, it is possible for a single WC lump-sum settlement agreement to be both a WC compromise case and a WC commutation case.

Generally, parties to WC commutation cases agree on a lump sum amount in exchange for giving up the usual continuing payments by WC for lost wages and for lifetime medical care related to the injuries. Such lump sum amounts are usually requested because the beneficiary wishes to use the funds for some specific purpose. For example, the individual's home may need to be remodeled to accommodate a wheelchair or, more typically, he or she is so disabled that lifetime attendant care is needed. In these latter cases, the injured individual seeks a lump sum payment so that such care can be arranged with certainty in the future. The amount of the lump sum is typically established by using a life care plan[2] and actuarial methods to determine the individual's life expectancy. When WC has accepted full liability in a case prior to the creation of a set-aside arrangement, the likelihood of any Medicare conditional payments being made is reduced.

Set-aside arrangements are most often used in those cases in which the beneficiary is comparatively young and has an impairment that seriously restricts his or her daily living activity. These set-aside arrangements are typically not created until the individual's

---

[2] If a life care plan is not used to justify the injured individual's future medical expenses, then the injured individual or his/her representative **must** present other alternative evidence that sufficiently justifies the amounts set-aside for Medicare.
expenses may be.

Page 4 - All Associate Regional Administrators

condition has stabilized so that it can be determined, based on past experience, what the future medical expenses may be.

Medicare regulations at 42 CFR 411.46 state that:

> If a lump-sum compensation award stipulates that the amount paid is intended to compensate the individual for all future medical expenses required because of the work-related injury or disease, Medicare payments for such services are excluded until medical expenses related to the injury or disease equal the amount of the lump-sum payment.

In addition the Medicare manuals (3407.8 of the MIM, 2370.8 of the MCM) state:

> When a beneficiary accepts a lump-sum payment that represents a commutation of all future medical expenses and disability benefits, and the lump-sum amount is reasonable considering the future medical services that can be anticipated for the condition, Medicare does not pay for any items or services directly related to the injury or illness for which the commutation lump-sum is made, until the beneficiary presents medical bills related to the injury equal to the total amount of the lump-sum settlement allocated to medical treatment.

Questions that have been raised are paraphrased below.

Question 1:

(a) **Does the Medicare program have a claim against a lump sum WC payment before an individual's Medicare entitlement?**
(b) **If not, can the Medicare program give a written opinion on the sufficiency of a set-aside arrangement even if the individual is not as yet entitled to Medicare?**
(c) **In WC cases involving injured individuals who are not yet Medicare beneficiaries, when must Medicare's interests be considered before the parties can settle the case?**

Answer:

These questions have been raised by attorneys who wish to devise set-aside arrangements, which represent amounts for medical items, and services that would ordinarily be covered by Medicare and are specified for future medical treatment for work-related illness or injuries. The attorneys are concerned that Medicare will not pay once the individual becomes entitled to Medicare, because the lump-sum included payment for future medical treatment.

Page 5 - All Associate Regional Administrators

The answer to Question 1(a) is no, Medicare cannot make a formal determination until the individual actually becomes entitled to Medicare. However, the attorneys are correct that once the individual becomes entitled, Medicare payment may not be made to the extent of Medicare's interests in the lump sum payment per 42 CFR 411.46 or a set-aside arrangement that adequately considers Medicare's interests in the lump sum payment.

The answer to Question 1(b) is that the RO (with consultation from the Regional OGC, if necessary) can review a proposed settlement including a set-aside arrangement and can give a written opinion on which the potential beneficiary and the attorney can rely, regarding whether the WC settlement has adequately considered Medicare's interests per 42 CFR 411.46. These settlements should all be handled on a case-by-case basis, as each situation is different. If there are several years prior to Medicare entitlement, the RO should use its best judgment regarding what Medicare utilization might be once there is Medicare entitlement. This decision should be based on the documentation obtained as stated in the answer to Question 10. Once the RO has given written assurance that the set-aside arrangement is sufficient to satisfy the requirements at 42 CFR 411.46, when the set-aside arrangement is established and the settlement is approved, the RO, should then set up a procedure to follow the case.

The answer to question 1(c) is, it is not in Medicare's best interests to review every WC settlement nationwide in order to protect Medicare's interests per 42 CFR 411.46. Injured individuals (who are not yet Medicare beneficiaries) should only consider Medicare's interests when the injured individual has a "reasonable expectation" of Medicare enrollment within 30 months of the settlement date, **and** the anticipated **total** settlement amount for future medical expenses **and** disability/lost wages over the life or duration of the settlement agreement is expected to be greater than $250,000.[3]

For example, if the injured individual is designated by WC as a Permanent Total disabled individual, has filed for Social Security disability, and the settlement apportions $25,000 per year (combined for both future medical expenses **and** disability/lost wages) for the next 20 years, then the RO should review that WC settlement because the total settlement amount over the life of the settlement agreement is greater than $250,000 ($25,000 x 20 years = $500,000) and the injured individual has a "reasonable expectation" of Medicare enrollment within 30 months of the settlement date. If the injured individual in this example fails to consider Medicare's interests, then Medicare may preclude its payments pursuant to 42 CFR 411.46 once the injured individual actually becomes entitled to Medicare.

---

[3] Please note that the review thresholds (i.e., 30 months and $250,000) will be subject to adjustment once CMS has experience reviewing these matters under these instructions.

NOTE: Injured individuals who are already Medicare beneficiaries **must** always consider
Medicare's interests prior to settling their WC claim regardless of whether or not the total settlement amount exceeds $250,000. That is, **ALL WC PAYMENTS** regardless of amount **must** be considered for current Medicare beneficiaries.

Question 2:

Should a system of records be established for the documentation that the RO and contractors receive/collect concerning these set-aside arrangements?

Answer:

Yes. CMS' Division of Benefit Coordination is in the process of establishing a system of records via the Federal Register process, which will provide legal authority to maintain records on individuals that are not enrolled in Medicare. The RO will be responsible for maintaining or housing the records for every arrangement on which the RO provides a written opinion. Please note that these records are not subject to Freedom of Information Act requests and may not be disseminated to the public.

Question 3:

Once the set-aside arrangement has been approved by the RO (with consultation from the Regional OGC, if necessary), what is the subsequent role of the ROs and contractors?

Answer:

When the RO approves a set-aside arrangement (with consultation from the regional OGC, if necessary), the RO will check on a monthly basis the National Medicare Enrollment database in order to determine when an injured individual actually becomes enrolled in Medicare. Once the RO verifies that the injured individual has actually been enrolled in Medicare, the RO will assign a contractor responsible for monitoring the individual's case. The RO will assign the contractor based on the injured individual's State of residence.

When the injured individual has actually been enrolled in Medicare, the RO **must** provide the Coordination of Benefits Contractor (COBC) with identifying information to add a WC record to Common Working File. The RO must exercise one of the following options: 1) Fax the information to the COBC; or 2) Submit through an Electronic

Page 7 - All Associate Regional Administrators

Correspondence Referral System (ECRS) inquiry. At a minimum, the RO must indicate that this is a WC set-aside arrangement case, and include the following information:

Beneficiary Name Beneficiary HIC Date of Incident DX code(s): If you do not have dx codes readily available, you must include a description of the illness/injury. **Note:** Do not forward to COB without a dx or description.

Administrator of Trust

Claimant Attorney Information

The administrator of the set-aside arrangement must forward annual accounting summaries concerning the expenditures of the arrangement to the contractor responsible for monitoring the individual's case. The contractor responsible for monitoring the individual's case is then responsible for insuring/verifying that the funds allocated to the set-aside arrangement were expended on medical services for Medicare covered services only. Additionally, the contractor responsible for monitoring the individual's case will be responsible for ensuring that Medicare makes no payments related to the illness or accident until the set-aside arrangement has been exhausted.

Question 4:

What types of measures should the RO and the contractors take to ensure that Medicare makes no payments related to the illness or accident until the set-aside arrangement has been depleted?

Answer:

Generally, set-aside arrangements that are designed as lump sums (i.e., the arrangement is funded by the WC settlement all at once) present less of a problem to monitor than structured arrangements. Medicare would not make any payments for individuals that possess lump sum arrangements until all of the funds within the arrangement have been depleted. For example, if a set-aside arrangement were established for $90,000, Medicare would not make any payments until the entire $90,000 (plus interest, if applicable) were exhausted on the individual's medical care (for Medicare covered services only).

Structured set-aside arrangements generally apportion settlement monies over fixed or defined periods of time. For example, a structured arrangement may be designed to disburse $20,000 per year over the next ten years for an individual's medical care (for Medicare-covered services only). If the $20,000 allocated on January 1 for Year One were fully exhausted on August 31, Medicare may make payments for the services performed after August 31 once the contractor responsible for monitoring the individual's case can verify that the entire $20,000 (plus interest, if applicable) is exhausted. However, when the structured arrangement allocates money for the start of

Year Two (i.e., on January 1) Medicare would not make any payments for services performed until Year Two's allocation was completely exhausted.

In every set-aside arrangement case the contractor responsible for monitoring the individual's case (with assistance from the RO, if necessary) should ensure that Medicare does not make any payments until the contractor responsible for monitoring the individual's case can verify that the funds apportioned to the arrangement have truly been exhausted.

NOTE:

Until the individual actually becomes entitled to Medicare, the set-aside arrangement fund must **not** be used to pay the individual's expenses. That is, an individual's medical expenses must be paid from some other source besides the set-aside arrangement when the individual is not a Medicare beneficiary. Once the individual actually becomes entitled to Medicare, then the administrator of the arrangement is permitted to make payments for the individual's medical care (for Medicare-covered services only) from the arrangement.

ADDITIONAL NOTE: THE ABOVE PARAGRAPH OF THIS NOTE HAS BEEN REPLACED BY QUESTION 3 OF THE JULY 11, 2005 ARA MEMORANDUM

If the contractor monitoring the individual's case discovers that payments from the set-aside arrangement have been used to pay for services that are not covered by Medicare or for administrative expenses that exceed those approved by the RO (see Question 11), then the contractor will not pay the Medicare claims. The contractor must provide the evidence of the unauthorized expenditures to the RO for investigation. If the RO determines that the expenditures were contrary to the RO's written opinion on the sufficiency of the arrangement, then the RO will notify the administrator of the arrangement that the RO's informal approval of the arrangement is withdrawn until such time as the funds used for non-Medicare expenses and/or unapproved administrative expenses are restored to the set-aside arrangement.

Question 5:

What are the criteria that Medicare uses to determine whether the amount of a lump sum or structured settlement has sufficiently taken its interests into account?

Answer:

The following criteria should be used in evaluating the amount of a proposed settlement to determine whether there has been an attempt to shift liability for the

Page 9 – All Associate Regional Administrators

cost of a work-related injury or illness to Medicare. Specifically, is the amount allocated for future medical expenses reasonable? If Medicare has already made conditional payments their repayment also has to be taken into account.

1. Date of entitlement to Medicare.

2. Basis for Medicare entitlement (disability, ESRD or age)-- If the beneficiary has entitlement based on disability and would also be eligible on the basis of ESRD, this should be noted since the medical expenses would be higher. This would also be true for beneficiaries who are over 65 but had been entitled prior to attaining that age.

3. Type and severity of injury or illness-- Obtain diagnosis codes so injury or illness related expenses can be identified. Is full or partial recovery expected? What is the projected time frame if partial or full recovery is anticipated? As a result of the accident is the individual an amputee, paraplegic or quadriplegic? Is the beneficiary's condition stable or is there a possibility of medical deterioration?

4. Age of beneficiary-- Acquire an evaluation of whether his/her condition would shorten the life span.

5. WC classification of beneficiary (e.g., permanent partial, permanent total disability, or a combination of both).

6. Prior medical expenses paid by WC due to the injury or illness in the 1 or 2 year period after the condition has stabilized-- If Medicare has paid any amounts, they must be recovered. Also, this would indicate that the case may not purely be a commutation case, but may also entail some compromise aspects, e.g., the WC carrier or agency may have taken the position that the services were not covered by WC.

7. Amount of lump sum or amount of structured settlement-- Obtain as much information as possible regarding the allocation between income replacement, loss of limb or function, and medical benefits.

8. Is the commutation for the beneficiary's lifetime or for a specific time period? If not for lifetime, what is the basis?-- Medicare must insist that there is a reasonable relationship between the respective allocation for services covered by Medicare and services not covered by Medicare. For example, is it reasonable for the settlement agreement's allocation for services not covered by Medicare to be based on the beneficiary's life time while the agreement's allocation for services covered by Medicare is based on a lesser time period? What is the State law regarding how long WC is obligated to cover the items or services

related to the accident or illness?

9. Is the beneficiary living at home, in a nursing home, or receiving assisted living care, etc.?-- If the beneficiary is living in a nursing home, or receiving assisted living care, it should be determined who is expected to pay for such care, e.g., WC (for life time or a specified period) from the medical benefits allocation of lump sum settlement, Medicaid, etc.

10. Are the expected expenses for Medicare covered items and services appropriate in light of the beneficiary's condition?-- Estimated medical expenses should include an amount for hospital and/or SNF care during the time period for the commutation of the WC benefit. (Just one hospital stay that is related to the accident could cost $20,000.) For example, a quadriplegic may develop decubitus ulcers requiring possible surgery, urinary tract infections, kidney stones, pneumonia and/or thrombophlebitis. Although each case must be evaluated on its own merits, it may be helpful to ascertain for comparison purposes the average annual amounts of Part A and Part B spending for a disabled person in the appropriate State of residence. Keep in mind that these Fee-for-Service amounts are for all Medicare covered services, while our focus here only deals with services related to the WC accident or illness. Therefore, the RO should use appropriate judgment and seek input from a medical consultant when determining whether the amount of the lump sum or structured settlement has sufficiently taken Medicare's interests into account.

The attorney for the individual for whom the arrangement is set-up should be advised that Medicare applies a set of criteria to any WC settlement on a case-by-case basis in order to determine whether Medicare has an obligation for services provided after the settlement that originally were the responsibility of WC.

NOTE:
Before evaluating whether an arrangement reasonably covers/considers Medicare's interests, **the RO must know** whether the arrangement is based upon WC fee schedule amounts or full actual charge amounts.

Question 6:

Some attorneys have indicated that a set-aside arrangement should only contemplate three to five years of estimated Medicare covered items or services. Would this be reasonable?

Answer:

No. To protect the Medicare Trust Fund, a set-aside arrangement should be funded based on the expected life expectancy of the individual unless the State law specifically limits the length of time that WC covers work related conditions. If an estimate of the beneficiary's estimated longevity was not submitted, one must be obtained.

Question 7:

What other issues should be considered ?

Answer:

The lump sum amount should be interest bearing and indexed to account for inflation consistent with how Medicare calculates its growth in spending. Provision should also be made in the settlement agreement to provide for a mechanism so that items or services that were not covered by Medicare at the time, but later become covered, are transferred from the commutation specified for non-Medicare covered items and services to the set-aside arrangement. (For example if outpatient prescription drugs become more widely covered.) If the beneficiary belongs to a Health Maintenance Organization that may not be coordinating benefits based on WC entitlement, the settlement should still set-aside funds for Medicare covered services in case the beneficiary converts to a fee for service plan.

NOTE: THIS ANSWER WAS REPLACED BY QUESTION 4 OF THE OCTOBER 15, 2004 ARA MEMORANDUM AND LATER REPLACED BY QUESTION 15 OF THE JULY 11, 2005 ARA MEMORANDUM.

Question 8:

Is it permissible for Medicare to accept an up-front cash settlement instead of a set-aside arrangement?

Answer:

An up-front cash settlement is only appropriate in certain instances when Medicare agrees to a compromise in order to recover conditional payments made when WC did not pay promptly. Thus, when future benefits are included in a WC settlement agreement, Medicare cannot pay until the medical expenses related to the injury or disease equal the amount of the settlement allocated to future medical expenses or the amount included for medical expenses in the set-aside arrangement has been exhausted.

Question 9:

How do providers and suppliers obtain payment for the services covered by the set-aside arrangement?

Answer:

There are two distinct methods for providers, physicians and other suppliers to obtain payment for WC covered services when funds are held in a set-aside arrangement. Determining which distinct payment method applies depends on two factors: 1.) How the set-aside arrangement is constructed and 2.) Whether the arrangement was constructed by contemplating full actual charges or WC fee schedule amounts (i.e., were the injured individual's medical expenses determined based on full actual charge estimates or WC fee schedule estimates).

When a set-aside arrangement's settlement agreement contains specific provisions establishing that the WC carrier will ensure that the arrangement cannot be charged more than what would normally be payable under the WC plan, and when the RO reviews and approves the sufficiency of the arrangement based on the WC plan's WC fee schedules, then, providers, physicians and other suppliers will be paid based on what would normally be payable under the WC plan (i.e., under the WC fee schedule). Therefore, providers, physicians and other suppliers would not be permitted to bill the arrangement more than the WC fee schedule rate. For example, if a provider's full charge for a particular service is $100 and the WC carrier normally pays $65 for that particular service, then the arrangement should only pay $65. However, when an arrangement's settlement agreement does **not** contain specific provisions ensuring that the arrangement cannot be charged more than what would normally be payable under the WC plan, then providers, physicians and other suppliers are permitted to bill the arrangement their full charges. It is important to note that when an arrangement's settlement agreement does not contain specific provisions ensuring that providers, physicians and other suppliers cannot bill the arrangement more than the WC fee schedule amounts, then the RO must review the sufficiency of that particular arrangement based upon full actual charge estimates.

Before evaluating whether an arrangement reasonably covers/considers Medicare's interests, **the RO must know** whether the arrangement is based upon WC fee schedule amounts or full actual charge amounts. If the arrangement is based upon WC fee schedule amounts, then, the RO cannot provide a written opinion on the sufficiency of an arrangement until the arrangement's settlement agreement contains specific provisions that establish that the WC carrier can and will ensure that the arrangement cannot be charged more than what would normally be payable under the WC plan. The WC carrier must require all entities and individuals that accept WC payments to agree not to charge the arrangement more than what the WC plan would normally pay.

If a WC carrier is unable to enforce the requirement that the arrangement can only be charged the WC fee schedule rates, then the RO will evaluate whether an arrangement reasonably covers/considers Medicare's interest based on whether the future medical expenses billed to the arrangement are enough to cover the actual expenses for the services at issue. If State WC laws do not provide a particular WC carrier with the legal authority to enforce that requirement, then the RO can still provide a written opinion on the sufficiency of the arrangement so long as future medical expenses are evaluated by the RO using full actual charge estimates, not WC fee schedule amounts.
If the arrangement is constructed based upon full actual charge estimates, then the RO must determine whether the proposed amount to be placed in the arrangement for future medical expenses and administrative costs (see Question 11) is sufficient to cover the actual charges for the services at issue (rather than an amount equal to what would have been the Medicare approved amount for a particular service).

Once the arrangement has been depleted because of payments for otherwise Medicare covered services, a complete accounting must be provided to the contractor responsible for monitoring the individual's case and if the payments have been properly made Medicare can then be billed.

NOTE: THIS ANSWER HAS BEEN REPLACED BY QUESTION 1 OF THE OCTOBER 15, 2004 ARA MEMORANDUM

Question 10:

Are there documentation requirements that must be satisfied before the RO can provide a written opinion on the sufficiency of a set-aside arrangement?

Answer:

Yes. At a minimum, the following documentation must be obtained by the RO prior to the approval of any arrangement:

A copy of the settlement agreement, or proposed settlement agreement, a copy of the life care plan (if there is one), and, if the life care plan does not contain an estimate of the injured individual's estimated life span, then a rated age may be obtainable from life insurance companies for injuries/illnesses sustained by other similarly situated individuals. Also, documentation which gives the basis for the amounts of projected expenses for Medicare covered services and services not covered by Medicare (this could be a copy of letters from doctors/providers documenting the necessity of continued care).

Page 14 – All Associate Regional Administrators

The RO may require additional documentation, if necessary and approved by CO.

NOTE: THE ABOVE ANSWER WAS CLARIFIED BY QUESTION 5 OF THE OCTOBER 15, 2004 ARA MEMORANDUM

Question 11:

How does the RO determine whether or not the administrative fees and expenses charged to the arrangement are reasonable?

Answer:

Before a proposed arrangement can be approved, the RO must determine whether the administrative fees and expenses to be charged to the arrangement are reasonable. The RO must be notified (in writing) of all proposed administrative fees prior to the RO providing its written assurance that the set-aside arrangement is sufficient to satisfy the requirements of 42 CFR 411.46. If the administrative fees are determined to be unreasonable, the RO must withhold its approval of the set-aside arrangement. The amount of the approved arrangement must include both the estimated medical expenses plus the amount of administrative fees found to be reasonable.

NOTE: THE ABOVE ANSWER HAS BEEN REPLACED BY THE MAY 7, 2004 ARA MEMORANDUM

Question 12:

What impact will arrangements have on Medicare payment systems and procedures?

Answer:

Because an arrangement's purpose is to pay for all services related to the individual's work-related injury or disease, Medicare will not make any payments (as a primary, secondary or tertiary payer) for any services related to the work-related injury or disease until nothing remains in the set-aside arrangement. Arrangements are established in order to pay for **all** medical expenses resulting from work- related injuries or diseases; arrangements are not designed to simply pay portions of medical expenses for work-related injuries or diseases.

When arrangements are designed as lump sum commutations (i.e., the arrangement is designed in a manner that the WC settlement is paid into the arrangement all at once, see Question #4 above), Medicare would not make any payments for that individual's medical expenses (for work-related injuries or diseases) until all the funds (including interest) within the arrangement have been completely exhausted. These same basic principles also apply to structured commutations (see Question #4 above).

When providers, physicians and other suppliers submit claims to Medicare related to the individual's work-related injury or disease, claims processing contractors should deny those claims and instruct the entity or individual to seek payment from the administrator of the arrangement. Since the injured individual will be a Medicare beneficiary at the time when the provider, physician, or other supplier submits the claim to Medicare, the contractor responsible for monitoring the individual's case will have already updated the Common Working File to indicate that the injured individual's claims should be denied. However, when a provider, physician or other supplier submits any claims that are for injuries or diseases that **are not** work-related, then contractors should process those claims like they would any other claim for Medicare payment.

When the administrator of an arrangement refuses to make payment on a provider's, physician's or other supplier's claim because the administrator of the arrangement asserts the services are for injuries or diseases that are not work-related (or when the administrator of the arrangement denies the claim for any other reason), and the provider, physician or other supplier, subsequent to the administrator's denial, submits the claim to Medicare, then the contractor should consult the RO in order to determine whether Medicare should pay the claim. If a determination to deny the claim is made, then Medicare's regular administrative appeals process for claim denials would apply to the claim.

Please note that Central Office is planning to have a contractor assist ROs in monitoring and processing (however, not evaluating) these set-aside arrangement cases as early as possible in Fiscal Year 2002. Further instructions will be issued at that time.

Regional Office staff's questions on these issues should be directed to Fred Grabau at (410) 7860206. We will issue additional guidance as necessary.

/s/

Parashar B. Patel

cc: Regional Administrators Gerry Nicholson, Benefits Operations Group
Liz Richter, Financial Services Group
FARD3/F.Grabau/60206/final 7/11/01 Document: /g:/ppg/dids/araWC2.doc Typist: T. Cox x60750

APPENDIX 34

AAJ Bulletin, dated August 11, 2009

August 11, 2009 American Association for Justice (AAJ) Email Bulletin

EMERGENCY MEDICARE SET ASIDE INFORMATION

Dear Colleague:

In cases involving Medicare beneficiaries, attorneys for both the plaintiff and defendant are required to report certain information to the Centers for Medicare and Medicaid Services (CMS). In addition, any case settlement or judgment must reimburse Medicare where the Trust Fund has made conditional payments for medical costs. Under the Medicare Secondary Payer Act, attorneys have been settling cases involving liability claims without completing a Medicare Set Aside (MSAs) to account for future medical costs. However, attorneys representing claimants in workers' compensation cases have been preparing MSAs on a case-by-case basis.

It has come to our attention that some defense firms and insurance providers are now claiming that CMS requires MSAs in liability cases pursuant to Section 111 reporting requirements included in the Medicare, Medicaid & SCHIP Act of 2007 (MMSEA), Public Law No. 110-173. This is false. Section 111 contains reporting requirements for responsible reporting entities(1) (RREs) only. Section 111 does not impact or change the requirements for plaintiffs' attorneys.

Moreover, statements from CMS, and other federal entities, make clear that the agency does not require set-asides for liability claims. Since the MMSEA's passage, CMS has held several Town Hall teleconferences to discuss the Section 111 requirements. During the March 24, 2009 call, Barbara Wright, CMS' Acting Director of the Division of Medicare Debt Management, made several statements reiterating that Section 111 has no impact on liability MSAs.(2) For example:

In response to a question as to whether liability set-asides will be required under Section 111, she said "the point is the set-aside process is totally separate from the Section 111 reporting process. As we've said in more than one call we don't anticipate changing our routine recovery process." (Transcript, pg. 24)

When explaining that worker's compensation agreements use a formal review process which makes set-asides recommended, she said that was in contrast to liability agreements. Liability "does not have the same formal review process although our regional offices will consider review of proposed liability set-aside amounts depending on their particular work load and whether or not they believe significant dollars are at issue." (Transcript, pg. 24).

In addition, CMS also has released several Alerts explaining Section 111, which do not indicate any intent to require MSAs for liability claims. For example:

"Unless you are a business entity which qualifies as [a required reporting entity (RRE)] for purposes of Section 111, you do not need to initiate any specific actions in connection with Section 111." (CMS Alert, 2/23/09).(3)

"The new Section 111 requirements do not change or eliminate any existing obligations under the MSP statutory provisions or regulations." (CMS Alert, 2/23/09).

Moreover, the Congressional Research Service (CRS) provided Congress with an "objective and non-partisan analysis" analysis of the MMSEA. As there was no legislative history regarding the bill, the CRS research report is the most reliable analysis of the MMSEA, including the Section 111 reporting requirements.

CRS' analysis of the Section 111 reiterates that it is a reporting requirement, and makes no mention of the need for set-asides in liability cases. The Section 111 analysis states, in part:

This provision requires an insurer or third-party administrator for a group health plan (and in the case of a group health plan that is self-insured and self-administered, a plan administrator or fiduciary) to (1) secure from the plan sponsor and participants information required by the Secretary for the purpose of identifying situations where the group health plan is or has been a primary plan to Medicare, and (2) submit information specified by the Secretary. If an insurer or third-party administrator for a group health plan fails to comply, then a $1,000 per day civil monetary penalty will be imposed for each individual for which information should have been submitted.(4)

APPENDIX 35

Letter of Medicare's Refusal to Review LMSA

DEPARTMENT OF HEALTH & HUMAN SERVICES
Centers for Medicare & Medicaid Services

61 Forsyth Street, Suite 4T20
Atlanta, Georgia 30303-8909

May 29, 2012

Franco Signor
Attn: ███████████
2316 Delaware Avenue, # 281
Buffalo, New York 14216 - 2687

Re: Liability Medicare Set-Aside Arrangement
       Claimant: ████████████
       HICN: ███████████
       SSN: ████████
       DOI: ███████

Dear ███████████:

This letter is in response to your initial proposal submitted on May 15, 2012, regarding the amount of a liability Medicare set-aside arrangement on behalf of the above named individual.[1]

The Medicare Secondary Payer ("MSP") provisions, 42 USC § 1395y(b)(2), preclude Medicare payments for medical items and services to the extent that payment has been made or can reasonably be expected to be made under an automobile or liability insurance policy or plan (including self-insurance). 42 U.S.C. § 1395y(b)(2)(A)(ii). Liability insurance includes but is not limited to automobile liability insurance, uninsured motorist insurance, underinsured motorist insurance, homeowners' liability insurance, malpractice insurance, product liability insurance, and general casualty insurance. 42 CFR § 411.50(b).

You proposed that a liability Medicare set-aside arrangement in the amount of $███████ be made available for payment of future medical expenses for items and services otherwise reimbursable by Medicare (including prescription medications) related to the proposed settlement, judgment or award

---

[1] If you are receiving this letter in response to a request for review of a proposed set-aside amount related to an action brought pursuant to either the Jones Act or the Federal Employer's Liability Act (FELA), please be advised that those are actions seeking damages for tort liability, not claims for workers' compensation. Therefore, any proposed Medicare set-aside arrangements related to claims under the Jones Act or FELA are referred to as liability Medicare set-aside arrangements.

1

Page 2 – Franco Signor

between  and We note that the proposed amount includes $____ for future prescription drug treatment.

Due to resource constraints, CMS is not providing a review of this proposed liability Medicare set-aside arrangement amount. Please be advised that this does not constitute a release or a safe harbor from any obligations under any Federal law, including the MSP statute. All parties must ensure that Medicare is secondary to any other entity responsible for payment of medical items and services related to the liability settlement, judgment or award. In addition, any Medicare payments made on behalf of your client for medical items and services related to the liability settlement, judgment or award must be reimbursed to the Medicare Trust Funds. 42 U.S.C. § 1395y(b)(2)(B); 42 C.F.R. § 411.24. [2]

If you have any questions concerning this letter, please call _____ at _____.

Sincerely,

cc: _____
    MSPRC

---

[2] Please contact the Coordination of Benefits Contractor at 1-800-999-1118 to start the process of determining the amount of Medicare payments made on behalf of your client for items and services which are related to the liability settlement, judgment or award. For more information on reimbursement obligations under the MSP statute, please visit our website at http://www.cms.hhs.gov/home/medicare.asp and review the information in the section entitled "Medicare Secondary Payer Recovery".

APPENDIX 36A

Sample Standard Recovery/Initial Determination Letter

Dear Mr./Ms. _____ [1]

    This letter follows our earlier communication in which we advised you that you would be required to repay the Medicare program for the cost of medical care it paid relating to your liability recovery if you received money from a third party payer for a claim related to [insert date] accident/ incident/injury. (The term "recovery" includes a settlement, judgment, award or any other type of recovery.) We have now been advised that you have received such proceeds.

    This means that Medicare now has a claim against these proceeds in the amount of $_____, which represents Medicare's claim after reduction for procurement costs, in accordance with 42 CFR 411.37. The Medicare Secondary payer provisions of the statute, 42 U.S.C.1395y(b)(2), preclude Medicare from paying for a beneficiary's medical expenses when payment "has been made or can reasonably be expected to be made under an automobile or liability insurance policy or plan (including a self-insured plan) or under no-fault insurance." However, Medicare may pay for a beneficiary's covered medical expenses when the third party payer does not pay promptly, conditioned on reimbursement to Medicare from proceeds received from a third party liability settlement, award, judgment or recovery. In your case, Medicare made a conditional payment in the amount of $_____. A list of the claims used to arrive at this total is enclosed.

    Medicare's regulations require that you pay Medicare back within 60 days of your receipt of settlement or insurance proceeds. It is our understanding that 60 days have passed since you received the insurance proceeds. Therefore, please send a check or money order in the amount of $_____, made payable to (name of contractor) in the enclosed envelope.

    Exercising common law authority and consistent with the Federal Claims Collection Act and 45

    CFR 30.13, we will assess interest if this debt is not repaid in full within 60 days of the date of this letter. Additionally, 45 CFR 30.14(a) provides that a

---

[1] See Chapter 7 of the MSP Manual, pages 105-106. Exhibit 2 - Standard Recovery/ Initial Determination Letter to Beneficiary (Rev. 25, Issued: 02-25-05, Effective: 04-25-05, Implementation: 04-25-05).

debtor may either pay the debt, or be liable for interest on the un-collectable debt while a waiver determination, appeal, or a formal or informal review of the debt is pending. Therefore, assessment of interest may not be suspended solely because further review may be requested. Interest will be assessed at an annual rate of_____. It should be noted, however, that you may repay the debt to avoid accruing charges, but retain your right to dispute, appeal, or request waiver of the debt. If you succeed in your appeal or waiver request, Medicare will refund your money.

If you do not repay this overpayment, Medicare has the authority to refer it to the Social Security Administration or Railroad Retirement Board for further recovery action, which may result in the overpayment being deducted from any monthly Social Security or Railroad Retirement benefits to which you may be entitled.

If you are unable to refund this amount in one payment, you may ask us to consider whether to allow you to pay in regular installments. The law requires that you must repay an overpayment to Medicare unless both of the following conditions are met:

1. This overpayment was not your fault, because the information you gave us with your claim was correct and complete as far as you knew, and, when the Medicare payment was made, you thought that it was the right payment for your claim,

   AND

2. Paying back this money would cause financial hardship OR would be unfair for some other reason.

If you believe that BOTH of the conditions above apply in your case, please let us know, giving a brief statement of your reasons. You will be sent a form asking for information about your income, assets, and expenses, and requesting that you explain why you believe you are entitled to waiver of the overpayment. We will notify you if recovery of this overpayment can be waived.

You may appeal our decision if: you disagree that you received an overpayment; or you disagree with the amount of overpayment; or you disagree with our decision not to waive your repayment of the overpayment.

For Part A and Part B services, you must file an appeal within 120 days from the date of your receipt of this determination. Appeals should be requested in writing to _____. If you decide to appeal this determination further, and if you want help with your appeal, you can have a friend, lawyer, or someone else help you. Some lawyers do not charge unless you win your appeal. There are groups, such as lawyer referral services, that can help you find a lawyer.

There are also groups, such as legal aid services, who will provide free legal services if you qualify. If you have any questions about this letter, you may contact either this office or any Social Security office.

Sincerely,
ABC Contractor
Attachments: List of claims

APPENDIX 36B

MSPRC Standard Letter Acknowledging
Request for Waiver

 Learn about your letter at *www.msprc.info*

insert name
insert address 1
insert address 2
insert city, state, zip code

Beneficiary: insert name
Medicare Number: insert HICN
Date of Incident:
Debt Identification No:
Demand Amount:

Dear insert attorney or other representative name:

This letter acknowledges your client's request for waiver of recovery of a Medicare overpayment resulting from the liability settlement, judgment or award your client received.

In order to help us evaluate your client's request under §1870(c) of the Social Security Act (42 U.S.C. 1395gg(c)), please complete and return the enclosed Form SSA-632-BK, Request for Waiver of Overpayment Recovery. Also, please provide an explanation of your client's reasons for requesting a waiver. Your client is responsible for providing complete documentation substantiating the request, including documentation of procurement costs and out-of-pocket expenses incurred, if any. If your client claims that repaying Medicare will create a financial hardship, you should provide evidence to demonstrate such hardship.

If your client is able to refund a portion of the overpayment, please let us know how much your client is able to repay, with an explanation of why your client is unable to refund the entire amount. Please refer to our   letter, in which we explained the criteria that control our determination of whether waiver may be granted.

Any person who makes (or causes to be made) a false statement of representation of material fact in an application or for use in determining a right to payment under the Social Security Act, commits a crime punishable under Federal law and/or State law. In submitting the enclosed SSA-632-BK form and any material documentation, you are deemed to affirm that all information you have given is true.

 Learn about your letter at *www.msprc.info*

If you have any questions concerning this matter, please call the Medicare Secondary Payer Recovery Contractor (MSPRC) at 1-866-677-7220 (TTY/TDD: 1-866-677-7294 for the hearing and speech impaired) or you may contact us in writing at the address below. If you contact us in writing, please be sure to include the beneficiary's name and Medicare health insurance claim number.

Medicare Secondary Payer Recovery Contractor
Auto/Liability
PO Box 33828
Detroit, Michigan 48232-5828

Sincerely,

MSPRC insert title

insert cc:

insert site identifier

APPENDIX 36C

MSPRC Request for Waiver of Overpayment – Form SSA 632-BK

SOCIAL SECURITY ADMINISTRATION

Form Approved
OMB No. 0960-0037

Request For Waiver Of Overpayment Recovery Or Change In Repayment Rate

We will use your answers on this form to decide if we can waive collection of the overpayment or change the amount you must pay us back each month. If we can't waive collection, we may use this form to decide how you should repay the money.

Please answer the questions on this form as completely as you can. We will help you fill out the form if you want. If you are filling out this form for someone else, answer the questions as they apply to that person.

FOR SSA USE ONLY		
ROAR Input	☐ Yes	
	☐ No	
Input Date		
Waiver	☐ Approval	
	☐ Denial	
SSI	☐ Yes	☐ No
AMT OF OP $		
PERIOD (DATES) OF OP		
	-	
	-	

---

1. A. Name of person on whose record the overpayment occurred:

_____

B. Social Security Number

☐☐☐ — ☐☐ — ☐☐☐☐

C. Name of overpaid person(s) making this request and his/her Social Security Number(s):

_____ ☐☐☐ — ☐☐ — ☐☐☐☐

_____ ☐☐☐ — ☐☐ — ☐☐☐☐

_____ ☐☐☐ — ☐☐ — ☐☐☐☐

_____ ☐☐☐ — ☐☐ — ☐☐☐☐

---

2. Check any of the following that apply. (Also, fill in the dollar amount in B, C, or D.)

A. ☐ The overpayment was not my fault and I cannot afford to pay the money back and/or it is unfair for some other reasons.

B. ☐ I cannot afford to use all of my monthly benefit to pay back the overpayment. However I can afford to have $_____ withheld each month.

C. ☐ I am no longer receiving Supplement Security Income (SSI) payments. I want to pay back $_____ each month instead of paying all of the money at once.

D. ☐ I am receiving SSI payments. I want to pay back $_____ each month instead of paying 10% of my total income.

SECTION I-INFORMATION ABOUT RECEIVING THE OVERPAYMENT

3. A. Did you, as representative payee, receive the overpaid benefits to use for the beneficiary?

☐ Yes   ☐ No (Skip to Question 4)

B. Name and address of the beneficiary

C. How were the overpaid benefits used?

4. If we are asking you to repay someone else's overpayment:

A. Was the overpaid person living with you when he/she was overpaid?   ☐ Yes   ☐ No

B. Did you receive any of the overpaid money?   ☐ Yes   ☐ No

C. Explain what you know about the overpayment AND why it was not your fault.

5. Why did you think you were due the overpaid money and why do you think you were not at fault in causing the overpayment or accepting the money?

6. A. Did you tell us about the change or event that made you overpaid?   ☐ Yes   ☐ No
If no, why didn't you tell us?

B. If yes, how, when and where did you tell us? If you told us by phone or in person, who did you talk with and what was said?

C. If you did not hear from us after your report, and/or your benefits did not change, did you contact us again?   ☐ Yes   ☐ No

7. A. Have we ever overpaid you before?   ☐ Yes   ☐ No

If yes, on what Social Security number?   ☐☐☐ — ☐☐ — ☐☐☐☐

B. Why were you overpaid before? If the reason is similar to why you are overpaid now, explain what you did to try to prevent the present overpayment.

SECTION II-YOUR FINANCIAL STATEMENT

NAME:

SSN:

You need to complete this section if you are asking us either to waive the collection of the overpayment or to change the rate at which we asked you to repay it. Please answer all questions as fully and as carefully as possible. We may ask to see some documents to support your statements, so you should have them with you when you visit our office.

EXAMPLES ARE:

- Current Rent or Mortgage Books
- Savings Passbooks
- Pay Stubs
- Your most recent Tax Return

- 2 or 3 recent utility, medical, charge card, and insurance bills
- Cancelled checks
- Similar documents for your spouse or dependent family members

Please write only whole dollar amounts-round any cents to the nearest dollar. If you need more space for answers, use the "Remarks" section at the bottom of page 7.

8. A. Do you now have any of the overpaid checks or money in your possession (or in a savings or other type of account)?

☐ Yes   Amount:$ _____
Return this amount to SSA
☐ No

B. Did you have any of the overpaid checks or money in your possession (or in a savings or other type of account) at the time you received the overpayment notice?

☐ Yes   Amount:$ _____
Answer Question 9.
☐ No

9. Explain why you believe you should not have to return this amount.

_____
_____
_____

ANSWER 10 AND 11 ONLY IF THE OVERPAYMENT IS SUPPLEMENTAL SECURITY INCOME (SSI) PAYMENTS. IF NOT, SKIP TO 12.

10. A. Did you lend or give away any property or cash after notification of the overpayment?

☐ Yes (Answer Part B)

B. Who received it, relationship (if any), description and value:

☐ No (Go to question 11.)

11. A. Did you receive or sell any property or receive any cash (other than earnings) after notification of this overpayment?

☐ Yes (Answer Part B)

☐ No (Go to Question 12.)

B. Describe property and sale price or amount of cash received:

12. A. Are you now receiving cash public assistance such as Supplemental Security Income (SSI) payments?

☐ Yes   (Answer B and C and See note below)
☐ No

B. Name or kind of public assistance

C. Claim Number

_____   _____

IMPORTANT: If you answered "YES" to question 12, DO NOT answer any more questions on this form. Go to page 8, sign and date the form, and give your address and phone number(s). Bring or mail any papers that show you receive public assistance to your local Social Security office as soon as possible.

Members Of Household

13. List any person (child, parent, friend, etc.) who depends on you for support AND who lives with you.

NAME	AGE	RELATIONSHIP (If none, explain why the person is dependent on you)

Assets-Things You Have And Own

14.

A. How much money do you and any person(s) listed in question 13 above have
as cash on hand, in a checking account, or otherwise readily available?   **$**

B. Does your name, or that of any other member of your household appear,
either alone or with any other person, on any of the following?

TYPE OF ASSET	OWNER	BALANCE OR VALUE	PER MONTH	SHOW THE INCOME (interest, dividends) EARNED EACH MONTH. (If none, explain in spaces below. If paid quarterly, divide by 3).
SAVINGS (Bank, Savings and Loan, Credit Union)		$	$	
		$	$	
CERTIFICATES OF DEPOSIT (CD)		$	$	
INDIVIDUAL RETIREMENT ACCOUNT (IRA)		$	$	
MONEY OR MUTUAL FUNDS		$	$	
BONDS, STOCKS		$	$	
TRUST FUND		$	$	
CHECKING ACCOUNT		$	$	
OTHER (EXPLAIN)		$	$	
TOTALS ➤		$	$	Enter the "Per Month" total on line (k) of question 18.

15.

A. If you or a member of your household own a car, (other than the family vehicle), van, truck, camper, motorcycle, or any other vehicle or a boat, list below.

OWNER	YEAR/MAKE/MODEL	PRESENT VALUE	LOAN BALANCE (if any)	MAIN PURPOSE FOR USE
		$	$	
		$	$	
		$	$	

B. If you or a member of your household own any real estate (buildings or land), OTHER than where you live, or own or have an interest in, any business, property, or valuables, describe below.

OWNER	DESCRIPTION	MARKET VALUE	LOAN BALANCE (if any)	USAGE-INCOME (rent etc.)
		$	$	
		$	$	
		$	$	
		$	$	

Monthly Household Income

If paid weekly, multiply by 4.33 (4 1/3) to figure monthly pay. If paid every 2 weeks, multiply by 2.166 (2 1/6). If self-employed, enter 1/12 of net earnings. Enter monthly TAKE HOME amounts on line A of question 18 also.

16. A. Are you employed?   ☐ YES (Provide information below)   ☐ NO (Skip to B)

| Employer name, address, and phone: (Write "self" if self-employed) | Monthly pay before deduction (Gross) | $ |
| | Monthly TAKE-HOME pay (NET) | $ |

B. Is your spouse employed?   ☐ YES (Provide information below)   ☐ NO (Skip to C)

| Employer(s) name, address, and phone: (Write "self" if self-employed) | Monthly pay before deduction (Gross) | $ |
| | Monthly TAKE-HOME pay (NET) | $ |

C. Is any other person listed in Question 13 employed?   ☐ YES   ☐ NO (Go to Question 17)   Name(s)

| Employer(s) name, address, and phone: (Write "self" if self-employed) | Monthly pay before deduction (Gross) | $ |
| | Monthly TAKE-HOME pay (NET) | $ |

17. A. Do you, your spouse or any dependent member of your household receive support or contributions from any person or organization?   ☐ YES (Answer B)   ☐ NO (Go to question 18)

B. How much money is received each month? $_____   SOURCE
(Show this amount on line (J) of question 18)

BE SURE TO SHOW **MONTHLY** AMOUNTS BELOW - If received weekly or every 2 weeks, read the instruction at the top of this page.

18.

INCOME FROM #16 AND #17 ABOVE AND OTHER INCOME TO YOUR HOUSEHOLD	YOURS	√	SPOUSE'S	√	OTHER HOUSEHOLD MEMBERS	√	SSA USE ONLY
A. TAKE HOME Pay (Net) (From #16 A, B, C, above)	$	☐	$	☐	$	☐	
B. Social Security Benefits		☐		☐		☐	
C. Supplemental Security Income (SSI)		☐		☐		☐	
D. Pension(s) (VA, Military, Civil Service, Railroad, etc.) TYPE / TYPE		☐		☐		☐	
E. Public Assistance (Other than SSI) TYPE		☐		☐		☐	
F. Food Stamps (Show full face value of stamps received)		☐		☐		☐	
G. Income from real estate (rent, etc.) (From question 15B)		☐		☐		☐	
H. Room and/or Board Payments (Explain in remarks below)		☐		☐		☐	
I. Child Support/Alimony		☐		☐		☐	
J. Other Support (From #17 (B) above)		☐		☐		☐	
K. Income From Assets (From question 14)		☐		☐		☐	
L. Other (From any source, explain below)		☐		☐		☐	
REMARKS TOTALS	$		$		$		

GRAND TOTAL $_____
(Add 3 total blocks above)

Monthly Household Expenses

If the expense is paid weekly or every 2 weeks, read the instruction at the top of Page 5. Do NOT list an expense that is withheld from income (Such as Medical Insurance). Only take home pay is used to figure income.

Show "CC" as the expense amount if the expense (such as clothing) is part of CREDIT CARD EXPENSE SHOWN ON LINE (F).

			$ PER MONTH	SSA USE ONLY
19.	A.	Rent or Mortgage (If mortgage payment includes property or other local taxes, insurance, etc. DO NOT list again below.)		
	B.	Food (Groceries (include the value of food stamps) and food at restaurants, work, etc.)		
	C.	Utilities (Gas, electric, telephone)		
	D.	Other Heating/Cooking Fuel (Oil, propane, coal, wood, etc.)		
	E.	Clothing		
	F.	Credit Card Payments (show minimum monthly payment allowed)		
	G.	Property Tax (State and local)		
	H.	Other taxes or fees related to your home (trash collection, water-sewer fees)		
	I.	Insurance (Life, health, fire, homeowner, renter, car, and any other casualty or liability policies)		
	J.	Medical-Dental (After amount, if any, paid by insurance)		
	K.	Car operation and maintenance (Show any car loan payment in (N) below)		
	L.	Other transportation		
	M.	Church-charity cash donations		
	N.	Loan, credit, lay-away payments (If payment amount is optional, show minimum)		
	O.	Support to someone NOT in household (Show name, age, relationship (if any) and address)		
	P.	Any expense not shown above (Specify)		
	EXPENSE REMARKS (Also explain any unusual or very large expenses, such as medical, college, etc.)	TOTAL	$	

Income And Expenses Comparison

20. A. Monthly income
(Write the amount here from the "Grand Total" of #18.) ————————⟩ $

B. Monthly Expenses
(Write the amount here from the "Total" of #19.) ————————⟩ $

C. Adjusted Household Expenses ————————⟩ + $25

D. Adjusted Monthly Expenses (Add (B) and (C)) ————————⟩ $

21. If your expenses (D) are more than your income (A), explain how you are paying your bills.

FOR SSA USE ONLY	
☐ INC. **EXCEEDS** ADJ EXPENSE	$ +
☐ INC **LESS THAN** ADJ EXPENSE	$ −

Financial Expectation And Funds Availability

22. A. Do you, your spouse or any dependent member of your household expect your or their financial situation to change (for the better or worse) in the next 6 months? (For example: a tax refund, pay raise or full repayment of a current bill for the better-major house repairs for the worse).

☐ YES (Explain on line below)
☐ NO

B. If there is an amount of cash on hand or in checking accounts shown in item 14A, is it being held for a special purpose?

☐ NO (Amount on hand)
☐ NO (Money available for any use)
☐ YES (Explain on line below)

C. Is there any reason you CANNOT convert to cash the "Balance or Value" of any financial asset shown in item 14B.

☐ YES (Explain on line below)
☐ NO

D. Is there any reason you CANNOT SELL or otherwise convert to cash any of the assets shown in items 15A and B?

☐ YES (Explain on line below)
☐ NO

Remarks Space — If you are continuing an answer to a question, please write the number (and letter, if any) of the question first.

_____
_____
_____
_____
_____

(MORE SPACE ON NEXT PAGE)

REMARKS SPACE (Continued)

PENALTY CLAUSE, CERTIFICATION AND PRIVACY ACT STATEMENT

I declare under penalty of perjury that I have examined all the information on this form, and on any accompanying statements or forms, and it is true and correct to the best of my knowledge. I understand that anyone who knowingly gives a false or misleading statement about a material fact in this information, or causes someone else to do so, commits a crime and may be sent to prison, or may face other penalties, or both.

SIGNATURE OF OVERPAID PERSON OR REPRESENTATIVE PAYEE

SIGNATURE (First name, middle initial, last name) (Write in ink)	DATE (Month, Day, Year)
	HOME TELEPHONE NUMBER (Include area code) ( ) –
SIGN ▶ **HERE**	WORK TELEPHONE NUMBER IF WE MAY CALL YOU AT WORK (Include area code) ( ) –

MAILING ADDRESS (Number and street, Apt. No., P.O. Box, or Rural Route)

CITY AND STATE	ZIP CODE	ENTER NAME OF COUNTY (IF ANY) IN WHICH YOU NOW LIVE
	–	

Witnesses are required ONLY if this statement has been signed by mark (X) above. If signed by mark (X), two witnesses to the signing who know the individual must sign below, giving their full addresses.

SIGNATURE OF WITNESS	SIGNATURE OF WITNESS
ADDRESS (Number and street, City, State, and ZIP Code)	ADDRESS (Number and street, City, State, and ZIP Code)

Privacy Act Statement

Collection and Use of Personal Information

Sections 204, 1631(b), and 1870 of the Social Security Act, as amended, and the Federal Coal Mine Health and Safety Act of 1969 authorize us to collect this information. The information you provide will be used to make a determination on waiving overpayment recovery or changing your repayment rate.

The information you furnish on this form is voluntary. However, failure to provide the requested information may prevent us from approving your request.

We rarely use the information you supply for any purpose other than for determining waiver or a change in the repayment rate of an overpayment recovery. However, we may use it for the administration and integrity of Social Security programs. We may also disclose information to another person or to another agency in accordance with approved routine uses, which include but are not limited to the following:

To enable a third party or an agency to assist Social Security in establishing rights to Social Security benefits and/or coverage; To comply with Federal laws requiring the release of information from Social Security records (e.g., to the Government Accountability Office and Department of Veterans' Affairs);

To facilitate statistical research, audit or investigative activities necessary to assure the integrity of Social Security programs; and To the Department of Justice when representing the Social Security Administration in litigation.

We may also use the information you provide in computer matching programs. Matching programs compare our records with records kept by other Federal, state or local government agencies. Information from these matching programs can be used to establish or verify a person's eligibility for Federally funded or administered benefit programs and for repayment of payments or delinquent debts under these programs.

Additional information regarding this form, routine uses of information, and our programs and systems, is available on-line at www.socialsecurity.gov or at your local Social Security office.

Paperwork Reduction Act Statement - This information collection meets the requirements of 44 U.S.C. § 3507, as amended by section 2 of the Paperwork Reduction Act of 1995. You do not need to answer these questions unless we display a valid Office of Management and Budget control number. We estimate that it will take about 2 hours to read the instructions, gather the facts, and answer the questions. **SEND OR BRING THE COMPLETED FORM TO YOUR LOCAL SOCIAL SECURITY OFFICE. To find the nearest office, call 1-800-772-1213 (TTY 1-800-325-0778).** Send only comments on our time estimate above to: SSA, 6401 Security Blvd., Baltimore, MD 21235-6401.

APPENDIX 36D

Standard Letter for Granting Full Waiver

If granting a full waiver, the contractor sends the Standard Letter Granting Full Waiver shown below. Use of this letter is mandatory. Substitutes may not be used. The contractor retains copies for the file.[1]

Re: Name of Beneficiary HIC #

Dear Beneficiary/Attorney:

We have reviewed your/your client's request to waive the amount owed to Medicare and have determined that you qualify for a full waiver.

This qualification is based upon the requirements of §1870(c) of the Act (42 U.S.C. 1395gg(c)), and the regulations found at 42 CFR 405.355-405.356, and 20 CFR 404.506 et seq. These regulations provide that a beneficiary's overpayment may be waived if the beneficiary is without fault in causing the overpayment, **and** if recovery would either defeat the purpose of the Social Security Act or Medicare program, **or** if recovery would be against equity and good conscience. Because you/your client meet(s) these qualifications, we are granting a full waiver.

You have shown [include explanation of the reasons the qualifications for waiver have been met]. The Medicare conditional payment in this case was $_____. You (Your client) received a settlement of $_____. The procurement costs in this case, including attorney fees were $_____. After allowing $_____ as Medicare's share of procurement costs, the amount which would have been due to Medicare is $_____.

However, for the reasons stated above, Medicare is waiving recovery of this amount.

Please sign the enclosed release agreement form within 10 days and return it to this office.

Should you/your client have any questions concerning this letter, please contact _____ on _____.

Medicare Contractor

Enclosure(s): Release Agreement

---

[1] See Chapter 7 of the MSP Manual, pages 125-126. Letter for Granting a Full Waiver (Exhibit 4) (Rev. 1, 10-01-03)

APPENDIX 36E

Standard Letter for Granting Partial Waiver

If granting a partial waiver, the contractor sends the Standard Letter Granting Partial Waiver shown below. Use of this letter is mandatory. Substitutes may not be used. The contractor retains copies for the file.[1]

Re: Name of Beneficiary HIC #

Dear Beneficiary/Attorney:

We have completed our review of your/your client's request to waive monies owed to Medicare.

It is our decision to partially waive Medicare's claim.

The authority to waive recovery of a Medicare overpayment is found in §1870(c) of the Social Security Act (42 U.S.C. 1395gg(c)). Under this provision, and the regulations found at 42 CFR 405.355-405.356, if a beneficiary is without fault in causing the overpayment **and** recovery would either defeat the purpose of the Social Security Act or Medicare program, **or** would be against equity and good conscience, recovery may be waived. In making these decisions, Medicare applies the rules found in Social Security regulations at 20 CFR 404.506-404.509, 404.510a, and 404.512.

In applying these rules, we found the following:

The contractor enters reasons for partial deductions:

Example

This partial waiver is granted because it would be against equity and good conscience to recover the full amount of the claim. The settlement proceeds in this particular case were very small considering the injuries suffered; therefore, it would be against equity and good conscience for Medicare to take the entire settlement.

OR

---

[1] See Chapter 7 of the MSP Manual, pages 127-128. Letter for Granting a Partial Waiver (Exhibit 5) (Rev. 1, 10-01-03)

Example

You have documented financial hardship and we have determined that it would defeat the purpose of the Social Security Act to request repayment of the entire claim. Therefore, we are granting a partial waiver in the amount of _____, and _____must be repaid to Medicare.

Medicare's conditional payment in this case was _____. You (your client) received a settlement of $_____. The procurement costs in this case, including attorney fees were

$_____. After allowing $_____ as Medicare's share of procurement costs per 42

CFR 411.37, Medicare's net conditional claim was $_____.

However, in accordance with this determination, we are granting a partial waiver in the amount of _____. The total amount now due to Medicare is $(principle and interest).

In accordance with this determination, a check in the amount of $_____, made payable to Medicare, should be sent to:

Medicare contractor
Address
Your/the beneficiary's name and health insurance claim number should be included on the check made payable to Medicare.

On (date that exhibit 2 was sent)_____, we notified you that interest would be assessed on any debt not repaid in full within 60 days of that date, regardless of whether you chose to appeal or to seek waiver of the debt. We advised you that repaying the debt would not affect your right to dispute, appeal, or request waiver of the debt. Because you did not repay the debt within 60 days of (the date that exhibit 2 was sent), you owe Medicare $_____, in interest charges.

Please sign the enclosed release agreement form within 10 days and return it to this office.

If you disagree with the decision not to grant a full waiver of recovery of this overpayment, you have 60 days from the date you receive this letter to request a reconsideration. The request can be submitted directly to the address above.

If you decide to exercise your appeal rights, and if you want help with your appeal, you can have a friend, lawyer, or someone else help you. There are groups, such as lawyer referral services and public interest advocacy groups that can help you find a lawyer.

There are also groups, such as legal aide services, who provide free legal services if you meet eligibility requirements. Should you/your client have any questions concerning this letter, please contact _____ on _____.

Medicare Contractor

Enclosure(s): Release Agreement Form

Pre-addressed envelope

If you decide to appeal this determination, and if you want help with your appeal, you can have a friend, lawyer, or someone else help you. There are groups, such as lawyer referral services and public interest advocacy groups, that can help you find a lawyer. There are also groups, such as legal aide services, who will provide free legal services if you meet eligibility requirements.

Copies of the law, regulations and guidelines upon which we based this determination are available upon request. If you have any questions about this reconsideration determination and/or the request for hearing, please contact: [name of contact person].

Medicare Contractor

APPENDIX 36H

MSPRC Final Settlement Detail Form

 **MSPRC**

 Learn about your letter at *www.msprc.info*

Final Settlement Detail Document

Beneficiary Name:
Medicare Number:
Date of Incident:

42 CFR 411.37(c) stipulates that Medicare will recognize a proportionate share of the necessary procurement costs incurred in obtaining a settlement. In order for Medicare to properly calculate the net refund it is due, please supply the information outlined below. This information will also be used to update the beneficiary's records to show resolution of this matter.

Total Amount of the Settlement: _____

Attorney Fee Amount: _____

Additional Procurement Expenses: _____
(Please submit an itemized listing of these expenses)

Date the Case Was Settled: _____

Settlement Information Provided By: _____

Date: _____

The completed form should be sent to:

Medicare Secondary Payer Recovery Contractor
Auto/Liability
PO Box 33828
Detroit, Michigan 48232-5828

If you have any questions concerning this matter, please call the Medicare Secondary Payer Recovery Contractor (MSPRC) at 1-866-677-7220 (TTY/TDD: 1-866-677-7294 for the hearing and speech impaired) or you may contact us in writing at the address below. If you contact us in writing, please be sure to include the beneficiary's name and Medicare health insurance claim number.

Region III

Philadelphia Regional Office of the Centers for Medicare and Medicaid Services, covering the States of Delaware, Maryland, Pennsylvania, Virginia and West Virginia and the District of Columbia.

Centers for Medicare & Medicaid Services (CMS)
Region III
Public Ledger Building, Suite 216
150 South Independence Mall West
Philadelphia, Pennsylvania 19106

Phone: (215) 861-4140

For Inquiries Regarding:	Contact	Phone	E-Mail
Medicare	Division of Beneficiaries, Health Plans and Providers	215-861-4226	rophihpp@cms.hhs.gov
Medicare Managed Care	Division of Beneficiaries, Health Plans & Providers	215-861-4224	rophihpp@cms.hhs.gov
Medicaid	Division of Medicaid and State Operations	215-861-4196	rophimso@cms.hhs.gov
State Children's Health Insurance Program (SCHIP)	Division of Medicaid and State Operations	215-861-4278	rophimso@cms.hhs.gov
Medicare Financial Questions	Division of Financial Management	215-861-4739	rophifm@cms.hhs.gov
Quality of Care Issues	Division of Medicaid and State Operations	215-861-4317	rophimso@cms.hhs.gov
Medicare Certification	Division of Medicaid and State Operations	215-861-4317	rophimso@cms.hhs.gov
Medicare Contractors	Consortium Contractor Management	215-861-4698	

Region IV

Atlanta Regional Office of the Centers for Medicare and Medicaid Services covering the States of Alabama, North Carolina, South Carolina, Florida, Georgia, Kentucky, Mississippi and Tennessee.

Centers for Medicare & Medicaid Services (CMS)
Region IV
Atlanta Federal Center
61 Forsyth Street, S.W., Suite 4T20
Atlanta, Georgia 30303-8909

Phone: (404) 562-7500

For Inquiries Regarding:	Contact	Phone	E-Mail
Medicare	Division of Beneficiary Services - Beneficiary Customer Service Line	404-562-7500	roatlbs@cms.hhs.gov
Medicare Managed Care	Division of Medicare Operations Customer Service Line	404-562-7360	roatlhpp@cms.hhs.gov
Medicaid and State Children's Health Insurance Program	Division of Medicaid and State Children's Health Insurance Program Customer Service Line	404-562-7359	roatlmso@cms.hhs.gov
Medicare Certification	Division of Survey and Certification Customer Service Line	404-562-7400	roatlmso@cms.hhs.gov
Medicare Financial Management and Program Integrity	Division of Financial Management Customer Service Line	404-562-7300	roatlfmpi@cms.hhs.gov
Medicare Contractors	Consortium Contractor Management Customer Service Line	404-562-7230	OCASouth@cms.hhs.gov

Medicaid Eligibility	Division of Medicaid & Children's Health	816-426-3406	rokcmmch@cms.hhs.gov
Medicaid Home & Community Based Services Waivers	Division of Medicaid & Children's Health	816-426-3406	rokcmmch@cms.hhs.gov
State Children's Health Insurance Program (SCHIP)	Division of Medicaid & Children's Health	816-426-3406	rokcmmch@cms.hhs.gov
Quality of Care Issues	Division of Quality Improvement	816-426-5746	rokcmcsq@cms.hhs.gov
End Stage Renal Disease	Division of Quality Improvement	816-426-5746	rokcmcsq@cms.hhs.gov
Survey & Certification	Consortium Division of Survey & Certification	816-426-5925	rokcmscb@cms.hhs.gov
Nursing Home Reform	Consortium Division of Survey & Certification	816-426-5925	rokcmscb@cms.hhs.gov
Organ Procurement	Consortium Division of Survey & Certification	816-426-5925	rokcmscb@cms.hhs.gov
Health Insurance Portability	Office of the Regional Administrator	816-426-5472	rokcmora@cms.hhs.gov
Statistics	Office of the Regional Administrator	816-426-5233	rokcmora@cms.hhs.gov

Region VIII

Denver Regional Office of the Centers for Medicare & Medicaid Services, including the administration of the Medicare, Medicaid and the State Children's Health Insurance Program in the six states of Colorado, Montana, North Dakota, South Dakota, Utah and Wyoming.

Centers for Medicare & Medicaid Services (CMS)
Region VIII
Colorado State Bank Building
1600 Broadway, Suite 700
Denver, CO 80202

Phone: (303) 844-2111

Inquiries Regarding	Contact	Phone	Mail
Medicare	Division of Medicare Operations	303-844-1568	rodenpub@cms.hhs.gov
Medicare Managed Care	Division of Medicare Operations	303-844-1568	rodenpub@cms.hhs.gov
Medicare Financial Questions	Division of Financial Management	303-844-7096	rodenpub@cms.hhs.gov
Medicare Fraud	Division of Financial Management	303-844-7096	rodenpub@cms.hhs.gov
Medicare Certification	Division of Survey & Certification	303-844-7715	rodenpub@cms.hhs.gov
Medicare Contractors	Consortium Contractor Management Staff	303-844-1568	rodenpub@cms.hhs.gov
State Children's Health Insurance Program (SCHIP)	Division of Medicaid and Children's Health	303-844-7715	rodenpub@cms.hhs.gov
Medicaid	Division of Medicaid and Children's Health	303-844-7715	rodenpub@cms.hhs.gov
Quality of Care Complaints	Division of Survey & Certification	303-844-7715	rodenpub@cms.hhs.gov

12

defend settlement that might be offered in a case without a Medicare component. If the court does not control the way in which past and future medical costs are awarded at trial, if at all, then there is a distinct likelihood that whatever award is entered will be completely consumed by Medicare and that Company X, to protect itself, will be forced to tender payment to Medicare in the full amount of Medicare's lien.

DATED: January ___, 2010
          [Insert City & State]

                    AB LAW FIRM, LLP

                    By: _____

TO:

      Attorney for Plaintiffs

APPENDIX 39

Proposed Scheduling Order

STATE COURT OF NEW YORK
ANY JURISDICTION, USA

Jane Doe Beneficiary,

      Plaintiff,   **SCHEDULING ORDER**

v.

Corporate CEO,

                Index No.:

      Defendant.

In the event any plaintiff is a Medicare beneficiary or Medicare eligible, plaintiff's counsel must inform counsel for the defendants of this fact, and plaintiff(s) shall provide the following information to all defendants:

a. Health Identification Card Number;

b. Address of beneficiary;

c. Date of Birth;

d. Properly executed Consent to Release Form entitling counsel for defendants to communicate with the Federal Government and its contractors (MSPRC and COBC);

e. Properly executed Medicare Section 111 form, found at the Centers for Medicare and Medicaid Services website: http://www.cms.hhs.gov/MandatoryInsRep/Downloads/NGHHICNSSNNGHPForm.pdf ; and,

f. Tax Identification Number of the Estate, if applicable.

Plaintiff's counsel shall be assigned as the "lead" to seek the appropriate information from the Medicare contractor.

Any plaintiff who is a Medicare beneficiary shall sign-up for MyMedicare.gov so that he or she can manage, on-line, the conditional payment information under the My MSP tab;

Throughout the duration of the case, plaintiffs have the following ongoing obligations with respect to Medicare:

    a. Continuous obligation to identify himself or herself as a Medicare beneficiary or Medicare eligible;

    b. Within 90 days of the service of this Order, the "lead" counsel shall make contact the Medicare contractor, and the parties shall use that 90-day period to agree upon the appropriate ICD-9 codes related to the claim;

    c. Within 120 days, the "lead" counsel shall notify the Medicare contractor and provide updates to the parties as to the progress;

    d. Within 60 days after receipt of the initial Payment Summary Form, all parties to the lawsuit shall be provided with the Payment Summary Form to determine whether it is appropriate to enter into relatedness discussions with Medicare; and,

    e. The Court shall be notified when conditional payment information is available.

All depositions to be completed by   _____

IME scheduled by   _____

IME completed by   _____

All expert information exchanged by   _____

Next pre-trial conference with the Court   _____

Section 111 Reporting Checklist

Franco Signature

Field No.	Field Name	Description	Check List: Data to Report
65	Self-Insured Type	Identifies whether the self insured is an organization or individual. Values: I=Individual O=Other (e.g. business, corporation, company). **Required** and must contain a value of I or O if Field 64 is Y. If N the field must equal space.	
66	Policyholder Last Name	If Field 65=I, first position must be a letter. If Field 65 does not equal I, must be all spaces	
67	Policyholder First Name	If Field 65=I, first position must be a letter. If Field 65 does not equal I, must be all spaces	
68	DBA Name	"Doing Business As" name of self-insured business. **Required if Field 65=O and Field 69 equals spaces.** If Field 65=I, field must be black	
69	Legal Name	Legal Name of self-insured business. **Required if Field 65=O and Field 68 not provided.** If Field 65=I, must be blank.	
71	Plan Insurance Type	Type of insurance coverage or line of business provided by plan policy or self-insurance. Values: D=No-Fault, E=Workers' Compensation, L=Liability **Required**	
72	TIN	"Tax Identification Number" of the plan used by the RRE. Must contain 9 digits. **Required**	
74	Policy Number	Identifier for the policy under which the underlying claim was filed. If liability self-insurance or workers' compensation self-insurance fill with 0s if you do not have a number reference. Must be at least 3 characters. **Required**	
75	Claim Number	Identifier by which the primary plan identifies the claim. If liability self-insurance or workers' compensation self-insurance fill with 0s if you do not have. May not be equal to all spaces. **Required**	
81	No-Fault Insurance Limit	Dollar amount of limit on no-fault insurance. Fields must not be black, all spaces. **Required if Field 71=D.** If Field 71=D and there is no dollar limit, fill with all zeroes or 9s. If Field 71=E or L, fill with all zeroes	
82	Exhaust Date for Dollar Limit for No-Fault Insurance	Date on which limit was reached or benefits exhausted for No-Fault Insurance Limit. Format: MMDDYYYY. Fields may not be blank, must have date or all zeroes. Where there is a valid date, the same date should be supplied in Field 99. If Field 71=D and the limit has not been reached, fill with zeroes. If Field 71=E or L fill with zeroes.	

Section 111 Reporting Checklist

Franco Signature

Field No.	Field Name	Description	Check List: Data to Report
84	Injured Party Representative Indicator	Code indicating the type of Representation provided. Values: A=Attorney, G=Guardian/Conservator, P=Power of Attorney, O=Other, Space=None. If injured party has more than one representative provide the attorney's information. **Required if Injured Party has representation.**	
85	Representative Last Name	**Either last and first name or firm name is required if injured party is represented.** Must be blank if Field 84 is blank.	
86	Representative First Name	**Either last and first name or firm name is required if injured party is represented.** Must be blank if Field 84 is blank.	
87	Representative Firm Name	**Either last and first name or firm name is required if injured party is represented.** Must be blank if Field 84 is blank.	
89	Representative Mailing Address Line 1	Street number and name should be placed on one address line field, while other information such as suite number should be placed on other. If US address is not available fill with spaces and supply 'FC' in the corresponding state code. **Required if injured party is represented.** Must be blank if Field 84 is blank.	
90	Representative Mailing Address Line 2	Street number and name should be placed on one address line field, while other information such as suite number should be placed on other. If US address is not available fill with spaces and supply 'FC' in the corresponding state code. Must be blank if Field 84 is blank	
91	Representative City	**Required if injured party is represented.** Must be blank if Field 84 is blank.	
92	Representative State	US Postal abbreviation state code. **Required if injured party is represented.** Must be blank if Field 84 is blank.	
93	Representative Zip Code	5 digit zip code **Required if injured party is represented.** Must be blank if Field 84 is blank.	
95	Representative Phone	Format: 1112223333. **Required if injured party is represented.** Must be blank or zeroes if Field 84 is blank.	
98	ORM Indicator	Indicates whether there is on-going responsibility for medicals. Values: Y=Yes N=No The Y value remains in this fie3ld even when Field 99 is submitted in this same record. **Required**	

Section 111 Reporting Checklist

Field No.	Field Name	Description	Check List: Data to Report
99	ORM Termination Date	Date ongoing responsibility for medicals ended. Only applies to records previously submitted with ORM Indicator=Y. ORM Termination Date not applicable if claimant retains the ability to submit/apply for payment for additional medicals related to claim. When ORM date is submitted Field 98 must=Y. Format:MMDDYYYY Fill with zeroes if Field 98=N or if date has not been established.	
100	TPOC Date 1	Date of association Total Payment Obligation without regard to ongoing responsibility for medicals. Date payment obligation was established, the date the obligation is signed if there is a written agreement. If court approval is required it is the later of the date the obligation is signed or the date of court approval. If there is no written agreement it is the date the payment is issued. Format: MMDDYYYY. Not required for the initial report of a claim reflecting ORM. If there is a TPOC date reportable at the time ORM termination is reported, report the TPOC fields on the second report for the ORM. Fill with zeroes if there is no TPOC to report. **Required for all other claims.**	
101	TPOC Amount 1	Amount of Total Payment Obligation to Claimant. When record includes ORM fill with zeroes unless there is a TPOC date/amount for payment in addition to the information which must be reported with respect to ORM. Not required for the initial report of a claim reflecting ORM. If there is a TPOC date reportable at the time ORM termination is reported, report the TPOC fields on the second report for the ORM. Fill with zeroes if there is no TPOC to report. **Required for all other claims.**	
102	Funding Delayed Beyond TPOC Start Date 1	If funding for the TPOC Amount 1 is delayed, provide actual or estimated date of funding. Format: MMDDYYYY. Fill with zeroes if not applicable.	
		Only Fill Out if Claimant is Deceased	
104	Claimant 1 Relationship	Relationship of claimant to the injured party. Values: E=Estate, Individual Name Provided, F=Family Member, Individual Name Provided, O=Other, Individual Name Provided, X=Estate, Entity Name Provided, Y=Family, Entity Name Provided, Z=Other, Entity Name Provided, Space= Not applicable. **Required if injured party is deceased and claimant is not the injured party**	
105	Claimant 1 TIN	Tax Identification Number, Employer Identification Number or Social Security Number. **Required if injured party is deceased and claimant is not injured party.** If Field 104 equals space, must contain all zeroes or spaces.	

Section 111 Reporting Checklist

Field No.	Field Name	Description	Check List: Data to Report
106	Claimant 1 Last Name	**Required if injured party is deceased and claimant is not the injured party and Claimant 1 Relationship=E, F, or O.** If Field 104 equals space, must contain all spaces	
107	Claimant 1 First Name	**Required if injured party is deceased and claimant is not the injured party and Claimant 1 Relationship=E, F, or O.** If Field 104 equals space, must contain all spaces	
108	Claimant 1 Middle Initial	**Required if injured party is deceased and claimant is not the injured party and Claimant 1 Relationship=E, F, or O.** If Field 104 equals space, must contain all spaces	
109	Claimant 1 Entity	**Required if injured party is deceased and claimant is not the injured party and Claimant 1 Relationship=X, Y, or Z.** If Field 104 equals space, must contain all spaces	
110	Claimant 1 Mailing Address Line 1	First line should include street name and number while other information such as suite number should be placed on other line. **Required if injured party is deceased and claimant is not the injured party.** If Field 104 equals space, must contain all spaces	
111	Claimant 1 Mailing Address Line 2	First line should include street name and number while other information such as suite number should be placed on other line. **Required if injured party is deceased and claimant is not the injured party.** If Field 104 equals space, must contain all spaces	
112	Claimant 1 City	**Required if injured party is deceased and claimant is not the injured party.** If Field 104 equals space, must contain all spaces	
113	Claimant 1 State	US Postal abbreviation State Code. **Required if injured party is deceased and claimant is not the injured party.** If Field 104 equals space, must contain all spaces	
114	Claimant 1 Zip	5-digit Zip Code. **Required if injured party is deceased claimant and is not the injured party.** If Field 104 equals space, must contain all spaces or zeroes	
115	Claimant 1 Zip+4	4-digit Zip+4. If unknown or not applicable fill with zeroes. If Field 104 equals space, must contain all spaces or zeroes	
116	Claimant 1 Phone	**Required if injured party is deceased and claimant is not the injured party.** If Field 104 equals space, must contain all spaces	
117	Claimant 1 Phone Ext.	Fill with spaces if unknown or not applicable. If Field 104 equals space, must be all spaces.	
119	Claimant 1 Representative Indicator	Code indicating the type of Representation provided. Values: A=Attorney, G=Guardian/Conservator, P=Power of Attorney, O=Other, Space=None. If injured party has more than one representative provide the attorney's information. **Required if Claimant 1 is represented.**	

Section 111 Reporting Checklist

Franco ~~Signor~~

Field No.	Field Name	Description	Check List: Data to Report
120	Claimant 1 Representative Last Name	**Either last and first name or firm name is required if injured party is represented.** Must be all spaces if Field 119 is spaces.	
121	Claimant 1 Representative First Name	**Either last and first name or firm name is required if injured party is represented.** Must be all spaces if Field 119 is spaces.	
122	Claimant 1 Representative Firm Name.	**Either last and first name or firm name is required if injured party is represented.** Must be all spaces if Field 119 is spaces.	
123	Claimant 1 Representative TIN	Tax Identification Number, Employer Identification Number or Social Security Number. If none is available fill with spaces or zeroes. If Field 119 is equal to space, must contain all zeroes or spaces. **Optional**	
124	Claimant 1 Representative Mailing Address 1	First line should include street name and number while other information such as suite number should be placed on other line. **Required if Claimant 1 has representation.** If Field 119 is equal to space, must contain all spaces.	
125	Claimant 1 Representative Mailing Address 2	First line should include street name and number while other information such as suite number should be placed on other line. If Field 119 is equal to space, must contain all spaces.	
126	Claimant 1 Representative City	**Required if Claimant 1 has representation.** If Field 119 is equal to space, must contain all spaces.	
127	Claimant 1 Representative State	US Postal abbreviation State Code. **Required if Claimant 1 has representation.** If Field 119 is equal to space, must contain all spaces.	
128	Claimant 1 Representative Zip Code	5 digit Zip **Required if Claimant 1 has representation.** If Field 119 is equal to space, must contain all spaces.	
130	Claimant Representative Phone	Format: 1113332222 **Required if Claimant 1 has representation.** If Field 119 is equal to space, must contain all spaces.	

APPENDIX 41

Proposed Discovery Demands

STATE COURT OF NEW YORK
ANY JURISDICTION, USA

_____

Jane Doe Beneficiary,

      Plaintiff,

                        DISCOVERY DEMANDS

v.

Corporate CEO,

                  Index No.:

      Defendant.

_____

Answers to the below discovery demands are hereby requested within 30 days of the date of this pleading. All questions are directed to the allegedly injured claimant with respect to the above-captioned action:

1. Name.

2. Address.

3. Date of Birth.

4. Date of Death, if applicable.

5. Tax Identification Number of the Estate, if applicable.

6. Gender.

7. Age.

8. Medicare HIC Number, if applicable.

9. Social Security Number.

10. Date of Injury.

11. Enrolled in Medicare Part A?

12. Enrolled in Medicare Part B?

13. Medicare benefits obtained as a result of the underlying incident.

14. Provide any communications to and from Medicare with respect to the incident in question.

15. Has the claimant applied for Social Security Disability Benefits?

    a. If so, when?

    b. Was the application denied?

    c. Is claimant appealing or re-filing for Social Security Disability benefits?

16. Has claimant recent treatment for kidney dialysis?

17. Has claimant received treatment for End-Stage Renal Disease?

18. Please provide information with respect to the current status of injuries resulting from the tort (physical and psychological) so as to evaluate the possibility of future treatment stemming from the underlying incident.

19. Please provide the defense with a properly executed Consent to Release Form entitling counsel for defendants to communicate with the Federal Government and its contractors (MSPRC and COBC).

20. If claimant is not a Medicare beneficiary, please provide a properly executed Medicare Section 111 form, found at the Centers for Medicare and Medicaid Services website: http://www.cms.hhs.gov/MandatoryInsRep/Downloads/NGHHI CNSSNNGHPForm.pdf

TABLE OF AUTHORITIES

Statutes

Federal Codes

Case Law

Guidance Memorandums, Town Hall Transcripts, Alerts

Congressional Bills